THE SPIRIT-PERSON

AND

THE SPIRIT-WORLD

THE SPIRIT-PERSON

AND

THE SPIRIT-WORLD

AN OTHERDIMENSIONAL PRIMER

KERRY POBANZ

HSA Publications
4 West 43rd Street, New York, NY 10036
www.hsabooks.com

ISBN: 1-931166-04-8

CONTENTS

Part I:
The Human Being as an
Inherently Spiritual Being

According to St. Paul, human beings are meant to become
aware that they not only have a physical body but also a
spiritual body. If we all possess these two bodies, how are
they related to each other?

As physical persons, we recognize that we have 5 physical
senses. Does the non-physical spirit-person also have
senses?

In what way and to what extent does the spirit-person
retain a record of his or her life on earth?

How does the spirit-person travel in
the otherdimensional spirit-world?

What is the "silver cord" and how does the silver cord
connect the spirit-self to the physical self?

Given that the human person is essentially a spiritual
being, then in what sense is the human person also a
"microcosm of the macrocosm"?

Part II:
Life in the Spiritual World:
Seven Critical Aspects

This book is dedicated to my spiritual mentor,
one of the wisest and most loving spiritual
teachers of all time—Rev. Sun Myung Moon

FOREWORD

This book has been written as a contribution toward guiding human beings into a twenty-first century of expanded spiritual awareness.

After all of our monumental struggles with money, power and knowledge, it has by now become abundantly clear that these things, in and of themselves, can never yield the ontological fulfillment we seek as human beings. Scientific advancement and sophisticated technological development, as brilliantly important as they are in facilitating an enlightened global culture and even in alleviating certain kinds of human suffering, are not and can never be the answer to the deepest quest of human being. Artistic creation, as profoundly important as it is to the realization of our humanity, is not the answer and can never be the answer that would enable us to become the fully human human beings that we desire to be.

Even world religions like Christianity, Islam, Judaism, Buddhism, Hinduism, etc., which have for many centuries occupied the high ground in claiming to reveal human ultimacy in God and in divine reality, and which have effectively comforted and inspired millions, have today, with the best of intentions, devolved into institutions of cultural complacency. Yet, despite the religious/moral lethargy of the present age, we can and should be reminded that, historically, all religious enterprises, whether mainstream, alternative or esoteric, have tirelessly attempted to help us understand the significance of a single fundamental reality: *that human beings are, by nature, spiritual creatures;* that we are more than just our physical bodies and physical lives; that unbeknownst to ourselves generally, we have awaiting us an unimaginably vital future beyond death.

Thus, this book is dedicated to the purpose of generating a renaissance of understanding about how exactly human beings exist as spiritual creatures, both structurally and functionally, individually and socially. It is meant further to provide rational and political understanding of the life one is introduced to after death, an understanding that is specifically corroborated in the affirmations of some of the world's greatest religious/mystical teachers, including Jesus, St. Paul, Emanuel Swedenborg, Rudolf Steiner, Paramahansa Yogananda, and Sun Myung Moon, as well as other noteworthy contemporary mystics and psychics.

The hope here is, among other things, that readers of this book can come to appreciate that an enlightened discussion of the spiritual reality of life after death can yield important practical insights into our life before death. In fact, we should know that if we do not try to understand the nature of spiritual reality, we have thereby forfeited the depth and full dimensionality that rightfully belongs to our lives as human beings, and that we continue an ignorance that is not bliss but can only serve to prolong the great suffering of both people on earth as well as in the spiritual world.

Thus, again, the following descriptions and explanations of spiritual reality are offered, not as some occult transmittal, but as a practical guide and as a means of timely education as humankind enters a new age of civilization.

PREFACE

My hope in writing this book has been all along that it would serve to stimulate the reader's imagination regarding the nature of spiritual reality, and that it would finally offer "food for thought" to those seeking the core of reality in God's love. That is to say, while this text is deliberately more metaphysical than it is theological, it also acknowledges that, without God, and God's love in particular, the foundations of the universe remain unknowable, and even unimaginable.

Emanuel Swedenborg, for instance, recognizes God as the ground of physical and spiritual reality throughout his thousands of pages of descriptions of the spiritual world. It is important for the reader to know that in referencing Swedenborg's works in each Section's Notes, the title of Swedenborg's particular work is followed by a number which is the section number where the passage is to be found; if the section number is followed by another number in brackets, this refers to a certain paragraph within the section.

Throughout this book I have avoided using, for the most part, the self-referential pronoun "I" and have instead adopted the convention of referring to the author as "We"—for good reason. First off, I would not hesitate to affirm that God has supported and guided me in this project. Moreover, during the past 10 years that were required to write this book, I have been acutely and continuously aware that I have been receiving both psychological support and intellectual assistance from unknown others in the spiritual world. Thus, the writing of this book surely has not been a solitary endeavor. Rather, this book represents a cooperative effort which I have chosen to acknowledge by using "We," instead of "I." But, at the same time, while "we" have composed this book together, I also want to be clear that I take full responsibility for any errors and inaccuracies herein.

Finally, I want to acknowledge those who have invested time and energy to read and critique various parts of the developing manuscript, with special thanks to Regis Hanna, Martin and Marian Porter, Nina Magnin, June Saunders and Matt Pugh. In addition, I am indebted to Michael Inglis for his spiritual counsel, to Jonathan Gullery for his meticulous and creative design, and to Louise Perlowitz for her precise proofreading. And, of course, I offer my deep gratitude to Carol, my wife, and to our four boys, all of whom encouraged me and persevered together with me in the writing of this book.

Kerry Pobanz
Nutley, New Jersey
July, 2001

If I have told you earthly things and you do not believe, how can you believe if I tell you heavenly things?

—Jesus of Nazareth

1

THE HUMAN PERSON AS AN INHERENTLY SPIRITUAL BEING

Section 1

According to St. Paul, human beings are meant to become aware that they not only have a physical body but also a spiritual body. If we all possess these two bodies, how are they related to each other?

It is sown a physical body, it is raised a spiritual body. If there is a physical body, there is also a spiritual body.
—I Corinthians 15:44

And yet, man after death is as much a man as he was before, so much so as to be unaware that he is not still in the former world. He has sight, hearing and speech as in the former world. He walks, runs and sits as in the former world. He lies down, sleeps and awakes, as in the former world. He eats and drinks as in the former world. He enjoys marriage delight as in the former world. In a word, he is a man in each and every respect. From all this it is clear that death is not the extinction but the continuation of life, and it is merely a transition.[1]
—Emanuel Swedenborg

Where is your spirit now? When you sleep, where is it? In your head? Where? Once you leave your physical body, you are in the spiritual realm. This is like coming out of water into the air. God is omnipresent, He is everywhere. So you can be everywhere in spirit. . . . After you die, your spirit can come back right here, but it does not occupy space in this air as you do now. Your physical being occupies so much space in the air. But your spirit can go right through my body and out the other side. It still has form, but it can go through anything material. It is not restricted by the physical. . . . You may see spirit forms as life-size. But that spirit can live and work in the realm of an atom.[2]
—Sun Myung Moon

3

discussion

It is probably best to begin by pointing out here that many of the world's major religious traditions incorporate the notion of the human person possessing, in addition to the physical body, some kind of ethereal, non-physical soul-body that continues to survive after death. In Christian mysticism, as aforementioned in St. Paul's writings, it is the spiritual body; in Tibetan Buddhism, it is the *bardo*-body; in Judiasm, the *coach-ha-guf*; in Hinduism, the *linga-sharira*; in Sufism, the *jismi-i-misal*; in Theosophy, the *astral* body. Clearly, spiritual experience around the world and across the ages affirms the existence of a distinct spirit-self which indwells the physical self during life on earth, and which continues to exist and grow after the death of the physical self. Our major questions here, then, are: *How is this true?* and *Why is this true?*

Let us begin by proposing that the universe is structured on the principle of *expression*, that is, of an inner dimension that is present through an outer expression, or of an invisible internal which becomes manifest through a visible external. Thus, we know that the mind, which is invisible, exists because it is expressed or represented through our external facial expressions and bodily gestures, as well as through our manifest efforts to communicate using certain words and ideas.

As it turns out, the mind-body relationship in human beings, in more general perspective, exists as the spirit-flesh relationship, or as the cosmic relationship between spirit-self and physical self. The spirit-self, which is eternal and causal, is designed to achieve critical expression through the phenomenal physical self, and while on earth, the human person lives through the dynamic give-and-take relationship between these selves, otherwise existing as the unity of these selves.

The spirit-self, while ethereal, is not at all insubstantial but is, rather, composed of the same subtle substance as one's thoughts and feelings. Again, it is probably best to *begin* by recognizing that the spirit-self has the same shape as the physical self and its vibrational quality is so refined that it directly and wholly interpenetrates and indwells the physical body, though as Sun Myung Moon and many others have noted, the spirit-self has an astonishingly protean nature, enabling it to indwell molecular, atomic and even subatomic spaces. For instance, Peter Thompkins in *The Secret Life of Plants* (1973) reviews an anecdotal account, first related by Marcel Vogel, of how a young girl psychically/spiritually projected herself into the circulatory system of a plant and traveled throughout the plant body; she and numerous others participating in this research demonstrated the ability to make remarkably consistent and scientifically accurate observations of the plant's internal structure, which otherwise could only be verified through using a high-powered microscope. From these experiments, Vogel concluded: "We can move into individual cells in our own bodies and, depending on our state of mind, affect them in various ways. One day this may explain the cause of disease."[3]

It is important here to further appreciate that there is a one-to-one correspondence between every point in the physical body and every point in the spiritual body (an insight, for instance, especially utilized by Tibetan Buddhists, Chinese acupuncturists and many of the New Age healing therapies).

At death, the spirit-self is detached from the physical body and, ideally, continues its growth and development in a higher dimension, though this option for growth is not chosen in certain cases, as we will describe in greater detail in later discussions. In brief, however, the foregoing sketches the "how" of the relationship between the spirit and flesh.

Why human beings are designed to function via this relationship between spirit-self and physical self is a question of cosmic importance, and deserves to be elaborated in a larger context. While it may be difficult for some people to accept, we must here affirm, together with Jesus and all great founders of religions, that the core of human being is **love**. Far beyond recognizing the human being as simply "homo sapiens" (man of wisdom) or "homo habilis" (tool-using man), we affirm that humans are in their origin and most essentially *homo amans, i.e., beings of love.* Swedenborg and Sun Myung Moon both affirm that, since humans are made in God's image, the highest realization of human being is the realization of true love and, on that foundation, the achievement of wisdom. The foundational meaning of the understanding that human beings are made in God's image is that they are designed with the potential to love as God loves which, further translated, means that human beings are designed to *grow* in such a way that they can fulfill a divine potential for loving, thereby authentically participating in God's divinity. Just as the physical self requires definite physical nutriments, like air, food and water, to develop, so also in parallel, the spirit-self requires certain spiritual nutriments to mature. Spiritual growth is, in reality, the growth of *character*, which most fundamentally is growth in one's ability to love and care for others. (This, however, also necessarily entails the concurrent development of one's knowledge and wisdom.)

It almost goes without saying that the spirit needs to receive and digest God's love and truth in order to develop. But, beyond this, it is most critical to grasp here that spiritual growth is not a matter of the spirit alone; it is not designed to take place (at least initially) apart from the physical self and physical life on earth. The spirit-self, or spirit-person, grows through receiving nutriments, called "vitality elements," from the quality of life lived while possessing a physical body. In other words, the stunning realization here is that the human person can only grow spiritually by receiving both nutriments created by God *and* the "vitality" nutriments created by the person throughout his or her life on earth. Hence, we arrive at a paramount insight—the understanding that the spirit-self matures on the foundation of the physical body and one's physical life on earth. From a *cosmic* perspective, then, we must acknowledge that the purpose of the physical body is to provide the means for the maturation of the spirit-self; the overarching purpose of life on earth is to *practice loving and serving other people.* In truth, a human person's physical lifetime represents the most precious opportunity he or she will ever have—the opportunity to love and serve others. In this way, to the extent we have spent our time unselfishly caring for others, and in loving service to others, we will have fulfilled our most fundamental purpose as human beings made in God's image.[4]

Section 2

As physical persons, we recognize that we have five physical senses. Does the non-physical spirit-person also have senses?

Unless there were interior vision the eye could never see. The sight of the eye springs from an inner sight; and therefore a man sees equally well after death, nay much better, than while he lived in the body, —not indeed worldly or corporeal objects, but those which are in the other life. They who were blind in the life of the body see in the other life equally with those who were quick-sighted; for the same reason also a man sees while he sleeps and in his dreams, as well as when he is awake. . . . From these considerations, it is evident that external vision springs from interior vision. The case is the same with every other sense.[1]

—Emanuel Swedenborg

'Unlike the spatial three-dimensional physical world cognized only by the five senses, the astral spheres are visible to the all-inclusive sixth sense—intuition,' Sri Yukteswar went on. 'By sheer intuitional feeling, all astral beings see, hear, smell, taste and touch. . . . [They] have all the outer sensory organs—ears, eyes, nose, tongue and skin—but they employ the intuitional sense to experience sensations through any part of the body; they can see through the ear, or nose, or skin. They are able to hear through the eyes or tongue . . . and so forth.'[2]

—Paramahansa Yogananda

discussion

In the directly preceding quote, Yogananda shares his own spiritual teacher's, i.e., Sri Yukteswar's, description of sensory experience in the world after death, noting that this is a profound and holistic "intuitional" experience, in which perception occurs as a multidimensional synesthesia. While synesthesia (i.e., perceiving through the cross-connection of the senses) is recognized as a rare form of sensibility (e.g., notably in someone like Helen Keller, as well as in others whose five physical senses are otherwise functioning normally) in the life before death, this is the standard operating perception one experiences in the life after death. Thus, the abilities, for instance, of hearing colors or tasting sounds are directly available to a spirit-person.

From a different yet complementary perspective, both Swedenborg and Sun Myung Moon affirm that human beings have five "outer" physical senses because they first have five "inner" spiritual senses. Because the universe is structured through an original cause-effect correspondence between inner and outer dimensions, the physical body is the manifest expression of the spirit-body, and the physical senses likewise resemble by correspondence the spiritual senses. Thus, seeing and hearing in the physical world resemble and correlate with spiritual sight, or clairvoyance, and spiritual hearing, or clairaudience, i.e., abilities for seeing and hearing people and events in the spiritual dimension. For instance, Jesus' disciples Peter, James and John at the Transfiguration (Mt. 17:1-3) were able to clairvoyantly see Jesus speaking with the spirit-men, Moses and Elijah. Further, in a well-known anecdote, Swedenborg shared that he himself, while sitting down to dinner in Gothenburg, Germany (July, 1759) clairvoyantly saw and elaborated before 15 witnesses, a raging fire that had broken out in Stockholm, 300 miles away. Two days later a letter arrived from Stockholm, confirming every detail of the fire he had reported.[3]

As with the examples of clairvoyance above, let us now briefly consider the functioning of the other spiritual senses, in the context of life *before* death. A clairaudient person is spiritually open through his/her sense of hearing, having the ability to hear spirits who may be attempting to communicate. This is, in fact, the ability to hear the thoughts of deceased persons who are communicating through/across the spiritual dimension, which is otherwise best understood as a dimension of *thought*. All human beings have at least latent clairaudience, which may serve, constructively, as a medium for receiving positive guidance or artistic inspiration. Unfortunately, in the present turbulent era of human civilization, clairaudient abilities may become an easy prey for destructive spirits. Such clairaudience occurs oftentimes in those who are clinically schizophrenic, who cannot control their mental openness to low spirits, and who thereby are tormented by having to hear unceasing accusations, insults and threats from these spirits. Psychic mediums, if they are authentic, are those few who can, in a deliberate and disciplined way, engage their clairaudient and clairvoyant abilities to receive messages from those in the spiritual world trying to communicate with relatives and friends on earth.

The spiritual sense of smell can enable a person to smell, for instance, the sweet fragrance of a loving environment or, on the other hand, the putrefaction of a criminal's spirit, which is no longer growing but rather decaying amidst selfish and violent deeds. The spiritual sense of taste, if active, makes it possible for a customer to "taste" the temperament or vibrational quality of mood of the cook as she prepares the food. Thus, if a customer is especially spiritually open through his sense of taste, and the salad is prepared by an angry chef, the customer may very well experience the salad as "sour," even if the physical ingredients of the salad were fresh. Oftentimes it is this spiritual sense that becomes active in vegetarians, who cannot bear the taste of fear experienced by animals that have been violently slaughtered.

Finally, the spiritual sense of touch is that unique sensitivity, latent in all persons, to indwell or "touch" the thoughts and feelings of another person, thereby manifesting itself as a kind of deep empathy or, in a higher octave, as compassion. It seems important, especially at this point, to emphasize that the spiritual senses, not surprisingly, are designed to function at their peak efficiency in the experience of true love, or that is, in the God-centered context of giving and receiving true love. As Rev. Moon has explained, one of the astonishing consequences of the fact that the universe was designed in accordance with God's love is that all things in the creation are designed to be known most fully by human beings exercising God's love. Because love is the power to become one with other persons or things, it is also the ability to spiritually enter into them and to know them from the inside out via an original empathy based upon love. Thus the sense of spiritual touch experienced during life on earth is often a loving experience of directly touching, therefore knowing, the feelings and even sometimes specific thoughts of another person. Such loving thought, as the basis of spiritual touching, or empathetic knowing, helps us to grasp that the universe is *essentially* structured symbiotically—such that, not only are human beings designed to know reality most completely through exercising God's love but, reciprocally, all things in creation are designed to automatically reveal themselves in response to being loved with God's love.[4]

Thus, the sense of spiritual touch, realized as loving thought or compassionate intuition is, for instance, markedly exemplified in a person like George Washington Carver, an agricultural chemist of such genius that he finally became known as the "Black Leonardo." Carver used his extraordinary scientific and intuitive skills to transform the humble peanut (used previously only as hog food) and the unknown sweet potato "into hundreds of separate products, ranging from cosmetics to axle grease to printer's ink and coffee." As a child, Carver, in explaining his ability to "heal" sick plants, said: "All flowers talk to me and so do hundreds of little living things in the woods."[5] When he was much older, and widely heralded as a genius, he described his apparently miraculous capacity for scientific discovery: "The secrets are in the plants. To elicit them you have to love them enough." Carver also went on to especially attribute his ability of fathoming secrets of the natural world to his love for God and the Bible, always emphasizing *love* to be his deepest way of knowing.[6]

Yet another closely related example of how the sense of loving spiritual touch may operate to elicit information is given by Hans Gebert, an Anthroposophist, who documents a relevant incident in Wolfgang von Goethe's life:

> During his stay in Strasbourg, Goethe had been fascinated by the cathedral. He had examined it under all possible lighting conditions. . . . He tried to experience the building in as many ways as he could. He also sketched what it would have looked like had it been finished. One of the friends confirmed from the original plans that Goethe was right in his projections. When asked who told him about the original design, Goethe replied: "*I bestowed on it so much affection that it decided at the end to reveal to me its manifest secret.*" Through observation, exercise, and mental effort he had penetrated to an imperceptible reality, to the idea of the architect.[7] (Emphasis added)

This example, then, further emphasizes that the sense of spiritual touch together with all the other spiritual senses, operating in the context of God's love, afford the deepest-possible knowing of reality.

In the present condition of human culture, the sense of spiritual touch unfortunately often operates as a liability. Consider that it is this sense that operates when we unavoidably interface with and assimilate the fears and anxieties of a friend we may be trying to counsel. Often we may end up feeling that we have absorbed the spiritual heaviness or depression of the person we have been trying to help.

As demonstrated above, it is possible to recognize that humans possess five spiritual senses that correspond to their five physical senses, or 10 senses altogether, and then to give a separate explanation of each of these two sets of senses. But now it is important to state that, from an original and unfallen point of view, the physical and spiritual senses were never meant to be separate, or to be understood separately, but rather to function as resonating complements to each other in complete harmonization. Up until the present historical moment, because native human spiritual senses have operated almost entirely latently and often with unconscious subtlety, it has been difficult to admit their authenticity, difficult to discern that they originally inform human being. But with the advent of the twenty-first century, it becomes possible to systematically and publicly acknowledge the existence of the spiritual senses.

Section 3

In what way and to what extent does the spirit-person retain a record of his or her life on earth?

Man has an outer and an inner memory, the outer one belonging to his natural person, and the inner one belonging to his spiritual memory. The details which a person has thought, intended, said, done—even what he has heard and seen—are written on his inner or spiritual memory. There is no way to destroy the things that are there because they are written at once on the spirit itself and on the members of its body. . . . So the spirit is formed in keeping with the thoughts and acts of its intention.

I know these things seem very strange, and on this account are almost impossible to believe; still they are true.

Let no one then believe that there is anything a person has thought within himself or done in secret that remains hidden after death. Let him rather believe that each and every thing will then be visible as in broad daylight.[1]
                    —Emanuel Swedenborg

I discovered that my mind was a veritable storehouse of facts concerning my earthly life. Every act I had performed, and every word that I had uttered, every impression I had received; every fact that I had read about, and every incident I had witnessed, all these, I found, were indelibly registered in my subconscious mind. And that is common to every spirit person who had an incarnate life.[2]
                    —Anthony Borgia

12

Since everything a man does is transformed into vitality elements and transmitted to his spirit man, all of one's life is recorded in the spirit man. The spirit man is like a video tape recorder on which a man's entire life may be seen.[3]
—Sun Myung Moon

discussion

Because the spirit-person automatically records all the events of one's life on earth, Swedenborg also refers to this phenomenon as the "Book of Life."[4] It is, in fact, this Book of Life that is opened and examined in the period immediately after death and, according to Swedenborg and many others, the results of this examination determine how and where the spirit-person chooses to live in the spiritual world. Often this examination reveals personal actions that have been selfish and self-serving in the sense that they have been consciously committed to the detriment and harm of others, and which are thereby deserving of *judgement.* Interestingly enough, however, this is *not* God's judgement, but it is the judgement rendered by one's own *conscience,* which is discovered to have an unquestionable and compelling reality.

This examination of the Book of Life is well-likened to the viewing and hearing of a videotape recording of one's entire life. That this "playing back" of one's life at the time of death does occur is confirmed for us in the multitude of contemporary testimonies of near-death experiencers (NDErs). Almost every one of these testimonies recounts a "life-review" phase in which the NDEr witnesses a playback, often in exact and minute detail, of all of their thoughts thought and actions done during their life on earth.

A further example demonstrating that the spirit-person does record one's life may be discerned in an experience related by Malachi Martin in *Hostage to the Devil* (1976). Therein, Martin, a former Jesuit priest, describes the event of an exorcism presided over by a Catholic priest attempting to cast the evil spirit(s) out of a middle-aged man. The priest, however, who had apparently indulged certain violations of conscience in his past, instantly came under attack of the possessing spirit, an attack that took the form of nastily accusing the priest of these specific violations, which the possessing spirit could read directly off of the priest's spirit-person.[5] It is also well-known among exorcists that, if a person has anything in his past which he desires to remain undisclosed, he should not attend an exorcism, since the possessing spirits will invariably use such "secrets" as fodder for their virulent accusations.

Swedenborg even specifically describes that, in the life after death, "each evil spirit is shown clearly all his evil deeds, his crimes, thefts, deceits, and devices. These are brought out of his own memory and proven; there is no room left out for denial, since all the attendant circumstances are visible at once."[6] But our question here must be this: Simply because an evil person can be brought to recognize that his or her actions were incontrovertibly evil, does that mean the person will necessarily repent or apologize for these actions? Unfortunately the answer is very often "No." Often, selfish people, both before and after death, are simply incapable of repenting and, after death, end up by default in some lower and darker part of the spiritual world, a phenomenon that we will later address more substantially.

Section 4

How does the spirit-person travel in the otherdimensional spirit-world?

He who is not acquainted with the arcana of heaven, cannot believe that a man can see earths that are so far distant, and give any account of them from sensuous experience. But let him know that spaces and distances, and therefore the progressions, which exist in the natural world, in their origin and first cause are changes of the state of the interiors, and that with angels and spirits they appear according to these changes; *and that through changes of state they may be apparently translated from one place to another, and from one earth to another, even to earths which are at the end of the universe: so likewise may man as to his spirit, his body still remaining in its own place.* This has been the case with me, since, by the Lord's Divine Mercy, it has been given to me to speak with spirits as a spirit, and at the same time with men as a man. That a man, as to his spirit, can be translated in this manner, is inconceivable to the sensual man, since he is in space and time, and measures his progressions according to them.[1] (Emphasis added)

—Emanuel Swedenborg

The spirit world is a world of thought; to think is to act, and thought is instantaneous. If we think ourselves into a certain place, we shall travel with the rapidity of that thought, and that is as near instantaneous as it is possible to imagine.[2]

—Anthony Borgia

The first thing he [a person who has died] realizes is that in the spirit-world he is released from the bonds of physical life, and the bonds of time and space no longer exist for him. In the spirit-world, travel from one corner of the universe to the other is *instantaneous,* like a spark flashing between two electrical poles. Like finding a station on the radio, all you have to do is tune yourself to the proper wavelength and everything you want to experience will come to you.[3] (Emphasis added)

A spirit-man can easily reach stars which are at a distance of several hundred thousands or several million light years away.[4]
—Sun Myung Moon

discussion

As evidenced in the foregoing quotes, travel in and through the spiritual world is a remarkably liberating experience. Swedenborg, Rev. Moon and others affirm that the world of mind/thought (consciousness)/spirit is as vast as the universe itself, even in unimaginable ways encompassing the universe. Whether or not anyone can grasp *how* it is done, we should know at least that mind/thought/spirit is capable of achieving what can only be described as a kind of interdimensional "translation" across astronomical and cosmic expanses. This interdimensional translation is accomplished through "changes of the state of the interiors," by which Swedenborg means that mind/thought/spirit undergoes special metamorphosis, enabling experience in the spiritual world, e.g., travel, and communication with spirit-people.

Complementing Swedenborg, Borgia and Rev. Moon also affirm that travel in the spirit-world is instantaneous, since thought itself is instantaneous. Spirit-persons literally think themselves from "place" to "place" in the spirit-world, with an instantaneity potentially greater than the speed of light. Paramahansa Yogananda describes this extraordinary travel in the spirit world in this way:

There are many astral planets teeming with astral beings. The inhabitants use astral planes, or masses of light, to travel from one planet to another, faster than electricity and radioactive energies.[5]

Thus, it is the case that the spirit-person is capable of travelling instanta-neously both to planets/stars in the macrocosm or, that is, the plenum con-stituted of the physical universe and the spiritual universe, across vast distances measurable even in millions of light years. This may be hard for many people to grasp who are presently living physically on earth, but it is nevertheless true and is potentially verifiable by all persons in the life after death.

Finally, we are well-advised to consider here that, in the last analysis, a spirit-person's *actual* mobility and locomotion in the spirit-world are determined in the context of the development of his or her own *thought*. The highest development of thought, or the most exalted sophistication of wis-dom in the spirit-world, in its turn, results from the greatest realization or accomplishment of *love*. Rev. Moon provides an excellent summary descrip-tion of this reality:

> The means and speed of travel in the spirit-world are very dif-ferent from here on earth. Each individual enters the spirit-world with a different level of accomplishment in love, a different love record. Thus, each has a different quality of power in his movements. . . .
>
> Although the distances between the stars and planets are vast, you can still traverse them within one second, if you are moving at God's speed. It is the power of God's love that enables Him to move so rapidly.[6]

Section 5

What is the "silver cord" and how does the "silver cord" connect the spirit-self to the physical self?

Remember your Creator in the days of your youth, before the evil days come, and the years draw nigh, . . . before the silver cord is snapped, or the golden bowl is broken, or the pitcher is broken at the fountain, or the wheel broken at the cistern, and the dust returns to the earth as it was, and the spirit returns to God who gave it.

—Ecclesiastes 12:1-7

You must know that when the physical body sleeps, the spirit body temporarily withdraws from it, while still remaining connected to it by a magnetic cord. This cord is the veritable lifeline between the spirit body and the earth body. The spirit thus situated will either remain in the vicinity of the earth body, or it will gravitate to that sphere which its earthly life, so far, has entitled it to enter. The spirit body will thus spend part of the lifetime of the earthly body in spirit lands.[1]

—Anthony Borgia

As I reached the back of my head, my hand brushed against something and I felt behind me with both hands. Whatever it was extended out from a spot in my back directly between my shoulder blades, as nearly as I can determine, not from the head, as I expected. I felt the base, and it felt exactly like the spread-out roots of a tree radiating out from the basic trunk. The roots slanted outward and into my back down as far as the middle of my torso, up to my neck, and into my shoulders on each side. I reached outward, and it formed into a "cord," if you could call a two-inch-thick cable a "cord." It was hanging loosely, and I could feel its texture very definitely. It was body-warm to the touch and seemed to be composed of hundreds (thousands?) of tendonlike strands packed neatly together, but not twisted or spiraled. It was flexible, and seemed to have no skin covering. Satisfied that it did exist, I took off and went.[2]

—Robert Monroe

discussion

As indicated above, the term "silver cord" is originally referred to in scripture and, as Borgia points out, this cord is probably best conceptualized as a *life-line,* inasmuch as once the cord is severed, the death of the physical self occurs. However, recalling the earlier explanation (Section 1) that the spirit-self matures on the foundation of the physical body, it is useful to think of the silver cord as a kind of *umbilical cord* that is meant to be severed once a certain maturation of the spirit is achieved. This is not at all unlike the situation of a baby in the womb connected to its mother via the umbilical cord which is rightfully severed once life/growth in the womb is finished, thereby enabling birth into a more dynamic state of being. It needs to be understood here, then, that the death of the physical body is *literally* a kind of birth into a higher dimension of *life,* and it is in this sense that we profoundly agree with the American-trained psychiatrist, Elizabeth Kübler-Ross, when she avers:

> Death is simply the shedding of the physical body, like a butterfly coming out of its cocoon. . . . And the only thing you lose is something you don't need anymore—your physical body.[3]

Thus, the physical self is immediately nourished by the spirit-self during life on earth. It is the case that, at certain times during sleeping and/or dreaming, the spirit-self detaches itself from the physical body and may travel, at the speed of thought, to visit friends, family and locations of personal emotional importance anywhere on the planet earth or, otherwise, the spirit-self may visit, as Borgia notes, certain regions of the spiritual world, meeting with deceased loved ones or participating in various kinds of educational experiences. The other instances in which the spirit-self may detach itself from the physical are those in which a person experiences severe trauma of some sort, whether emotional or physical, e.g., such as being in a deadly car accident, or undergoing life-saving surgery. In these latter cases, the detached spirit-self is often in a position to observe other earthly people who are working to save and repair its physical body. Raymond Moody in *Life After Life* has documented many of these cases.

The silver cord itself is composed of spiritual substance and, as such, is capable of stretching out indefinitely, e.g., to the other side of the earth, across millions of miles to the nearest planets, or even across innumerable light years to the stars themselves. As long as the cord remains intact, the person can continue life in his or her physical body. Once the cord is severed, whether from natural causes or as a result of an accident, "death" occurs.

Section 6

Given that the human person is essentially a spiritual being, then in what sense is the human person also a "microcosm of the macrocosm"?

Man was called a microcosm by the ancients, because he resembled the macrocosm, which is the universe in the whole complex. . . . The ancients called man a microcosm, or little universe, from the knowledge of correspondences which the most ancient people possessed, and from their communication with the angels of heaven; for the angels of heaven know, from the visible things about them, that all things in the universe, *viewed as to uses,* represent man in an image.

But that man is a microcosm, or little universe, because the created universe viewed as to uses is man in an image, cannot enter the thought and knowledge of anyone, except from an idea of the universe *as seen in the spiritual world.* It cannot therefore be shown but by some angel in the spiritual world, or by some one to whom it has been granted to be in that world, and to see the things therein. As this has been granted to me, I am enabled, by what I have seen there to reveal this arcanum.[1] (Emphasis added)

—Emanuel Swedenborg

The human spirit encapsulates all the elements found in the spirit world as the unfolding of the spirit's internal nature and external form. The human body encapsulates all the elements of the physical world, since God created the material realm as the unfolding of the body's internal nature and external form. Accordingly, since human beings contain within themselves the essence of all things in the cosmos, each person is a microcosm.[2]

—Sun Myung Moon

discussion

In essence, this truth that each human person is a substantial encapsulation of the whole universe, or is a universe in miniature, is also found in all the mystical traditions of the great world religions, i.e., in Islam, Christianity, Judaism, Buddhism and Hinduism. Both Swedenborg and Rev. Moon understand, in fact, that the cosmos is deliberately created in the image of the human being, meaning that not only is the physical world designed after the pattern of the structure and function of the physical body, but the spiritual world has also, likewise, been created in the pattern of the structure and function of the human mind or spirit.

Further, as aforementioned, just as the physical *self* exists in direct correspondence and resemblance to the spirit-*self,* so also at this point we are able to understand that the spiritual *world* closely resembles the physical *world.* With great clarity, Swedenborg describes what this means:

> Let us then first state the nature of correspondence. The whole natural world corresponds to the spiritual world—not just the natural world in general, but actually in details. . . . It is vital to understand that the natural world emerges and endures from the spiritual world, like an effect from the cause that produces it.[3]
>
> Be it known that the spiritual world in external appearance is altogether similar to the natural world. Lands, mountains, hills, valleys, fields, lakes, rivers and fountains appear there, consequently all things of the mineral kingdom, also paradises, gardens, groves, woods, with trees and shrubs of all kinds; and animals, birds, and fishes of all kinds, thus all things of the animal kingdom appear there. Man there is an angel or a spirit. This is premised that it may be known that the universe of the spiritual world is altogether similar to the universe of the natural world.[4]

To sum up, then, we acknowledge that while human beings have been made in the *direct* image of God, all other beings and things in the universe are made in the human image or, that is, in the *indirect* image of God.

In addition, the idea that the human image is a prototype for all things has other very tantalizing and profound implications. We should consider, for instance, that the *human form* is, in appropriate consideration, an integral part of the human image, as explained here by Sun Myung Moon (and otherwise generally corroborated by Swedenborg):

The whole being [human being], physical and spiritual, is created in God's image. In the spirit world, the form or image of God is not visible. *But the entire spirit world appears like a human form.* Some people belong to the part which represents the eye, some people belong to the part which represents the feet, etc. The huge cosmos is in human form. The entire universe appears in the form of a man; yet each individual according to his inclinations or specific mission or personality belongs to some specific part of the whole—some to the eye, some to the heart, some to the feet, the lung or brain, or hands. Those who are active with their hands may belong to the part of the universe which appears as hands; those who like to think more than other people may belong to the brain, and so on. Agricultural or industrial people may belong to hands or feet. The characteristics of individual men make up the macrocosm.

Also, the earth spiritually appears in the form of a man. Each nation and each society may appear as the form of a man. Each family as well as each individual appears in the form of a man.

Judging from this, the individual God is still in the form of a man, and vice versa. Each cell of your body is in the image of you yourself.[5] (Emphasis added)

Thus, since all things are made in the human image, the human form informs the appearance of the cosmos and the spiritual world in its entirety. The earth, nations and societies, the nuclear family and the human individual are all directly spiritually represented in the human form (perhaps not unlike the way in which, in the business world, corporations are treated legally as "persons"). Given this understanding, the reality of God takes the form of a human being. Even cellular and atomic realities exist in accordance with the human image.

In this regard, both Swedenborg and Rev. Moon *specifically* describe that *heaven itself* is organized in accord with the human image, i.e., in accord with the harmonious structure and functioning of the human body. Swedenborg reveals that heaven is constituted like a person, both in general and in particular, and is thereby rightfully understood as the "Grand Man" or "Universal Human":

Since God is a Person, the entire angelic heaven, taken in a single grasp, resolves into one person. This entity is divided into realms and sections that follow the members, organs, and viscera of a human being.

There are actually communities of heaven that make up a section including everything that belongs to the brain, and everything that belongs to the parts of the face, and everything that belongs to the body's inner organs. These sections are marked off from each other just the way they are in a person. Angels even know what section of the person they are in.[6]

This extraordinary and provocative insight is corroborated by Rev. Moon, who affirms that heaven ultimately consists in an ideal world which functions in the total constructive harmony that is the full realization of God's love. Such an ideal world is the "big man," composed of vital organs, or God-centered communities which, in their turn, are composed of healthy cells, or individual persons practicing true love.

The body is the most vivid example of a microcosm of the future [ideal] world. Ultimately our universe will be like one God-centered man. In that one body you will perform some role somewhere, like a cell. You will have your own universe, your own world, own tribe, nation and clan, but all within this one harmonized body. If this one man with the heart of God is rejoicing and ecstatic in the world, what about you? You cannot be separate from that joy. When the whole is happy, each individual has to enjoy and share in that same happiness. Each cell is connected to the big man, breathing on the same wavelength. The entire universe is ultimately like one man, and each of us individually will act as one cell. When the big man is accomplished in the love and heart of God and rejoicing in God's love, each cell has got to be breathing on the same wavelength.[7]

In summary here, it is important to keep in mind that the human person is indeed a microcosm of the macrocosm because all things are designed after the patterns of the human physical and spiritual selves. Human beings occupy such a profoundly central position in the scheme of the cosmos because they have been created as sons and daughters of God, and thereby are uniquely designed to carry the Heart of God and to fulfill God's love. Nevertheless, it is fashionable in this age of radical skepticism and scientific materialism to see this affirmation of the human person as cosmic prototype as naive anthropocentrism which should otherwise be readily dismissed. Yet, we would maintain that if one is able to grasp this affirmation in the larger context of original and authentic love (that is, God's love), this truth is, far from being naive, a recondite insight into the nature of reality.

Section 7

From a cosmic perspective, how does the human person exist in both the physical world and the spirit-world at the same time?

Man is the means by which the natural world and the spiritual world are conjoined. Man is the medium of conjunction, because in him there is a natural world and there is a spiritual world. To the extent that man is spiritual he is the medium of conjunction, but to the extent that a man is natural, and not spiritual, he is not a medium of conjunction.[1]
—Emanuel Swedenborg

When a person's flesh and spirit unite through give and take action . . . , the physical and spiritual worlds can also begin give and take action with that person as their center. They thus achieve harmonious integration to construct a cosmos that is responsive to God. Like the air that enables two tuning forks to resonate with each other, a true person acts as the mediator and center of harmony between the two worlds.[2]
—Sun Myung Moon

discussion

As Swedenborg points out, it is *because* the human person is a microcosm, possessing both a physical world and a spiritual world in oneself, that he or she has the potential to stand as the mediating link that unites these two worlds or dimensions. We here arrive at the understanding that the human person is designed, in accordance with God's love, as an authentically cosmic being, one that God intends should rightfully stand as mediator and center of harmonization between the two worlds. Thus, the macro-cosmos was meant to find its greatest integration and harmonization via the microcosmos of the human being who is fully realized in God's love.

Clearly, however, it is not enough to recognize the *cosmic potential* of the human person. Rather, we need to ask here: Why, if human beings possess such aforementioned potential, have they been so historically unable to understand and fulfill this potential?

When we say that God designed the human person to stand as mediator and center of harmony in the universe, we mean that the spiritual and physical worlds are not designed to be able to relate harmoniously with each other *except through* the proper and harmonious relationship between the spirit and flesh of the individual person. In other words, it is the *correct relationship* between the human spirit-self and physical self that is the *point of interface* between the two worlds or dimensions.

In this way, we gain new insight into the meaning of the separation from God's love experienced by human beings at the time of the Fall. In fact, the human person's separation from God instantly translated into the dis-harmonization and un-synchronization of the human spirit and flesh. Perhaps in broader perspective, we might better describe that the human person's loss of original relationship with God was synonymous with the loss of *all* properly-ordered relationships, e.g., with other human beings and all of nature as well, beginning with the destruction of the true relationship between the human spirit and flesh.

The consequences of this primordial disordering of the relationship between the spirit-self and the physical self have been devastating. Human beings, first and foremost, lost the awareness of themselves as authentic sons and daughters of God, who were otherwise originally designed to exercise a *dominion of true love* over the vast physical and spiritual realms. In an instant, they lost their awareness of and sensitivity to the spiritual world. After the Fall, human beings were no longer capable of standing as mediators through which the two worlds could relate, and thus physical and spiritual realms necessarily became almost completely unsynchronized, or separated from each other. To this day there exist very few people who are spiritually awake to the world before death, and even fewer who have any accurate grasp at all of human life beyond physical death.

If human beings had not lost their original connection to God, but instead had grown to their rightfully intended spiritual maturity in God's love, they would indeed have dynamically bridged the physical and spiritual worlds.[3] In this case, having full use of his or her spiritual senses, for instance, the human person could have easily seen and conversed with his or her ancestors, even ones thousands of years old, living in the spiritual dimension. Swedenborg often affirms such an original existential status for human beings:

> Man was so created by the Lord as to be able while living in the body to speak with spirits and angels, as in fact was done in the most ancient times; for, being a spirit clothed with a body, he is one of them. But because in process of time men so immersed themselves in corporeal and worldly things as to care almost nothing for aught besides, the way was closed. Yet as soon as corporeal things recede, in which man is immersed, the way is again opened, and he is among spirits, and in a common life with them.[4]

Thus, what this would mean practically is that one would be able to talk with one's great-great-great-great-great-grandmother in the spirit-world just as easily and directly as one could speak with his or her brother or sister currently living on earth. If such immediate interaction were possible between people on earth and in the spiritual world, we can realistically imagine that the constructive development of culture, rooted in God's love, could proceed dramatically in both worlds.

11.

LIFE IN THE SPIRITUAL WORLD: SEVEN CRITICAL ASPECTS

Section 8

"Where" is the spiritual world and how is it situated?

In my Father's house are many mansions; if it were not so,
I would have told you. I go to prepare a place for you.
—John 14:2

I am talking about using the OBE [out-of-body experience] to
explore new levels of reality, new dimensions of time and space
within the universe. All of the great astral projectors have been
aware of these spheres of existence, these "higher worlds," and
have glimpsed them. Hugh Callaway, Marcel Louis Forham,
Robert Monroe, J.H.M. Whiteman, and many others have
described these parallel worlds and spiritual dimensions in
their autobiographies. Some have been able to interact with
their residents. Keith Harary has personally told me about
these "higher worlds" and their inhabitants. . . . Many parapsychologists would prefer to believe that these dimensions are
merely inner worlds created by and within the mind. I contend
that they are real but metaethereal planes of existence that
interface with our own, but that can be contacted only while
one is out-of-body.[1]
—Scott Rogo

Spirits and/or angels live on the stars. Spirits of a different
stage or degree will group by themselves and dwell there.
Spirits on some stars may be higher than those on other
planes. They look like they are all related to one center—God.
Just as your heart or mind is at one place, and yet is free to go

everywhere. Spiritually gifted people can see your spirit-form right where you are, and yet that spirit-form can go everywhere.[2]

—Sun Myung Moon

The spheres [or realms] of the spirit world are ranged in a series of bands forming a number of concentric circles around the earth. . . .

An exemplification of the concentric circles is afforded us when we are told a visitant from a higher sphere is coming *down* to us. He is relatively above us, both spiritually and spatially.

The low realms of darkness are situated close to the earth-plane, and interpenetrate it at their lowest. . . .

With the spirit world made up of a series of concentric circles, having the earth world approximately at the centre, we find that the spheres are subdivided laterally to correspond broadly with the various nations of the earth, each subdivision being situated immediately over its kindred nation.[3]

—Anthony Borgia

discussion

Throughout history and right through the twentieth century, many saints and spiritual teachers have proffered unambiguous testimony of other worlds of existence beyond the death of the physical body. Clearly, the spiritual world has actual existence **somewhere.** In the effort to describe "where" the spiritual world is, especially in relation to where the conventionally recognized physical world is, these spiritual teachers have employed numerous seminal conceptualizations, including mansions, dimensions, planets, worlds, stars, spheres, realms, levels and planes. While, at first consideration, some of these conceptions might seem to be mutually exclusive, it can and will be shown here that they are all in fact complementary. In particular, we have chosen to discuss these various conceptualizations of the spirit-world, not in terms of their chronological emphasis, but rather from the perspective of their progressively greater completeness. Thus, for instance, the subsections treating the spirit-world structured as "mansions" (its oldest characterization) and as "dimensions" (its most contemporary representation) are presented first, since they afford less information about the situatedness of the spirit-world than does the concentric-spherical explanation, which is given third and which, in its turn, is less informative than Swedenborg's or Rev. Moon's delineations. This discussion, then, seeks to render needed metaphysical clarification of how the spiritual world is situated, especially acknowledging that an ecumenical, eclectical, yet integral understanding of spiritual reality is required for the advent of a new age of human civilization.

I.   The Spirit-World as "Mansions"

Ever since Jesus declared 2,000 years ago that "In my Father's house are many mansions. . .", Christian scholars have believed that he was referring to numerous, distinct areas of dwelling in the world after death. Exactly what these promised "dwelling places" might be, or where they might be, was never further elaborated by Jesus beyond giving at least one of them a specific name, that is, "Paradise." Swedenborg offers that "mansions" are specific divisions only of *Heaven* (or, in his terms, the "Universal Human") which are indwelt by those spirits of a corresponding spiritual development or character development:

> But the people who are within the Universal Human have a
> freedom of breathing when they are involved in the good of
> their love. Yet they are all different as regards the quality and
> amount of the good, which is why there are so many heavens,
> called "mansions" in the Word (John 14:2).[4]

Thus, this larger multitude of dwelling places for people in the spirit-world is initially described by Anthony Borgia as "realms of differing vibration," a characterization that continues, for instance, to be employed by the famous twentieth-century Indian yogi, Paramahansa Yogananda, in relating the descriptions of his resurrected spiritual master, Sri Yukteswar, in *Autobiography of a Yogi:*

> Various spheric mansions or vibratory regions are provided for
> good and evil spirits. Good ones can travel freely, but the evil
> spirits are confined to limited zones.[5]

Yogananda here specifies that mansions are actually numerous "vibratory regions" of the spirit-world that exist to accommodate spirits of corresponding degrees of spiritual development. Good spirits who embody love and wisdom are, by definition, those manifesting highest vibration and greatest radiance, while evil spirits, whose vibrational quality is necessarily very low, are ensconced in various degrees of darkness.

II.   The Spirit-World as "Dimensions"

Yogananda, above, usefully explains that such vibratory regions are distinct regions characterized by differing rates of vibration which, in turn, determine different manifestations of time and space. Such a description then facilitates the transition to the contemporary grasping of the spirit-world as constituted in terms of "new dimensions of time and space in the universe," acknowledged by Scott Rogo in the Opening Quotes to this Section.

The "dimensional" interpretation of the spirit-world is *primarily* important because it plausibly affirms to twentieth-century scientifically oriented persons that *the spirit-world, while otherdimensional, also ubiquitously coincides with the physical world.* Anthony Borgia, for instance, describes the location of the spirit-world in this way:

> Where is the boundary between the earth world and the spirit-world? Upon the instant of my passing, of which, you will remember, I was fully conscious, when I arose from my bed in response to a very distinctive urge, *at that moment I was in the spirit world.* The two worlds, then, must interpenetrate one another.[6]

That there is more than one dimension or plane constituting the spiritual world is further elaborated by Swami Panchadasi:

> The [astral or spiritual] planes do not lie one above the other, in space. . . . They interpenetrate each other in the same point of space. A single point of space may have its manifestations of each and all of the seven planes. . . . A plane of being is not a place, but a state of being.[7]

This description is remarkably corroborated by that of Robert Monroe, a reputable Virginia businessman who became a widely respected consciousness researcher and investigator of out-of-body experiences in the 1970s and 1980s. In *Journeys Out of the Body,* he suggests that perhaps many worlds can occupy the same area occupied by our physical matter world, much as the various wave frequencies in the electromagnetic spectrum can simultaneously occupy the same space with a minimum of interaction. Under rare circumstances these worlds may interfere with each other. Thus, if we wonder *where* these worlds are, *"where is here,"* Monroe says.[8]

Gary Zukav clearly agrees with Monroe that the universe is a multi-dimensional reality and is filled with intellegent life:

Other intelligences inhabit other ranges of frequency. These forms of life do not exist elsewhere from us. Just as infrared light, ultraviolet light, microwave light and many, many other frequencies and ranges of frequencies coexist with the visible light spectrum, but are invisible to us, the Life forms that are characterized by different frequency ranges of nonphysical light coexist with us, but are invisible to us. In the place that you now sit exist many different beings, or groups of beings, each active and evolving in its own way. These realities comingle with yours in the same way that microwave radiation exists alongside of visible light, but is undetectable to the human eye.[9]

This relatively recent elaboration by Zukav is a strong echo of an even more scientifically imaginative presentation of otherdimensional inhabitants by Dr. Roger Wescott. Dr. Westcott, Professor and Chairman of the Anthropology Department at Drew University, has put forth some intriguing and scientifically plausible speculations about the general nature of reality:

Time—as Western man has conceived it at least since the Renaissance—is single in dimension, uniform in pace and irreversible in direction. If time should turn out to have more than one dimension, discontinuity of pace, or reversibility of direction, or if space should turn out to have more than three dimensions, then it would be quite possible for solidly and prosaically material beings from the "real" world to pass through our illusively constricted space-time continuum as a needle passes through a piece of cloth.[10]

Dr. Wescott further suggests that perhaps many different beings, even seemingly fantastical ones from our folklore, might appear and disappear suddenly as part of this interdimensional traffic. Unbeknownst to ourselves, the planet Earth may actually exist in "'hyperspace' and/or 'hypertime'" as a "hypersphere" of some sort.[11]

It is probably important to recognize here that there are some who will be disposed to discount the abovementioned three more scientifically rendered accounts as illegitimate since they attempt to describe aspects of reality in terms of "physics" that otherwise can only rightfully be explained via "metaphysics." The only comment that we would make here, though it seem cryptic to some, is that there is a point at which physics and metaphysics coincide, not unlike the manner in which we finally realize that there is a point where the human body and the human mind exist in unity and, ontologically speaking, are even the same thing. That this is the case will be expanded on later in the book.

Westcott, Zukav, Monroe and Borgia all describe reality in terms of its inhabited multidimensionality, which is, interestingly, also otherwise directly evidenced in numerous reports of near-death experiences. In *The Eternal Journey,* for instance, near-death researchers Craig Lundahl and Harold Widdison aver:

> These accounts are representative of numerous accounts that suggest that the world[s] of the spirits and the living are very near—but in different dimensions. George Ritchie in his NDE [near-death experience] observed a city superimposed on our physical city. He also noticed that the beings of one city were not aware of the existence of the other.[12]

Finally, it seems valuable to note here that Emanuel Swedenborg, while not directly employing the notion of "dimensions" to describe the spirit-world, does strongly suggest that spiritual reality has a "dimensional" character. The earlier Section of this book discussing travel through the spiritual world highlights Swedenborg's description of his method of seeing/visiting other "earths in the universe." Swedenborg explains his method as one of "translation" via "changes in the states of one's interiors" which "appear to [the spirit] as progressions through spaces."[13] Through such translation, the spirit becomes able to traverse vast astronomical distances, "the body still remaining in its own place." We have, in turn, dubbed Swedenborg's method "interdimensional translation," since the transformation of consciousness Swedenborg describes enables a profound alteration of the conventional dimensions of time and space, thereby allowing the relevant translation.

Thus, in summary, "mansions," used by Jesus 2,000 years ago to metaphorically describe the structure of his Father's creation, has become reconceptualized in contemporary terms as "dimensions." We can acknowledge that such a dimensional interpretation of spiritual reality is useful and valuable in that it can accommodate the "horizontal" aspects of the general interconnectedness of all things, including mansions, or dimensions, in the universe. Yet, the dimensional interpretation is necessarily (and even deliberately) incomplete inasmuch as it neglects to recognize the vertical or hierarchic, aspects of spiritual reality and, to this extent, is inadequate. Eventually a major question arises: Are there not *higher* and *lower* manifestations or dimensions in the world after death, and, if so, what determines the difference between them? The short answer here is "Yes" and that all such difference derives from the primary difference in peoples' abilities to love God and to love each other. However, before we arrive at where this can be explained in detail, let us explore a final preliminary conception of the situatedness of the spirit-world in terms of planets and concentric spheres.

III. The Spirit-World as Planets, Stars and Concentric Situatedness

A. The Spirit-World as Planets and Stars

In *The Eternal Journey*, Lundahl and Widdison quote from a report of a near-death episode in which the experiencer, John Paul, recounts: "My spirit left my body and went with my guide who took me to the next planet. . . ."[14] In fact, many near-death experiencers, including Betty Eadie, have described traveling to other planets and stars. At this point, then, it is important to recognize that the spirit-world is not only *otherdimensional,* but that it is constituted as a spiritual cosmos, not unlike the physical cosmos. The resurrected Sri Yukteswar, speaking to his disciple Yogananda, describes this spiritual cosmos, or astral universe, in this way:

> There are many astral planets, teeming with astral beings. . . .
> Just as many physical suns and stars roam in space, so there
> are also countless astral solar and stellar systems. Their planets
> have astral suns and moons, more beautiful than the physical
> ones.[15]

In addition, in an Opening Quote to this Section, Sun Myung Moon declares that spirits naturally group together with others of like minds and hearts to dwell on particular stars and that spirits on some stars may be higher, or more highly developed, than those on others. Further, while the spiritual cosmos is incomprehensibly vast, for those knowing God's love, it is discernibly oriented toward a single metaphysical center, God.

Betty Eadie, in recounting part of her near-death experience, speaks of traveling across galaxies, finding God's children inhabiting many earths:

> I traveled to many other worlds—earths like our own but more
> glorious, and always filled with loving, intelligent people. We
> are *all* God's children, and he has filled the immensity of space
> for us. I traveled tremendous distances, knowing that the stars
> I saw were not visible from earth. I saw galaxies and traveled
> to them with ease and almost instantaneous speed, visiting
> their worlds and meeting more children of our God, all of
> them our spiritual brothers and sisters.[16]

A significant question arises, however, in regard to this passage. Is it possible that Eadie is describing other worlds in the *physical universe,* or are these worlds exclusively situated in the spiritual universe? While such a passage may be open to interpretation, at the very least we can understand that Eadie is encountering these other worlds as inhabited in the spiritual universe. Likewise, Swedenborg, in the following passage, is probably best and most accurately understood, not as affirming that spirits dwell on an actual planet like Mercury in our solar system, but rather as generally affirming that there are innumerable planets/earths throughout the spiritual cosmos where human spirits dwell:

> There are spirits whose sole study is the acquisition of knowledges, finding in them their only delight. These spirits are therefore permitted to wander about and even to pass beyond the solar system into others, and procure knowledges. They have stated that there are earths in immense numbers, inhabited by human beings, not only in the solar system, but in the starry heaven beyond it. These spirits are from the planet Mercury.[17]

Having then suggested that Swedenborg is most likely describing inhabited earths in the spiritual world, it must immediately be acknowledged, on balance, that Swedenborg *might actually* be explaining that, in fact, there are many planets connected to many stars throughout the *physical universe* that are populated by human beings. Evidence for this interpretation can be seen in the following quote where he asserts that the spirits of deceased human beings reside near (around?) their respective planets.

> The spirits of every earth are near their own earth, because they are from its inhabitants (for every man after death becomes a spirit), and because they are thus of a similar genius, and can be with the inhabitants and be of service to them.[18]

To recap, we began by recognizing that "mansions" most likely refers to the multidimensional or otherdimensional nature of the universe. This otherdimensionality has been more specifically conceptualized as the simultaneous or parallel existence of the spiritual cosmos, which contains countless inhabited spiritual stars/planets. Next, we will explore the situatedness of the spirit-world in even more specific terms, that is, in terms of its existence in a series of subtle, concentric spheres surrounding our own planet Earth.

B.   The Spirit-World as Concentric Situatedness

While Anthony Borgia does not directly discuss other planets and stars in the spiritual world, he *does* suggest that such entities would exist, located in the concentric realms radiating out from the earth itself "into the infinity of space":

> The spheres of the spirit world are ranged in a series of bands around the earth. These circles reach out into the infinity of

space, and they are invisibly linked with the earth world in its lesser revolution upon its axis, and, of course, in its greater revolution round the sun. The [physical] sun has no influence whatever upon the spirit world. We have no consciousness of it at all since it is purely material.[19]

From the above description, we are led to appreciate that the earth stands as a kind of cosmic center, spiritually speaking. The extended passage by Borgia presented in the Opening Quotes to this Section, clarifies that the spirit-world has both a horizontal or lateral ordering and a vertical or hierarchical ordering to it. The lateral ordering consists in adjacent spiritual regions corresponding to particular nations, with each region generally located over its respective nation. Thus, there is a certain sense in which cultural and/or geographic boundaries are carried over into the architecture of the spirit-world; yet it is also the case that, within limits, every spirit person has certain individual freedom to choose to live amongst *any* particular grouping or nationality of spirits. The vertical ordering of the concentric spheres means that they are situated hierarchically, with the lowest, darkest, most hellish parts of the spirit world most closely surrounding the earth and interpenetrating the earth. Borgia relates here the relevant testimony of deceased Monsignor Robert Hugh Benson, who all along has been communicating to him the nature of the spirit-world:

> It was through these [lower realms closest to the earth] that I
> passed with Edwin when he came to take me to my spirit
> home, and it was for that reason that he recommended that I
> keep my eyes firmly closed until he should tell me to open
> them again. I was sufficiently alert—too much so, because I
> was fully conscious—otherwise to see some of the hideousness
> that the earth world has cast into these dark places.[20]

That this is, indeed, an accurate depiction of how the spirit world is organized has been confirmed by numerous spiritualists and psychic investigators. Consciousness researcher, Robert Monroe, for instance, describes this above-mentioned reality in similar but very contemporary terms, noting that anyone journeying in their spirit body ("Second Body") must go through the emotionally distorted realms of the spirit-world ("Locale II") before entering the higher, brighter realms:

> This implies that the areas of Locale II "nearest" the physical
> world (in vibratory frequency?) are peopled for the most part
> with insane or near-insane, emotionally driven beings. . . .
> They include those alive but asleep or drugged and out in their
> Second Bodies, and quite probably those who are "dead" but

still emotionally driven. . . . The principal motivation for these
near inhabitants is sexual release in all forms.[21]

Of special note in this passage is Monroe's observation that the "insane" spirits dwelling in the darkest regions are enslaved to the acting out of distorted sexual compulsions, a fact of no small importance in the consideration
of the nature of certain relationships between people on earth and people
in the lower spiritual world. This subject will be addressed more fully in a
later Section.

Finally, having briefly looked at the concentric situatedness of Hell in
the spirit-world, let us consider Swedenborg's more exacting discernment of
the concentric situatedness of Heaven. As mentioned previously, Swedenborg
insists that Heaven exists generally in the structure of the "Universal
Human," meaning that Heaven is constituted in *correspondence* to all internal and external anatomical aspects of the human body. In other words, as
Swedenborg understood the notion of the human person and all things created in God's image, because there is a part of God, and a part of the perfection which is Heaven, that originates as a "heart," so also a heart exists
correspondingly in humans as well as in all other parts of the Creation;
because there is a part of God, and the perfection which is Heaven, that originates as "feet," so also humans have feet, and the rest of the creation
"stands" correspondingly on "feet," etc. In a similar manner, in the following remarkable passage, Swedenborg describes that the originally divine
circular and rotational form of Heaven is uniquely patterned as the concentric
circularity of brain convolutions in the human person:

> Heaven's form is awesome, and utterly surpasses all human
> understanding. It in fact is far loftier than any concepts of form
> that anyone can possibly grasp even by analysis of earthly mat-
> ters. All the heavenly communities are arranged according to
> this form. And marvelous as it is, there is an orbiting accord-
> ing to the forms, which angels and spirits do not feel. It is like
> the earth's daily rotation on its axis and its annual orbit of the
> sun, which its inhabitants do not notice.
>
> I have been shown what the heavenly form is like in a
> lower sphere. It is like the form of the convolutions we see in
> the human cerebrum. I was allowed to see this rotation or
> these orbits graphically. This lasted for several days. I could see
> from this that the brain is formed in accord with the form of
> heaven's rotation. But deeper regions of the brain, which are
> not visible to the eye, are in accord with the forms of more
> inward heavens, which are wholly beyond comprehension. I
> was also told by angels that this enables us to see that man was

created in accord with the forms of these heavens, and that in this way an image of heaven was stamped on him, so that man is a tiny heaven in miniature. I was also told that this is the source of his correspondence with the heavens.[22]

Thus, Swedenborg sees the heavenly spirit-world as situated in accordance with original, sophisticated concentric circularity best represented by the convolutional form of human brain tissue.

The most important insights to be gained from the discussion in this subsection, then, are that the spirit-world exists as a spiritual cosmos, that the spiritual cosmos, while having God as its metaphysical center, is locally centered on the planet earth, and that there is a hierarchy of concentric spiritual spheres radiating outward from the earth, from lowest to highest. In Part IV immediately following, we will consider the most definitive perspective on the situatedness of the spirit-world, in terms of its most completely specified hierarchical organization.

IV. Realms and Levels in the Spirit-World

St. Paul's description in 2 Cor. 12:2 sets the stage for a more detailed understanding of how the spirit-world is divided up:

> I know a man in Christ who fourteen years ago—whether in the body I do not know, or whether out of the body I do not know, God knows—such a one was caught up to the third heaven.

Most Biblical scholars accept that St. Paul in this passage is relating his *own* spiritual experience of having glimpsed the "third heaven." Mainstream Christianity has never clarified how or why there might be *three* heavens. However, both Swedenborg and the Unification teaching of Rev. Moon have independently elaborated, not only that there exist three recognizably heavenly realms, but also three fundamentally hellish realms. In both elaborations, the heavenly realms stand above, and the hellish realms stand below, an *intermediate realm* where deceased persons first enter and are first received into the spiritual world.

Swedenborg explains that Heaven is divided vertically or "regionally" into three parts or three necessarily distinguishable levels, which he then refers to as three distinct heavens:

> . . . an inmost or third heaven, an intermediate or second, and an outmost or first. They follow each other and are independent—just like the top of a person, called his head, his middle or body, and his extremities or feet—or like the top, middle, and bottom of a house. The Divine that comes forth and down

from the Lord is similar in design, so by requirement of design, heaven has three parts.[23]

Thus, Swedenborg names these three heavens the "natural" (or "natural-spiritual") heaven (outermost), the "spiritual" heaven (mediate), and the "celestial" heaven (inmost) which, again, represent the three basic "noncontinuous" levels of Heaven. Swedenborg here offers a very insightful way of comprehending the nature of these three discrete or noncontinuous levels serving to establish the divisions of Heaven:

No one can grasp how the heavens are divided, or even what the inner and outer person are, if he does not know the arrangement of the Divine design in levels. The only idea many people in this world have about inner and outer or higher and lower levels, is a rough idea of something uninterrupted, or something that goes along without a break from purer to more crude. But inner and outer things are arranged as distinct, not continuous.

Levels are of two kinds. There are continuous levels and noncontinuous levels. With continuous levels, it is like the lessening of light from blazing to dark, or the lessening of sight from things in the light to things in the shade, or like levels of air purity from bottom to top. These levels are assigned spatial units.

Levels which are not continuous, but are distinct, are marked off rather as "leading" and "following," like cause and effect or like producer and product. Anyone who looks carefully will see that there are these levels in every single thing in the whole world, levels of production and composition with one thing obviously resulting from another, a third from that, and so on.[24]

Swedenborg affirms that when a person dies, his or her first place of residence in the spirit-world is almost always the "world of spirits." The world of spirits is the intermediate realm between Heaven and Hell, which is, in fact, a kind of halfway house for spirits in which they are able to become generally oriented to their new state of existence and to become prepared to finally choose what realm in the spirit-world they are most suited to dwell in. Often in the state immediately after death, a person will meet many deceased relatives and close friends from his or her life on earth. As Swedenborg notes, married partners will often greet each other with great joy and may dwell together for a time but, if their "ruling loves" (or principally governing motivations) are different in the last analysis, they go their separate ways. In effect, this kind of phenomenon exemplifies one of the absolute laws governing life in the spirit-world: *Like attracts like; similarity conjoins, dissimilarity separates.* Thus, in the end, a spirit-person *necessarily* gravitates to a society of others with similar characters, similar motivations, similar intentions, similar desires. If one has held murderous intentions, amplified all the more because of actually having committed murders in his/her life on earth, he or she is inescapably drawn into some appropriate community of murderers in hell in the spirit-world. If, on the other hand, one has always tried to love and serve others in one's life on earth, or has tried to alleviate the suffering of others, such a person finally comes to dwell in a community of like-hearted spirits in the spiritual world. In summary, the world of spirits, then, is a place of true self-discovery inasmuch as one unavoidably becomes fully aware of one's own inmost motivations and, on that basis, receives appropriate instruction preparing one for a substantially more permanent kind of dwelling in the spirit-world together with like-minded spirits.

Finally, Swedenborg affirms that, according to a law of cosmic balance, there are three fundamental hells that correspond to the three levels of heaven—an outermost hell, which is least hellish, an intermediate hell, and an inmost hell which is the absolutely miserable dwelling place of the most cruel, depraved spirits of all.

A culminating and inclusive view of realms and levels constituting the spiritual world is given by Rev. Sun Myung Moon. The philosophical formulation of Rev. Moon's Unification worldview has been exclusively entrusted by Rev. Moon to Dr. Sang Hun Lee. Dr. Lee, who died in 1995, has continued his work in the spiritual world and has provided the following adumbration of the basic realms of the spirit-world.[25]

Again, similar to Swedenborg, Dr. Lee explains that when one dies, one first enters an intermediate realm called the "transitional spirit world," where he or she is welcomed by loving relatives and friends. In this place, the newly deceased person encounters the "mirror-of judgement" phenomenon, in which all of one's deeds during his lifetime on earth, including everything from achievements to carefully concealed violations, are publicly exposed for all to see, even those spirits dwelling in hell. Thus, the purpose of this mandatory initiation is to determine the status of heart of the spirit-person which, in turn, determines which level of the spirit-world the person will live in. Again, the governing principle for this determination is "like attracts like." Once this determination is completed, those spirits who first welcomed the newly deceased will lead him/her to his or her rightful dwelling, i.e., to either one of the heavens or one of the hells.

It is the case, according to Dr. Lee's observation, that spirits usually remain in the transitional realm for up to seven weeks before moving to their permanent dwelling. Under certain circumstances spirits may not follow this standard schedule. If, for instance, a spirit is severely emotionally disturbed, or otherwise seriously mentally unbalanced, he or she may end up wandering about in a kind of limbo or delusional state. Such spirits are known generally as "earth-bound" and may also act as poltergeists, or they may even try to possess people on earth for one reason or another. But it is important to understand here that this kind of situation presupposes that other designated helping spirits have been unable to reach (emotionally or intellectually) such a mentally unbalanced spirit-person. In this context, spirits may wander or become fixated for many years, until they are finally able to become open to receive positive spiritual guidance.

Hell, orientationally speaking, is located beneath the transitional spirit world and is populated by people who have led predominantly selfish lives, either actively or passively, and who have habitually sought to misuse or sacrifice other people in order to benefit themselves, i.e., engaging in deliberate deception and generally committing all manner of violence against others, both in thought and action. Unification teaching distinguishes three levels of hell, each progressively darker and more vile than the one before. On the first level reside, for instance, unrepentant thieves, adulterers, betrayers, hypocrites, misers, drunks, etc., whereas the second and third degrees of hell are reserved for those having committed the most heinous crimes of rape, murder, torture and mass-murder. Whereas those occupying the first realm of hell continue to exhibit a somewhat human appearance, those in the depths of hell often are not even identifiable as human beings, otherwise taking on various hideous or monstrous appearances.[26]

The three heavens standing above the transitional realm are known as the Lower Heaven (or the Form Spirit realm of the spirit-world), Paradise (or the Life Spirit realm of the spirit-world), and the Kingdom of Heaven (or the Divine Spirit realm). Conscientious people, the charitable, patriots, educators, etc., i.e., all those who sincerely tried to live a life of goodness *primarily* according to their conscience (whether or not they also held religious beliefs) are among those who have their dwelling in the Lower Heaven. This realm is bright with warm sunlight and with landscapes incomparably more beautiful than those found on earth. The people here are basically aware that love is the essence of life, without being fully cognizant of the original source of Love in God.

Paradise, by contrast, is the dwelling place of all those good religious people who, through their devotion to God, unreservedly dedicated themselves in love and service to others. Devotion to "God," however, here encompasses devotion to Allah, Krishna, Buddha, etc., as well as an unremitting devotion to Truth. For instance, authentic Christians who have assiduously practiced *agape* love, following a sacrificial path in imitation of

Christ (Jesus), are among those who reside here. Paradise is astonishingly brighter and more beautiful than the environments of the Lower Heaven.

In the higher realms of Paradise dwell those of advanced spirituality who have genuinely lived for the sake of humanity, in God-centered service to humanity, e.g., the founders of religions including Buddha, Confucius, and Mohammed. Finally, only Jesus, who brought the fullest-yet revelation of the meaning of God's love, is qualified to dwell in the highest realm of Paradise. In this regard, it should be carefully understood that Jesus was able to teach *agape* love, or the unconditional love of one's neighbor which, as profound as such is, remains a form or type of *brotherly love*. It was Jesus' hope that he would have been able to substantially reveal God's love in its highest dimension, as *unconditional parental love*.[27] The highest heavenly realm in the spiritual world, or the Kingdom of Heaven, will finally be opened with the fullest realization of God's love, accomplished via the establishment of genuinely God-centered nuclear families on earth. It is in the family and through the family that all fundamental forms of God's love, i.e., parental love, conjugal love, brother-sister love, and children's love, are meant to be realized. This is further to make the point that, with respect to these dynamics, before the Kingdom of Heaven can be opened in the spiritual world, it must *necessarily* be realized or opened on the earth through God-centered families. Thus, the Kingdom of Heaven is not more than, and can never be less than, the Kingdom of True Love.

Though we have not considered here Swedenborg's descriptions of Heaven and Hell in detail, it is correct to say that Swedenborg and Rev. Moon present some very similar descriptions of Heaven and Hell, especially regarding the division of each into three levels and separated by an intermediate realm for newly deceased persons. In other words, they both present the spiritual macrocosm as consistuted of seven basic realms. It also seems noteworthy to recognize that Anthony Borgia accepts the ordering of the spirit-world into seven basic inhabited concentric spheres. Further, Swami Panchadasi affirms that reality is generally organized in terms of seven cardinal inhabited interpenetrating planes.

In summary, we have tried to fathom the situatedness of the spirit-world by fleshing out a number of the ways that such situatedness has been traditionally conceptualized, i.e., in terms of mansions, dimensions, planes, planets, worlds, stars, spheres, realms and levels. Our intention here has been to demonstrate, in particular, that these conceptualizations are not at odds with each other, but are *complementary* and really represent different ways of talking about the same spiritual reality. The major conclusions regarding such spiritual reality that have been arrived at here might be finally characterized in this way: The term "mansions" that Jesus used to refer to the spirit-world has been recast as "dimensions" by contemporary writers. The otherdimensional spirit-world is revealed, via expanded analysis, to exist as a vast inhabited spiritual cosmos, situated in ubiquitous parallel to the physical cosmos. The spiritual cosmos, as locally positioned around the earth and other planets/stars, may be understood as hierarchically organized into concentric spheres. And from an overall vertical perspective, the seven basic realms of the spirit-world consist in the three levels of Hell, the "transitional" realm, and the three levels of Heaven.

Section 9

What is the nature of communication and language in the spirit-world?

Here, he said, was another instance of the concreteness of thought. If we can move ourselves by the power of thought, then it follows that we should also be able to send our thoughts by themselves, unhindered by ideas of distance. When we focus our thoughts upon some person in the spirit world, whether they be in the form of a definite message, or whether they are solely of an affectionate nature, these thoughts will reach their destination without fail, and they will be taken up by the percipient. That is what happens in the spirit world. . . . We had so far used our "organs of speech" in conversing with each other. It was quite natural, and we hardly gave the matter any thought. It had not occurred either to Ruth or myself that some means of communication at a distance must be available here.

Although we can thus send our thoughts, it must not be assumed that our minds are as an open book for all to read. By no means. We can, if we so will, deliberately keep our thoughts to ourselves.[1]

—Anthony Borgia

[5] Then as the bystanders had no wish to understand that spiritual thought so far exceeds natural thought as to be comparatively ineffable, I said to them, "Make an experiment; enter your spiritual society and think of some subject, retain it, and return and express it in my presence."

They entered, thought of a subject, retained it, and came out; and when they tried to give expression to it they could not; for they could find no idea of natural thought adequate to any idea of purely spiritual thought, and thus no words to express it; for the ideas of thought become words of speech. Afterwards they entered again, and returned; and became convinced that spiritual ideas are supernatural, inexpressible, ineffable and incomprehensible to a natural man; and they said that being so supereminent, spiritual ideas or thoughts in comparison with natural are ideas of ideas and thoughts of thoughts, and therefore by them the qualities of qualities and the affections of affections are expressed; consequently that spiritual thoughts are the beginnings and origins of natural thoughts; and from this it is evident that spiritual wisdom is the wisdom of wisdom, and is therefore inexpressible to any wise man in the natural world. [6] Then it was said from the higher heaven that there is a still more interior or higher wisdom which is called celestial, the relation of which to spiritual wisdom is like the relation of this to natural wisdom, and that these inflow in order according to the heavens from the Lord's Divine wisdom, which is infinite.

Thereupon, the man speaking with me said, "This I see because I perceive it, that one natural idea is the containant of many spiritual ideas; also that one spiritual idea is the containant of many celestial ideas. From this it follows as a consequence, that what is divided does not become more and more simple, but more and more manifold, because it approaches nearer and nearer to the infinite, which contains all things infinitely."[2]
—Emanuel Swedenborg

Language in the spirit world is versatile; people there communicate with song and dance as well as speech, and you have to answer them in singing and dancing. So for eternity you dance and sing, but you always feel new energy welling up. Furthermore, when you dance and sing, the entire universe will join in harmony with you. You will dance together forever with your eternal love.[3]
—Sun Myung Moon

discussion

As a general statement here, we can simply say that communication between people in the spirit-world is normally by means of telepathy, i.e., through the direct sending and receiving of thought. But in more particularized description, there is a great richness of detail characterizing such communication that rightfully should be noted if we are to gain some substantial appreciation of the extraordinary environment constituting the spiritual world. In this regard, Swedenborg's writings are most demonstrative and helpful, but both Anthony Borgia and Sun Myung Moon, in their Opening Quotes, also offer special and important insights which deserve to be elaborated.

Borgia notes, for instance, that upon first arriving in the spirit-world, there is a "natural," in the sense of *habitual*, tendency to continue to try to use the "organs of speech," i.e., the tongue, mouth, throat, etc., for conversing with others. But very quickly, after overcoming the habitual aspect, one discovers an even more natural, in the sense of *aboriginal*, tendency to speak via thought, enabling spontaneous "communication at a distance." This is widely corroborated by contemporary near-death testimonies, virtually all of which confirm that, once the person has moved out of the physical body and encountered other spirit-persons, the primary mode of communication is a direct exchange of thoughts:

> At the moment of death, many individuals report hearing doctors or others pronounce them dead. However, once they meet spirit beings, they report that communication is not through voice, but mind to mind. They know what the other person is thinking, so spoken communication is unnecessary.[4]

To this general description from near-death researchers, Borgia uniquely contributes his own description of two further facets of the after-death thought transmission/reception process—first, that the process is "instantaneous" and second, that the receiving of another's thought in the spirit-world is preceded by a "flash of light":

> As a prelude to hearing Edwin's voice, we had both perceived a bright flash to appear before the eyes. It was in no sense blinding or startling; indeed, the flash was too beautiful for that.

> And that, I think, describes briefly what happens to all of us when a thought is passed between one and another of us. The thought is invisible in transit, it arrives at its destination

instantaneously, when it manifests itself before us as a pleasant but compelling flash of clear light, and we can then hear the voice of our communicator speaking close to the ear, as it seems.[5]

First of all, then, the instantaneity of thought is, as we have recognized in earlier Sections, not only the means of locomotion for people in the spirit-world, but is also the general means of communication amongst spirit-persons. Thus, a spirit-person, with regard to contacting another spirit-person, has two basic options; either he can send himself, via thought, instantaneously, to visit the other person, or he can send a message, via thought, instantaneously, to the other person. Robert Monroe describes his own out-of-body exploration of an otherdimensional realm, "Locale II," in almost identical terms:

> In this environment, no mechanical supplements are found. No cars, boats, airplanes or rockets are needed for transportation. You think movement, and it is fact. No telephones, radio, television and other communication aids have value. Communication is instantaneous.[6]

Even more recently, Rupert Sheldrake in *The Physics of Angels* was prompted to meditate upon the instantaneity of thought from his consideration of the following passage by Christian mystic, Hildegard of Bingen: "Angels do not have wings as birds do, but fly many times as fast, at the same pace that human thoughts do."[7] In his discussion of this passage with Matthew Fox, Sheldrake conjectured:

> Hildegard is going beyond the common usage: angels move as fast as thought. Even today that is the best metaphor. We don't know how fast thoughts travel. If I telephone somebody in Australia, I can transmit a thought to that person at the speed of light. But maybe thoughts can move even faster than this. If I look at a distant star, there's a sense in which my thoughts reach out to touch that star, moving over literally astronomical distances with the utmost speed.[8]

From the above-quoted passages, it seems clear that the instantaneity of thought in the spirit-world is closely tied to what Borgia terms "communication at a distance." Swedenborg notes this phenomenon by saying, ". . . for in the spiritual world speech can be heard at a distance, just as in one's presence, extension of space there being merely an appearance."[9] Briefly, in explication, we should remember that the spirit-world is a dimension of "mentality," or even more generally, "interiority." Time and space are phenomena of "exteriority," that is, of our earthly waking reality. But when the dimensions of time and space are reduced, experientially, in the spirit-world to their *interiors,* space, or "distance," for example, is instantly consumed by thought, informed by desire or will. Thus, time and space have only an interior existence, or manifestation, in the spirit-world, i.e., an existence which is directly modulated by thought.

I. Swedenborg: Spiritual Communication as "Cogitative Speech"

In fact, Swedenborg's many detailed descriptions of the nature of communication in the spirit-world are genuinely fascinating and, for our purposes here, extremely relevant. In reviewing these descriptions, the reader should keep in mind that Swedenborg is speaking, not out of his imagination or creative intuition, but rather out of his direct experience of spiritual realities in the spirit-world. As such, Swedenborg's descriptions stand as a veritable treasure trove of phenomenological insights into the fundamentally spiritual character of human thought, speech and communication.

Swedenborg's most fundamental discovery, in all of his spiritual journeys, was that the core of reality is love, or "affection," itself. Hence, the ground or innermost essence of reality is, in a word, emotional, or affectual. This was an astonishing realization for Swedenborg, who otherwise had previously dedicated the first 54 years of his life to the development of his powers of rationality as the means to the highest discernment of truth. We, as appreciative on-lookers to Swedenborg's life, may also be rightfully astonished by this metamorphosis of Swedenborg's understanding. This insight, that love (or affection, or desire, or motivation) underlies and determines even rational thought, informs all of Swedenborg's investigations into the nature of spiritual reality. Thus, it is only fitting to begin here with Swedenborg's metaphysical declaration in *Arcana Coelestia*: "For in the other life hearts speak, and not lips."[10]

It is valuable to consider first Swedenborg's comments regarding some of the *general properties* of the speech of spirit-persons. The speech of spirits is "interior speech," or what Swedenborg often refers to as "cogitative speech," that is, "thought speaking."[11] Such speech-thought is also heard by spirits as if it had been otherwise physically vocalized; that is, it is audible in the same way in which a discussion between two people on earth is audible to both of them:

> It is sonorous, and as it were of words, but the words are what are called intellectual ideas. It is through speaking, such as is the interior thought from hearing when it passes into visual thought.[12]

Hence, the speech of spirits is actually a *speech of ideas*, which necessarily affords much clearer or more precise communication than that achievable through using earthly language:

> As man thinks from what is sensuous . . . he does not know
> what an idea is, and especially that thought is distinguished
> into ideas, as speech is into words; for thought appears to him
> continuous, and not discrete; when yet the ideas of thought are
> the words of spirits; and the ideas of thought still more interior
> are the words of angels. As ideas are the words of their speech,
> they are sonorous among spirits and angels. Hence the silent
> thought of man is audible to spirits and angels when the Lord
> so pleases. How perfect are the ideas of thought in comparison
> with the words of speech, may be evident from the fact, that a
> man can think more things in a minute than he can utter or
> write in an hour. . . .[13]

Again, Swedenborg notes that speech amongst spirits is capable of rendering profound distinctions of meaning:

> The speech of spirits with man is effected by means of words;
> but the speech among themselves, by means of ideas . . . not
> obscure ones like those of man, but distinct ones. . . . After
> death, the ideas of thought become discrete, so as to serve for
> distinct forms of speech.[14]

It is the case, then, that in the spiritual world, *thinking is speaking*, with ideas functioning as unique *forms of speech*. Swedenborg affirms, further, that such an extraordinary language of ideas is actually instinctive for all human beings, that it never has to be learned but is, rather, latent within the depths of every human being until the point of "death," whereupon it is spontaneously discovered and used by the spirit-person:

> A language like that of the spiritual world is instinctive in
> every individual, but it is in the realm of his more inward
> understanding. However, since this realm does not, in [earthly]
> man's case, find its way into words that parallel affections the
> way it does with angels, man is unaware that the language is
> there. Still this is why man is at home with this language of
> angels and spirits when he enters the other life, and knows
> how to speak it without being taught.[15]

Thus, since the spiritual world is constituted as dimensions of thought and since human beings discover that this is their fully natural habitation after passing out of the physical world, it is perhaps not difficult to imagine that human beings inevitably experience an amazing precision in their ability to manipulate thought generally, as well as to communicate via greatly enhanced ideational subtlety:

> Spirits think with much more clearness and distinctness than they had during their life in the body. There are more things contained within a single idea of their thought than in a thousand of the ideas they had possessed in this world. They speak together with so much acuteness, subtlety, sagacity, and distinctness, that if a man could perceive anything of it, it would excite his astonishment.[16]

While it is not our intention here to discuss the issue of the privacy of one's thoughts in the spirit-world, it is important to note that both Swedenborg and Borgia suggest that such privacy can be maintained in certain ways. However, in specifically considering the communicative relationship that spirits have with each other, it is sobering to recognize that, to a great extent, spirits cannot conceal their thoughts from each other. Speaking from personal experience in this matter, Swedenborg recorded in his *Spiritual Diary* on March 17, 1748:

> The state of spirits and angels is such that none of them can think anything which all the rest do not understand and perceive. For some years, I, too, have not been able to think anything which all present did not perceive; at which I at first felt indignant, and I supposed that I could never be in their company, because I could think nothing by myself without the knowledge of all. But afterwards, when I perceived that the Lord was leading the thoughts of all, it was no trouble to me.[17]

We may say that spirit-persons generally come to know each other through the mutual perception and liberated exchange of thoughts or ideas, not unlike the parallel process on earth, except that the discernment of a person's character takes place instantly and with absolute accuracy in the spirit-world. In the following passage, Swedenborg explains why such discernment is possible:

> This has been made evident to me by many experiences, as for example (to mention only one) that the quality of a spirit can be known in the other life from one single idea of his thought. Indeed, angels have from the Lord the power of knowing at once, when they look upon anyone, what his character is, nor is there any mistake. It is, therefore, evident that every single idea and every single affection of a man, even every least bit of his affection, has an image of him and a likeness of him, that

is, there is present therein, nearly and remotely, something from all his understanding and from all his will.[18]

In this way, a person's character may be divined from a single idea (or "word"), which necessarily bears the person's image, or unique spiritual imprint. For instance, Swedenborg points out that, for this reason, deception is all but impossible since it is instantly revealed, instantaneously perceived:

> . . . so that if they (spirits) are deceitful, even if there is no deceit while they are speaking, yet the genus and species of deceit are perceived in every word and idea . . . so there is no need of much exploration; for in every word and idea there is an image of it.[19]

While the above description stands as a stunning *general* truth, it is even more carefully articulated in the following passage. Here Swedenborg explains, through the specific example of the speech of hypocrites, that even though such a person's ideas or "words" may be proper or attractive, i.e., from an *external* perspective, these ideas in the spiritual world are instantly betrayed via the direct perception of their underlying, or internal, *affection* (i.e., motivation), which is manifest in the "sound" or "articulate" of the speech. Hence, in the spirit-world, the reality is that no one can speak other than they think:

> To this I will add that in the spiritual world there is a communication of affections and of thoughts from them, which results in no one's being able to speak except as he thinks; likewise, everyone changes facial expression and reflects his affection, and thus shows in his face what he is. Hypocrites are allowed sometimes to speak otherwise than they think, but the tone of the voice sounds utterly out of harmony with their interior thoughts, and they are recognized by the discord. It may be evident from this that the internal lies hidden in the tone of the voice, the speech, the face and gesture of the external, and that it is not perceived by men in the world, but plainly by angels in the spiritual world.[20]

In fact, even more detailed discernment of the speech of hypocrites reveals the striking quality of this abovementioned "discord":

> The language of hypocrites (the ones who can pretend to be angels of light) is like the language of angels as far as the words are concerned. But as to affections and resultant thought-concepts, it is wholly opposite. So when the inward quality of their speech is perceived, the speech itself sounds

like a grinding of teeth, and strikes horror.[21]

Thus, to be fully comprehensive in describing the nature of spiritual speech, it is the case that such speech is manifested, never simply as a speech of ideas but, rather, as a *speech of ideas informed by affections*, or informed by the inmost dimension of core attitude/desire/motivation. As Swedenborg notes, such speech flows from the "whole spirit":

> Spiritual speech is universal, from ideas; but its sound, or articulate, flows from the affection itself which is natural to the [speaker], so that the affection expresses itself by the sound, that is, the articulate, with them, just as every affection has natural gestures with it. Consequently, the sound of the speech, that is, their words, flows from the whole spirit.[22]

Further, Swedenborg carefully documents that, while spirits cannot "utter" (via vocal speech) the names of persons or places or, indeed, any word of earthly language, they are able in cogitative speech to spontaneously communicate the collective "sense" of these things, i.e., to instantly convey in thought a "whole" presentation containing the sights, sounds, smells and personal significance of a particular person or place:

> When spirits think of any person, city, or the like, of which they have had an idea derived from their experience in the world, they barely bring up the idea before them, that is, whatever they have heard or seen or conceived of a man, a kingdom, a city, which idea is sometimes simultaneous, sometimes ramified into many [i.e., sometimes successive], and from thence flows their speech and a full perception. Thus also I have often spoken with spirits, namely in their own speech, and they have perceived every thing distinctly, and more things indeed in a moment than could be uttered in an hour. . . .[23]

And, as we have already mentioned, such a direct mode of communication is vastly more efficacious than typical earthly speech, allowing spirits to speak among themselves "with marvelous acuteness and perspicacity, by as many series of reasons following in order . . . . "[24]

At this juncture, it seems correct to briefly describe, not only how spirits speak with each other, but also how spirits generally communicate or speak with men and women on earth. Swedenborg affirms that communication with a person on earth normally entails that the spirit's ideas become translated into the particular earthly language of the person. Such translation is not in any way labored, but is completely spontaneous and instantaneous. This process is so quick, smooth and subtle that an earthly person generally cannot discern, and is almost never aware, that he or she has received communications from spirit-persons. Swedenborg offers his sharp observations on this phenomenon in the following way:

> The speech of spirits with man is in his vernacular, which they speak as readily and skillfully as if they had been born in the same land. . . . They [spirits] know the various meanings of the words [which they take from man's memory], and apply them in a moment, without any premeditation; for the reason that the ideas of their language inflow into no other words than those which are fit . . . almost as when a [earthly] man is speaking, and thinks nothing about the words, but is solely in the meaning of the words; then, according thereto his thought falls readily and spontaneously into words: it is the internal meaning which produces the words. In such an internal meaning, but still more subtle and excellent, consists the speech of spirits; and by this a man, although unaware of the fact, communicates with spirits.[25]

Swedenborg's experiences with communication in the spiritual world were especially dramatic when he had the opportunity to try to grasp the nature of the thought and language of angels.[26] An appropriate prelude to discussing angelic speech is in first discussing the phenomenon of *ineffability,* characterized by Swedenborg in his Opening Quote to this Section. Basically, Swedenborg shares here his consummatory insights on the way in which thought and language function with greater and greater subtlety as one moves from lower to higher realms of the spirit-world. In order to grasp the full meaning of this quote, it is important to remember that Swedenborg has previously explained that Heaven is divided overall into two primary kingdoms, the spiritual and the celestial (and is otherwise divided *regionally* into three heavens). In this quote, Swedenborg, who has already explained to a certain group of spirits that he is dwelling intermediately in both a *natural* state and a *spiritual* state, tells these spirits to perform an experiment by departing from him in his natural state, then entering back into the realm of their spiritual society to think of a specific notion, and finally returning to the natural realm to tell Swedenborg what they have conceived. In this passage, Swedenborg gives remarkable articulation to the reality of the progressive refinement of thought that is operative in the spiritual world— "that spiritual ideas are *super*natural, inexpressible, ineffable and incomprehensible to a natural man," that such spiritual ideas and thoughts can only be grasped as "ideas of ideas and thoughts of thoughts," capable of expressing "qualities of qualities." Likewise, however, we should realize that the most profound interiority of thought, i.e., manifest in "celestial" thought, is a further quantum leap beyond the interiority of "spiritual" thought; that if spiritual wisdom is the "wisdom of wisdom," then celestial wisdom is the wisdom of wisdom of wisdom. Thus, the subtle refinement of thought suggested here (as also Swedenborg alludes to in a different context[27]) might be illustrated in this way: If a natural idea essentially contains 100 spiritual ideas, or spiritual shades of meaning, and each spiritual idea, in its turn, contains 100 celestial shades of meaning, we arrive at the astonishingly exponential realization that, in its deepest essence, a single natural idea may rightfully entail 10,000 celestial shades of meaning, 9,999 of which may well be otherwise ineffable for the natural person.[28] And, because Swedenborg is not content to just note the fact of ineffability, he offers the following further explication of why such ineffability is *necessarily* the case:

> Before we separated we talked about this matter, and I said, "These distinctions come solely from this, that you in the spiritual world are substantial but not material, and substantial things are the beginnings of material things. What is matter but an aggregation of substances? You therefore are in principles and thus in the least particles, while we are in derivatives and compounds; you are in particulars, while we are in generals; and as generals cannot enter into particulars, so neither can natural things, which are material, enter into spiritual things, which are substantial; just as a ship's cable cannot enter or be drawn through the eye of a sewing needle, or a nerve cannot be drawn into one of its fibers of which it is composed. This then is why the natural man cannot think the thoughts of the spiritual man, and therefore cannot utter them.[29]

The foregoing consideration of ineffability is also important because, in pointing up the progressive interiority of speech/language, it clearly suggests that our everyday natural speech is not just a serendipitous artifact of developing human civilization but, rather, is specifically spiritually derived from, and objectively condensed through, this aforementioned hierarchy of levels of interiority. As Swedenborg indicates in this passage, just as speech on the first level externally represents the more interior speech of the second level, so the second-level speech is the outer expression of the third, or inmost level of articulation:

> Thus there are speeches more [and more] interior, in order, but such that one comes forth from another in order, and one is in another in order. The speech of man is known, and also the thought from which this speech is. . . . The speech of the angels of the first heaven, and the thought from which it is, are more interior. . . . The speech and thought of the angels of the second heaven are still more interior. . . . And the speech and

thought of the angels of the third heaven are inmost. . . . And although they are all such speeches that they appear as if different and diverse, still the speech is one, because the one forms the other, and the one is in the other; but that which comes forth in the exterior is representative of the interior.[30]

And, in due course, we are led to the realization of the origins of human speech and language, led to grasp that our everyday speech is ultimately rooted in and founded upon an innermost interiority which is itself the primordial Speech:

That all languages derive their origins from the speech of spirits. Thus the speech of spirits is a universal speech. . . . And thus the speech of angels, which is still more universal, is as it were the mother of the speech of spirits. . . . It follows that there is a still more universal speech, to wit, that of the interior and inmost heaven, which is not intelligible to the angels of the interior [lesser] heaven, still less to spirits and men. . . . And thus the Lord Alone is Speech—*sermo*, and the Word.[31]

In particular, one can clearly sense Swedenborg's fascination throughout his writings with trying to grasp and describe angelic speech. In *Heaven and Hell,* for instance, on the one hand, he explains matter-of-factly that angels talk with each other about practical, political and spiritual matters, just as people do on earth, only more intelligently.[32] On the other hand, however—lest we overexaggerate our commonality with angels and otherwise fail to appreciate just *how* "intelligently" angels communicate—Swedenborg reminds us that "The ideas of a man in respect to those of an angel are like the light of a candle to that of the sun,"[33] and avers that he himself has often been overwhelmed in his exposure to angelic discourse:

As a result, their speech is so full of wisdom that they with a single word can express things that men could not compass in a thousand words. Then, too, their thought-concepts embrace things such as men cannot grasp, let alone verbalize. Consequently, the sounds and sights of heaven are called inexpressible, and such as ear has not heard, nor eye seen.

[2] I have been granted knowledge of this on the basis of experience. On occasion, I have been assigned to the state in which angels were, and in that state have talked with them. At such times I understood everything. But when I was sent back into my earlier state—hence to the natural thinking proper to man—and wanted to recall what I had heard, I could not. For

there were thousands of things that had no equivalent in concepts of natural thought, that were therefore inexpressible *except through shiftings of a heavenly light*—not at all by human words.[34] (Emphasis added)

Thus, angelic speech is so advanced, or refined, that it cannot but appear or be represented, on a lower level, except as "shiftings of heavenly light." Swedenborg repeats this general description of angelic speech in many places throughout his works, differentiating further that the speech of "spiritual" angels often appears as "vibration of light," whereas the speech of "celestial" angels manifests as "variegations of resplendent flame,"[35] in which the primal affectional (i.e., intentional and emotional) dimension of heavenly "heat" is the veritable origin of heavenly light. In addition, angelic speech often "sounds" like "flowing water."[36] Specifically, angelic *ideas* are spontaneously represented as "birds," or sometimes as "bright white clouds," in the intermediate World of Spirits.[37] Lastly, angelic language has written forms in the spiritual world; the alphabet used in the inmost heaven bears some resemblance to written Hebrew, while written works in the lesser heavens employ the same alphabets as those used on earth.[38]

II. Rev. Moon: Spiritual Communication as the Expression of True Love

In now considering the Opening Quote by Rev. Sun Myung Moon, we are afforded the opportunity, not only to understand that language, and thereby communication, take numerous forms in the spirit-world, but also to grasp something about the innermost purpose of communication generally. So that we can better appreciate the significance of these points, it is useful to re-state this Opening Quote:

> Language in the spirit world is versatile; people there communicate with song and dance as well as speech, and you have to answer them in singing and dancing. So for eternity you dance and sing, but you always feel new energy welling up.
> Furthermore, when you dance and sing, the entire universe will join in harmony with you. You will dance together forever with your eternal love.[39]

To address the first point, Rev. Moon affirms that communication in the higher realms of the spirit world takes place, not only through speech, but also through other significant symbolic offerings and receivings. While Rev. Moon mentions here only that singing and dancing serve as other distinct forms of (joyful) language, Swedenborg corroborates the versatility of language in the spiritual world, further exemplifying such in this passage:

> There is also a language that uses the face, trailing off into
> something audible that is altered by concepts. There is also a
> language in which representations of heaven are combined
> with concepts and one formed from concepts presented to
> sight. There is also a language using bodily motions correspon-
> ding to affections, and picturing things similar to those con-
> veyed by words. There is a language by means of shared
> elements of affection and shared elements of thought, there is
> a thundering language, and there are others.[40]

In one sense, we might simply recognize that these abovementioned forms
of language are not unique to the spirit-world but, in fact, also function in
a general communicative sense in human culture on earth, e.g., in various
art-forms like opera, theater, painting, etc. Yet, what is distinctive about these
abovementioned forms of language is that, in the spirit-world, their symbolic
nature translates with absolute precision and clarity into specific universal
meanings.

Finally, in his Opening Quote, Rev. Moon, not unlike Swedenborg, is
pointing to love as the ontological basis of communication. In the higher
realms of the spiritual world, it becomes absolutely evident that God's love,
or true love, as it were, is not only the ground of human happiness, but is
the ground of reality. Because true love is the original power to relate and
unite, such love is also the quintessential communication. In other words,
in a nutshell, the innermost purpose of communication is to participate in
true love, to share true love, to multiply God's love; and since the purpose
of true love itself is to render possible original experience of cosmic joy, we
may further say here that all communication is meant to facilitate loving rela-
tionality as well as loving acquisition of wisdom, both of which in the end
are not different from true joy.

As Rev. Moon points out in this passage, communication borne out of
true love is a sharing of joy, i.e., a reciprocation of singing and dancing. But
in this place we should understand that speech, as well, is an act of love.
Finally, even thought, all thinking, is necessarily an act of love, something
which is always clearly discernible in the heavenly spheres. In the
"Unification Thought" of Rev. Moon, one is reminded that the innermost,
core purpose of thinking (and all wisdom accruable thereby) is to understand
how to love more, i.e., how to love more deeply and more comprehensively.
Thus, again, all human thought, speech and communication, both on earth
and in the spiritual world, have always been meant to be the means of
expressing and sharing God's love, thereby enabling God's eternal sharing
of joy with human beings.

Section 10

question

What is the nature of human sexuality in the spirit-world?

answer

Love for the sex continues with every person as it was inwardly, that is, such as it was in the interior will and thought in the world. All one's love follows one after death, for love is the *esse* of man's life. The ruling love, which is the head of the rest, and subordinate loves along with it, persist with man to eternity. Loves persist because strictly they are of man's spirit, and of the body from the spirit, and after death the human becomes a spirit, and thus takes his love with him. . . . As for sexual love, it is the universal love, having been put by creation in man's very soul, which is his whole essence, and this for the sake of the propagation of the race. This love in particular remains, because a man after death is a man and a woman is a woman, and there is nothing in soul, mind or body, which is not masculine in the male and feminine in the female. The two have been so created, moreover, that they seek after conjunction, yes, to be one; this striving is the love of the sex, which precedes marital love. A conjunctive inclination which has been inscribed on each and all things of man and woman cannot be blotted out and perish with the body.[1]
— Emanuel Swedenborg

Sex was, at least in part, like sleep, a matter of the soul.[2]
— M. Scott Peck

The good man and good woman go forward to God and offer a full bow while receiving resplendent light within a beautiful melody. Within the bright radiance of that light, the husband and wife embrace each other. The appearance of the couple loving is as the world of light becoming one, and is very bright. Within the light, God embraces them and rejoices by radiating love in a stem [stream?] of light.[3]
—Sang Hun Lee

discussion

It is probably true that most people who believe in life beyond death have hardly even wondered if sex continues into the life after death. However, we need to be very clear here that authentic sexual love is indeed a special part of a person's life in the spiritual world. Far from the manifestation of sexuality in hell as the attempt to hurt and destroy others,[4] the realization of sexual union in the heavenly realms is one that includes God and is a consummation of cosmic joy. But before we get too far ahead of ourselves here, perhaps we should first carefully examine what Swedenborg describes in what we would consider to be part of Swedenborg's overall "spiritual anthropology."

Swedenborg goes to some considerable pains, in *Conjugial Love*, to explain that, as love is the essence of a human life, all forms of human loves are preserved in the "essential" life in the spirit-world. Not least of these loves is sexual love. The character of one's sexual desires carries with him or her into life in the spiritual world. Sexual desire, in particular, Swedenborg says, is implanted in the "very soul" of a human being at creation and is structured in accordance with the nature of the absolute genders of masculine and feminine, which have been designed with an aboriginal "conjunctive inclination" to attain oneness. Beyond this initial purpose of attaining oneness, the sexual union has the practical purpose of "the propagation of the race."

What is especially interesting here is Swedenborg's recognition that the sexual impulse, or sexual drive, in human beings is "the universal of all loves," and that sexual desire seems to originate as a desire or an impulse to join with many. He further recognizes that "this striving is the love of the sex which precedes conjugial love" or, that is, that physical sexuality, *per se*, is little more than blind animal instinct, though it manifests first in human development. Sexual love ultimately finds its rightful context or, that is, its truest and fullest realization only in authentic marital love centered upon God—which Swedenborg terms "conjugial love." Swedenborg does a better job in communicating his meaning here:

> Love of the sex is love towards many of the sex and with many;
> but conjugial love is love towards one of the sex and with one.
> Love towards many and with many is a natural love, for man
> has it in common with beasts and birds, and these are natural;
> but conjugial love is a spiritual love and peculiar and proper to
> men, because men were created and are therefore born to
> become spiritual. Therefore, so far as man becomes spiritual,
> he puts off love of the sex and puts on conjugial love. . . . From
> what has now been said, it is evident that love of the sex, being
> a love shared with many and in itself natural, yea, animal, is
> impure and unchaste; and being a roving and unlimited love, is
> scortatory [adulterous]; but it is wholly otherwise with conju-
> gial love. That conjugial love is spiritual and properly human,
> will be clearly evident from what follows.[5]

It is in the context of conjugial love, then, that the two previously mentioned
purposes of attaining oneness and propagating the race have, not just physical reference, but the profound spiritual significance involved in becoming
a fully human human being, i.e., coming to fully resemble God through
true love.

Suffice it to say, however, that sex in the spirit-world *is* considerably
different from sex in the physical world. Swedenborg, in his concern to
make plain these differences, shares a "Memorable Relation" detailing at least
one demonstrative conversation (or perhaps a number of condensed conversations) in which angelic spirits are instructing "novitiates," or newly
arrived spirits, answering their specific questions regarding the nature of spiritual sexuality. In this first passage, the angelic spirits have just explained that
angelic sexuality is "the chaste love of the sex," and is "devoid of all the
allurement of lust," which sexuality to the novitiates seems otherwise dis-
tressingly passionless and pale:

> To this the novitiates said: "If it is love of the sex without
> allurement, what then is love of the sex?" And, thinking of this
> love, they sighed and exclaimed: "Oh, how dry is the joy of
> heaven. What young man can then wish for heaven? Is not
> such a love barren and void of life?"
>
> The angelic spirits, laughing, made answer: "Yet the
> angelic love of the sex, being that love as it is in heaven, is full
> of inmost delights. It is a most pleasing expansion of all things
> of the mind, and thence of all things of the breast; and within
> the breast it is like the heart sporting with the lungs, from
> which sport comes respiration, sound, and speech. These

delights make the companionship between the sexes, that is, between young men and women, to be heavenly sweetness itself, which is pure."[6]

The "chaste love of the sex," Swedenborg explains, affords "delights which are too interior and too rich . . . to be described in words," and is necessarily at the heart of conjugial love. If the conjugial union of husband and wife on earth has notable joys, what about heavenly conjugiality? What might married partners, for instance, expect to experience sexually in the spirit-world?

Hearing this, the three novitiates asked whether there is the same love between married partners in heaven as on earth, and two angelic spirits answered that it is the same in every respect. Then, perceiving that they wished to know whether there were the same ultimate delights there, they said, "They are the same in every respect, but far more blessed, inasmuch as angelic perception and sensation is far more exquisite than human perception and sensation."[7]

Married love on earth often produces children. But what does conjugial love in the spirit world produce? —

The novitiates then asked whether offspring are born from the ultimate delights of that love; and, if offspring are not born, of what use are those delights? The angelic spirits replied that there are no natural offspring but spiritual offspring.

The novitiates then asked, "What are spiritual offspring?" They answered: "By means of ultimate delights, married partners become more united in the marriage of good and truth, and the marriage of good and truth is the marriage of love and wisdom. It is love and wisdom that are the offspring born of that marriage; and because both are spiritual, therefore no other offspring than spiritual offspring can be conceived and born there."[8]

In other words, and in summary, Swedenborg affirms that while married sexuality in the spirit-world is similar to married sexuality on earth, it is also different in two major ways. First, such incorporeal sexuality can achieve a profoundly more total, sensitive and ecstatic union of husband and wife, masculine and feminine, love and wisdom, than is normally possible through corporeal sexuality. Second, which in a way restates the first point, while earthly intercourse can produce other human beings, i.e., children, spiritual sexuality can result only in spiritual offspring, i.e., the deeper union of love and wisdom in both husband and wife (which Swedenborg also otherwise characterizes in part as "the most pleasing expansion of all things of the breast; . . . it is like the heart sporting with the lungs, from which sport comes respiration, sound and speech").

If we now jump forward 200 years into the present, we discover the contemporary out-of-body researcher, Robert Monroe, attempting to describe incorporeal sexuality in plausible scientific terms appropriate to the twentieth century, but which also, in at least one way, echo Swedenborg's descriptions of conjugial love in the spirit-world. In *Journeys Out of the Body*, Monroe proffers his observations on "Second State" sexuality in this way:

> First and most obvious, there is no evidence of the male-female interpenetration. Attempts to express the need in such a functional manner become pathetic in retrospect. One discovers in frustration that it just doesn't happen that way in the Second State. Next, sensuality produced by the physical form of the sex counterpart is entirely absent. There is no distinct pattern of physical shape, either visually or by touch.

> How, then? What then? The analogy of the opposite magnetic poles stills holds. There is an acute awareness of "difference," which is like radiation (as it may well be) from the sun, or a fire as felt by one shivering with cold. It is dynamically attractive and needed. This attraction varies in intensity with the individual. (Define what makes one person more sexually attractive than another; it is more than physical proportions.) It can be like magnetic lines of flux.

> The "act" itself is not an act at all, but an immobile, rigid state of shock where the two truly intermingle, not just at a surface level and at one or two specific body parts, but in full dimension, atom for atom, throughout the entire Second Body. There is a short, sustained electron (?) flow one to another. The moment reaches unbearable ecstasy, and then tranquility, equalization, and it is over.[9]

In contrasting Monroe with Swedenborg, it is clear that there are more differences between them than similarities. One of the first things to remember in considering this passage is that, unlike Swedenborg, Monroe is definitely *not* describing a form of exalted conjugal love. Rather, out of his own honest, though limited, out-of-body experience, Monroe is attempting to detail certain rudiments of heterosexual sexual engagement and then to conjecture regarding the nature of the resultant union of spirit-persons. Further, Swedenborg would decisively reject as incorrect Monroe's contention that spiritual sexuality does not involve male-female interpenetration; for Swedenborg, the earthly act of marital intercourse is explicitly paralleled in the spirit-world in conjugial love. But, *similar* to Swedenborg, Monroe is concerned to recognize that the profound sexual union that is possible through the absolute intermingling of spiritual bodies in the spirit-world is something that is far beyond the union typically achievable through sexual intercourse on earth. Specifically addressing this phenomenon, Monroe (platonically) suggests that physical sexuality is but a shadow of our primordial spiritual predisposition toward unification:

> The sexual action-reaction in the physical seems but a pale imitation or a feeble attempt to duplicate a very intimate Second State form of communion and communication which is not at all "sexual" as we understand the term. In the physical drive for sexual union, it is as if we are somehow remembering dimly the emotional peak that occurs among people in the Second State, and translating it into the sexual act.[10]

Monroe, it seems to us, makes several fruitful suggestions in the two above-quoted passages that may also yield some clarification of what Swedenborg describes in more philosophical/poetic stance. First, Monroe observes that heterosexual sexuality in the spirit-world takes the form of a kind of cosmic magnetic attraction into deep communion, characterized by "unbearable ecstasy." Swedenborg, for instance, also seems to be describing ecstatic spiritual communion when he explains that the "ultimate delights" of conjugial love result in the progressively deeper union of good and truth, and love and wisdom. Further, Monroe asserts that the experience of *sensuality*, usually evoked on earth by sight and touch of physical bodies, plays no part in spiritual sexuality. That is to say, sensuality as such belongs to the context of corporeal sexuality. This seems to be a restatement of Swedenborg's notion of "the chaste love of the sex" which lacks all "allurement of lust." Finally, Monroe's recognition that the sexual act is neither "sexual" nor an "act," in the last analysis, but is instead a kind of ecstatic intermingling of spiritual selves, bears some meaningful resemblance to the forthcoming description of spiritual conjugal union as transcendent "resplendence" by Dr. Sang Hun Lee.

What both Swedenborg and Monroe describe above has been fashionably translated into layman's terms by psychotherapist and popular writer, M. Scott Peck, who proposes that "Sex [is], at least in part, . . . a matter of the soul." Peck undoubtedly stated the point in this way out of deference to the sense that sex seems also to have a lot to do with the physical body. Yet, we would affirm that even a stronger statement than this is in order if we are to grasp the true wellsprings of human sexuality:

> Sexuality starts and ends in the soul. It is an illusion—an understandable one—that sexuality starts and ends in the body.[11]

This statement, I think, brings us closer to the truth. First, we should acknowledge that Swedenborg would probably not agree with this statement inasmuch as he describes initial "love of the sex" as a "natural" and purely instinctive impulse. Such an impulse only stops being "animal," and becomes "properly human," when consummated in the context of conjugial love. Second, we can agree that conjugial love, as defined by Swedenborg as necessarily spiritual, affords human beings the opportunity to discover their divine birthright as inherently spiritual beings. Yet, it is otherwise not so easy to understand that, if sexuality is planted so deeply in the human soul at creation, why it *initially* manifests in human development as only an "animal" or, that is, as a *non-human* impulse, and on this basis, why it then manifests as originally *unprincipled,* i.e., as "scortatory" or naturally adulterous. Rather, it seems to us that we are better served here to consider that sexuality and sexual desire, as originally in God, originate as perfectly ordered and balanced; that human sexual desire began as a perfectly ordered spiritual impulse which, as the result of a cosmically disordering event—the Fall—became reduced to the raw, violent, anti-spiritual instinctuality that it often appears to be in contemporary culture. From this standpoint, which is not only Augustinian in its thrust but is also theologically Unificationist, we would especially endorse the notion that sexuality, as an inherently spiritual impulse, does indeed "start and end in the soul," notwithstanding its transitory, though critical, intermediation through the physical body.

If Swedenborg offers us a vision of conjugial love via angelic sexuality, and Monroe "scientifically" conjectures an otherdimensional sexuality climaxed in "magnetic" communion, deceased Unificationist Dr. Sang Hun Lee channels to us, via psychic medium, remarkable images of liberated conjugal ecstasy in the heavenly realms—returning us to a Swedenborg-like perspective. In this passage, Dr. Lee describes the quality of the conjugal love of husband and wife who, always following God's heart, have lived and loved with pure hearts; such love achieves in its sublime union a state of being undreamt of on earth:

> Conjugal love is the love where men and women are connected physically. On earth, we can feel emotion when our bodies meet and love. But in heaven, a man and woman without bodies can love. The conjugal love between those high spirits (those who are close to God) is like a beautiful picture. Since the bodies of the two become totally one when they love, they can feel a strong emotion through their bodies and minds which goes beyond the feeling of love they felt on Earth. It is like creating a higher existence from the state of a complete absence of ego. It is like feeling you are in a magical world.
>
> Also, you can actually view the scene of making love with

your own eyes. Couples on Earth make love in their bedrooms most of the time. Here, in heaven, that is absolutely not the case. It is not a hidden love, which you can only perform in your bedroom. In heaven, you might love among wild flowers in a field, a beautiful land or on an ocean wave. You can even love in the mountains where the birds are singing and the scene is so beautiful that those who watch you become intoxicated. Rather than feeling shame or disgrace as you felt on earth, you can observe the scene with a peaceful mind, admiring the beauty.[12]

If we can grasp that the act of sexual union originates in God, as the most universal, i.e., *public* being of all, then the foregoing passage suggests that the final human realization of sexual union in the spirit-world should rightfully stand as an edifying, intoxicating public spectacle of Divine Joy. Needless to say, this idea probably seems contrary to conventional wisdom, but human beings, being what they are presently, do not understand that they are *inherently* spiritual beings and consequently that their futures hold unimaginable possibilities for growing to more completely resemble God.

Finally, in his graphic style, Dr. Lee describes that the conjugal love of husband and wife in heaven is really their union with God and, as such, is manifested as brilliantly radiant Light dancing to mellifluous harmonies:

The good man and good woman go forward to God and offer a full bow while receiving resplendent light within a beautiful melody. Within the bright radiance of that light, the husband and wife embrace each other. The appearance of the couple loving is as the world of light becoming one, and is very bright. Within the light, God embraces them and rejoices by radiating love in a stem [stream] of light.[13]

Thus, in overall consideration, we would side with those who believe that original love-making belongs to God, and that it then becomes God's precious gift to human beings. Such a gift has eternal significance, affording earthly immortality to endless generations of ancestors and their descendants, as well as the unending spiritual regeneration entailed in more and more completely fulfilling that Union who is God.

Section 11

What other beings, besides human beings, live in the spiritual world?

Now, God produces the creature by His intellect and will. Hence the perfection of the universe requires that there should be intellectual creatures. Now intelligence cannot be the action of a body, nor of any corporeal power, for every body is limited to here and now. Hence the perfection of the universe requires the existence of an incorporeal creature. . . . Incorporeal substances rank between God and corporeal creatures. Now the medium compared to one extreme appears to be the other extreme, as what is tepid compared to heat seems to be cold; and thus it is said that the angels, compared to God, are material and corporeal, not, however, as if anything corporeal existed in them.[1]

—St. Thomas Aquinas

The angels, archangels, and spirits of the age in our spiritual environment have put forth from themselves certain beings who descend . . . into the kingdoms of nature; [these] nature spirits are detached from the beings of the third hierarchy whom we have learned to know today. They are offspring, and to them has been allotted other service to humankind, namely, service to nature.[2]

—Rudolf Steiner

The UFO occupants, like the elves of old, are not extra-terrestrials. They are denizens of another reality. . . .

To put it bluntly, the UFO phenomenon does not give evidence of being extraterrestrial at all. Instead it appears to be interdimensional and to manipulate physical realities outside of our space-time continuum.[3]

—Jacques Vallee

If you love animals, you will have them in the spirit world. Your love toward Sheba [Questioner's dog] will be reflected to the spirit world, and it will be created there as Sheba for yourself. It will be a reflection of your attachment. It will not be Sheba herself, but a reflection of your mind. But it will still please you.[4]

—Sun Myung Moon

discussion

In presenting the following discussion, we address four spiritual topics of great popular interest and heated speculation upon our entrance into the twenty-first century. The first three topics or areas of discussion are: the nature of angels; the ontological character of mythological creatures like gnomes and sylphs; and the contemporary enigma of the UFO beings reported in thousands of sightings and encounters, especially in the second half of the twentieth century. These three topics, we shall discover, are rather closely interrelated in the last analysis. The fourth area of discussion concerns the way in which animals continue to exist after death in the spirit-world. Do animals have spirits in the same way as human beings? Many modern-day psychics and mediums popularly contend that this is the case. Yet, this is not accurate—the truth being more subtle and more profound. Needless to say, each of the aforementioned four topics could easily become a book in itself; but our hope here is that even a severely abbreviated treatment will serve to emphasize a macrocosmic perspective and a unified understanding of these four areas.

I.   Angels and the Angelic World

A.   General Introduction

Traditionally, angels are glorious, incorporeal, spiritual creatures, resembling human beings in appearance, created by the God of Abraham, Isaac and Jacob as a multitudinous Heavenly Host, whose mission it is both to glorify and serve God as well as to inspire and protect human beings. How do we know about the existence of angels, especially since they are naturally invisible to almost all human beings? Well, it turns out that over the past 6,000 Biblical years—according to the testimony of Jews, Christians and Moslems—angels have seemingly transformed themselves (or have been transformed by God) to enable numerous everyday, average persons to consciously see and hear them. Consider, for instance, the Biblical event in Judges 13:3-25, where an angel appears to Manoah's wife and then to Manoah, without either of them at first knowing that he is an angel, and thereby gives prenatal diet instructions to Manoah's wife to follow so that her prospective son, Samson, may be born to become a great deliverer of his people. This, then, is our earliest and foremost means of knowing about the angels. But there is a second, very important way in which the angels have become known to human civilization. This is through the descriptions of those rare human beings who have been able to view the angelic world *clairvoyantly.* That is to say, in contrast to the angels *making themselves visible,* clairvoyant visionaries, through the use of their own awakened spiritual senses, have been able to subjectively penetrate into and discern various aspects of angelic life. Thus, it is the project of this subsection first to consider the more traditional testimonies about angels. Second, after presenting the foundational angelology of Christian mystical thinker/theologian, Dionysius the Pseudo-Areopagite, we move to consider some of the profound descriptions of angels given by two notable clairvoyants in the history of Western civilization—Emanuel Swedenborg and Rudolph Steiner. This subsection is organized into two parts. The first part is somewhat introductory and is organized in terms of seven major questions and answers, which seek to provide general and historical background on the nature of angels. The second part is devoted to brief yet substantial explorations into the angelologies of Dionysius the Pseudo-Areopagite and the two above-mentioned clairvoyants.

Angels have been a subject of insatiable curiosity, never failing to capture our imagination. Why should this be? We would suggest that such widespread preoccupation with angels arises out of the fact that most human beings are instinctively or intuitively aware that they are, in their original nature, spiritual beings and, as such, that they have a natural kinship of sorts with other inherently spiritual beings—like angels. Many people worldwide, perhaps most people, feel that they have guardian angels, not unlike those featured on the very popular TV series, *Touched By An Angel.* Theologian Matthew Fox has commented that, at his public lectures, a stunning 60% to 80% of his audiences claim to have sensed or experienced angels.[5] Even random surveys of groups of Americans suggest that a third of the population has felt the presence of an angel at some time in their lives.

Angels, however, remain elusive creatures—thereby calling for elucidation. Thus, what follows is a series of brief questions and answers, set forth to provide a general description of angels.

1.   What are angels?

Again, in a nutshell, angels are usually highly intelligent, non-physical, non-human beings who, however, resemble human beings in appearance. And let us be clear from the outset: *angels do not have wings,* though they have been characterized as such in traditional religious scriptures and though they have been portrayed that way down through the history of religious art in order to emphasize their celestial bearing. Whereas Zoroastrianism, Hinduism and Buddhism make some reference to angelic beings, the angels we will specifically address here are those created by the God of Abraham, Isaac and Jacob and who are otherwise recorded in Hebrew, Christian and Islamic scriptures, with primary emphasis on Hebrew and Christian sources.

Angels, then, are created by God with the purpose of worshiping, glorifying and serving God, as well as having the responsibility to serve as messengers to, and caretakers for, the human race. These primary angelic missions are especially evident throughout the Bible. For example, two angels visiting Sodom are invited to supper by Lot, whereby they inform him that, because they are about to destroy Sodom, Lot should gather up his family and flee the city (Gen. 19:1-26). Consider also the story of Balaam's ass: God sends an angel to block Balaam's path; at first, only the donkey can see the sword-wielding angel and acts evasively to carry Balaam out of harm's way. But Balaam, who cannot initially see the angel, strikes his apparently obstinate and wayward donkey three times. God then speaks through the donkey's mouth to help Balaam realize that his abuse of the donkey is really quite unfair—at which point Balaam's eyes are opened so he also can see the angel, who informs him that the donkey has, in fact, saved Balaam's life (Numbers 22:22-35). And who can forget the description of the angel Gabriel announcing Mary's conception of Jesus (Luke 1:31). Finally, there is the sublime vision of multitudes of angels praising and worshiping God (Rev. 5:11-12, 7:11-12).

2.   What is the nature of angels?

This, of course, is a perennially intriguing question. In Genesis 6:2, the Bible refers to angels as "sons of God." But it should be pointed out here that the way in which angels are children of God is very different from the way in which human beings are God's children. While angels are understood to be glorious creatures, close to God, and are often imaged as standing on high above human beings, this is only accurate from the standpoint of realizing that human beings suffered a "fall" away from God. From an original, unfallen standpoint, God created human beings, in accord with His direct and complete image, with the cosmic potential to love as God loves, i.e., to grow to become like God—and, in this way, to fully resemble God as the authentic sons and daughters of God. Angels, on the other hand, were originally designed and birthed by God to function as helpers and servants, created in accord with an *indirect*, or symbolic, image of God. Thus, angels were created with a lesser potential to comprehend and to carry the heart of God, and to express God's love, than human beings, who were meant to grow up and actually be able to love as God loves. This pivotal distinction between angels and human beings is expressed by St. Paul in other terms: "Do you not know that we are to judge the angels?" (I Cor. 6:3). This insight, that human beings originally and rightfully stand above angels, is furthermore offered up from yet a different perspective by the renowned Indian spiritual teacher, Paramahansa Yogananda: "The man form is higher than the angel form; of all forms it is the highest. Man is the highest being in all creation, because he aspires to freedom."[6]

3.   Where do the angels live?

This is a query about the original home of the angels. As such, there are two distinctive ways of answering this question which may, in the last analysis, be the same answer. The first answer is that the angels originally reside in Heaven, or in the heavenly realms of the spiritual world. This is the traditional and, in itself, unproblematic, way of describing the home of the angels, and this is the description we will develop in our consideration of the angelologies of Dionysius, Swedenborg and Rudolf Steiner. There is, however, a second and rather intriguing description possible here. Emanuel Swedenborg (in his work, *Earths in the Universe*) as well as many contemporary psychics, mediums and near-death experiencers have alluded to the reality that spirits and angels *live on the stars.*

But this description is undoubtedly more complex than it sounds. In what sense, or in what way, do spirits and angels live on the stars? For instance, this author, back in the early 1980s, once attended a late night prayer vigil at a special Holy Ground near the Tarrytown, N.Y. family residence of Rev. Sun Myung Moon. On this occasion, before the prayer vigil began, Rev. Moon spoke briefly about God's love and the creation of the universe and, gazing up at the starry heavens, he concluded with the enigmatic assertion: "You know, the angels live on the stars." Interestingly, in the same spirit, *The Urantia Book* (a 2,100-page collection of papers allegedly composed by an angel) claims that vast angelic kingdoms originated in remote parts (i.e., distant galaxies and stars) of our physical universe. But, we are left asking: What do incorporeal creatures like angels have to do with corporeal stars? In what sense do spiritual beings dwell on physical stars? It turns out here, again, that we can offer two slightly different, tantalizing answers to *this* question, which may, in fact, again describe the same reality. Swedenborg, for instance, describes that spirits of different characters in the spirit-world gravitate to dwell in the spiritual space, corresponding to the physical space, that surrounds different physical planets in our own solar system (e.g., like Mercury, Venus, Mars, etc.), or that surrounds planets (stars?) in other parts of our galaxy, or in other galaxies.[7] On the other hand, Paramahansa Yogananda and numerous others record descriptions of an astral or spiritual cosmos teeming with *astral planets,* each of which is peopled with spirits of a particular degree of spiritual development. Along these same lines, Rev. Moon in 1965 answered the following questions:

Q: What about other planets? Do spirits live there?

A: Yes, spirits or angels.

Q: What realm would that be? Like ours, or a realm where relatively higher spirits reside?

A: Spirits of a different stage or degree will group by themselves and dwell there. Spirits on some stars may be higher than those on other planes.
    They look like they are floating everywhere, but they are all related to one center—God. Just as your heart or mind is at one place, and yet is free to go everywhere.[8]

Especially in light of the discussion presented in the earlier Section of this book regarding the situatedness of the spirit-world, we would re-state here what seems to be the most reasonable and plausible perspective: That there is a spiritual cosmos existing as a parallel dimensionality to the physical cosmos, and that there exist many incorporeal, yet substantial, stars upon which angels (and other spirits) dwell.

4. How many angels are there?

Unlike being able to provide a relatively accurate estimate of the earth's population in the year 2000, it is quite another story to consider estimating the population of all those presently in the spirit-world who have died throughout the history of all of earth's civilizations. Perhaps even more remote is our ability to imagine the population of angels, originally and forever incorporeal beings, who reside in the spiritual world. However, consulting Rev. 5:11, we are assured that there are at least *millions* of angels:

> Then I looked, and I heard the voice of many angels around
> the throne, the living creatures, and the elders; and the number
> of them was ten thousand times ten thousand, and thousands
> of thousands. . . . (NKJV)

John Milton very likely had this Biblical passage in mind when he wrote in Book IV of *Paradise Lost:* "Millions of creatures walk the earth unseen, both when we wake and when we sleep." The Medieval Age was the last period in the history of Western civilization when anyone seriously tried to speculate about the number of existing angels. Matthew Bunson shares a delightful and light-hearted description of this era:

> An aspect of the medieval fascination with the angels, this
> speculation included the idea that each of the nine choirs pos-
> sesses 6,666 members. This would give each choir 44,435,556
> angels; the entire heavenly host would boast an enormous
> body of 399,920,004 angels—give or take a few princes, stan-
> dard-bearers, and potential angels on probation or in training,
> if one wants to include Clarence Oddbody before he won his
> wings in the classic film *It's a Wonderful Life* (1946).[9]

Of course, if one accounts for the third of the angels that eventually followed Satan into the nether realms, that would leave only 266,613,336 angels remaining in heaven. So much for the putative mathematical definition of the Heavenly Host!

5. What do angels do? What are their missions?

Traditionally, as we have already mentioned, angels carry messages from God to human beings and otherwise function as intermediaries who serve God or, that is, who carry out God's instructions with regard to the universe, and with special regard to the human race. In particular, Judaism, Christianity and Islam all accept the idea of "guardian" angels, or "tutelary" angels. From the earliest times, Jewish belief held that every human being is assigned at least one guardian angel at birth who cares for and protects that person. Interestingly, the Talmud extravagantly avers that every person is attended by *11,000* ministering angels.[10]

Christians are confident that every child is protected by guardian angels, primarily due to Jesus' testimony in Mt. 18:10: "See that you do not despise one of these little ones; for I tell you that in heaven their angels always behold the face of my Father who is in heaven." St. Thomas Aquinas, foremost and renowned theologian of the Catholic Church, offered the edification that all humans, whether they are aware of it or not, have guardian angels who stay with them throughout their lives. Such angels do their best to encourage each soul toward goodness and God while, if they have lived sinfully, guiding them toward repentance. Yet, as Aquinas and numerous others affirm, angels cannot override any person's individual will or choice; rather, according to spiritual law, angels must guide via gentle suggestion and unobtrusive persuasion.[11] In addition, Emanuel Swedenborg knew firsthand that, without angelic support, human beings would be seriously liable to the intrusions of evil spirits: "Angels from the Lord lead and protect us every moment."[12]

Muslims as well cherish belief in guardian angels. Islam offers the teaching that the *hafaza* are not only angelic documenters, recording all deeds of each human being, but they also function as guardian angels. Two pairs of these angels stand by each earthly person in order to protect him or her from evil spirits.

"Tutelary" angels not only serve as guardians for each person, but particular angels also stand as "ethnarchs" who are assigned stewardship over the various nations of the earth. The ancient Jews, for instance, regarded the archangel Michael as the protecting angel of Israel, while recognizing Duma (or Rahab) as the angel of Egypt, Dubbiel as the angel of Persia and Samael as the angel of Rome.[13] Altogether, Jewish legend held there were 70 ethnarchs whose stewardship sometimes promoted the conflicting interests of their various nations. The history of Christianity has also endorsed the recognition of tutelary angels for nations, cities, churches and particular (holy) geographic locations. As Bunson notes, the English clairvoyant poet and artist, William Blake, once illustrated in his works the angel of the United States.

And, while *guardian angels* may rightfully be said to care only for human beings proper, it is interesting to note that, historically, angels are often understood to have missions as *patron angels*—angels who are entrusted with the responsibility of governing particular attributes or things, like patience or poetry, or of presiding over particular events, like war. Some examples of patron angels variously acknowledged in Judaism and/or Christianity are the following: Af (anger), Arael (birds), Raphael (compassion; knowledge; progress), Yroul (fear), Rashiel (earthquakes), Mumiel (health), Raphiel or Theliel (love), Achariah (patience), Radwerial (poetry),

Phanuel (penance), Matariel (rain) and Michael or Gabriel (war).[14] Again, Jewish lore mentions that every blade of grass has its own angel to nurture it to fruition. Needless to say, this assertion would suggest the total number of angels would be well beyond the millions mentioned earlier. But St. Augustine, in his *Eight Questions,* appears to second this truth: "Every visible thing in this world is put in charge of an angel."

In general, then, the task of guardian angels is to inspire and protect us. If that is true, however, why is it that our angels almost never present themselves to us, so that we can see them and address them? In fact, one discovers that guardian angels *do* reveal themselves, but only in extremely critical moments, usually when we *absolutely need to be assured* of their support. As Pierre Jovanovich expresses it:

> The guardian Angel's task is above all to guide us, to help us benefit from our existence on earth and not fear living. Of course the Angel will never put a coin in the parking meter if you have no change; But to go on from that to say that with the Angels, Life is rosy, kind, sweet, sugary, and full of flowers with birds singing in the fields—sweet chariot—is utterly false, enormously false, and makes Life and the Angels seem what they are not, a candy bar—but in 99 percent of cases they reveal themselves at a time of blood, tears and despair, since we have seen that guardian Angels only materialize fully when:
> 1) we are in an accident, or at the end of our rope
> 2) we die with a round-trip ticket (NDE [Near-Death Experience])
> 3) we die with a one way ticket (Deathbed Visions).[15]

While the foregoing descriptions give us the mainstream traditional conception of guardian angels, we must note that there is a second, and also very prominent, notion of guardian angels. This is the conception of tutelary angels who *became* angels only after having lived as human beings with physical bodies on earth. Swedenborg, Mormon prophet Joseph Smith and most contemporary psychic mediums subscribe to this understanding of guardian angels. For Swedenborg, whose notion of angels generally is non-traditional, there are no angels *at all* who did not first live as human beings on earth. He reiterates this somewhat curious notion in many places throughout his writings. Prophet Joseph Smith, President Brigham Young and Mormonism generally, have the view that all the angels guiding human beings *on earth* were once themselves human beings who lived on earth. Mormon *President* Joseph F. Smith (a different person from *Prophet* Joseph Smith) offers this description of guardian angels:

. . . We are told by the Prophet Joseph Smith that "there are no angels *who minister to the earth* but those who do belong or have belonged to it." Hence, when messengers are sent to minister to the inhabitants of this earth, they are not strangers, but from the ranks of our kindred, friends, and fellow-beings and fellow servants. . . . In like manner our fathers and mothers, brothers, sisters and friends who have passed away from this earth, having been faithful, and worthy to enjoy these rights and privileges, may have a mission given to them to visit their relatives and friends upon the earth, bringing from the divine Presence messages of love, of warning, of reproof and instruction to those whom they had learned to love in the flesh. . . .[16] (Emphasis added)

What is further interesting about this otherwise seemingly "humanistic" conception of guardian angels is that it corresponds exactly to the notion of "spirit guides" described by most psychic mediums, e.g., Anthony Borgia, Sylvia Browne and George Anderson. Borgia, who nowhere mentions angels per se in his channeled writings, describes the "guardian angel" mission of spirit-guides:

The principal guide is chosen for each individual on the earth plane in conformity with a fixed plan. Most guides are temperamentally similar to their charges in the latter's finer natures, but what is most important the guides understand and are in sympathy with their charges' failings. Many of them, indeed, had the same failings when they were incarnate, and among other useful services they try to help their charges overcome these failings and weaknesses.[17]

Contemporary psychic medium, George Anderson, in his recent book, *Lessons from the Light* (2000), describes a personal (psychic) reading done for a woman who was deeply in love with her 47-year-old husband, the victim of a sudden and unexpected massive heart attack. In the reading, her beloved deceased communicated to her that he was indeed watching over her as a guardian angel.[18] Sylvia Browne, another well-known psychic medium who does recognize the existence of angelic beings who have never been physically embodied, also acknowledges that almost all of the spiritual support we receive on earth comes through our spirit-guides who *were* once physically embodied persons. In particular, Sylvia's own spirit-guide, Francine, describes what seem otherwise to be traditionally angelic responsibilities:

The spirit guide's purpose is to research, suggest, nudge, and encourage the person whom he or she may be guiding through life. In most cases, the guides operate in the individual's subconscious, appearing as the "voice of conscience." They will illustrate lessons and speak of what the individual is here to learn, but they never interfere with choices. They are extremely careful never to preclude the opportunity for a person to learn a life lesson. If the subject is headed toward an event that will teach a valuable but difficult lesson, a spirit guide may point out an alternative route. The decision remains with the individual; if that choice involves pain and struggle, the guide won't prevent it.

. . . [S]pirit guides may use a variety of methods to communicate. They convey knowledge through dreams, or as a flash in the mind's eye, even occasionally as a voice. It's a frustrating task . . . because few people take time to really listen.[19]

Finally, in consideration of the foregoing, we should ask: Is it really the case that all angels and/or guardian angels were once human beings? Our opinion is that this is far too simplistic; rather, we consider the truth in this matter to be that there exist *both* never-incarnated angels who serve as guardian angels, *as well as* once-incarnated but now deceased human beings who often serve as spirit-guides for people on earth.

6. How do angels communicate? In what language do they speak?

In answer to the first question here, we would offer that angels communicate with us in a variety of ways. They *can* appear and speak to us personally, either in language or other symbolic presentations, while we are fully conscious—though, as mentioned earlier, this apparently doesn't happen very often. Otherwise, it seems to be the case that, most often, angels do not appear to us, but speak to us through both our conscious and subconscious thoughts. If angels communicate with us subconsciously and/or in our dreams, their communication is most often in the form of a series of symbols which we then have to be responsible to interpret. Even Swedenborg, in mediumistic trance, sometimes encountered higher-order angels who communicated via streams of complexly-layered symbols—communications which Swedenborg admits he often could not fully understand but could only marvel at.[20]

Less personally, angels may choose to speak to us through other people who either directly or indirectly communicate angelic messages. This possibility includes both the situations where the "other people" may be just other human beings, e.g., like family, friends or strangers, as well as the situation where these others are actually angels disguised as human beings—memorably alluded to by St. Paul: "Do not neglect to show hospitality to strangers, for thereby, some have entertained angels unawares." (Hebrews 13:2) Beyond this, angels may choose, when appropriate, a more direct method of delivering a message via guiding us through certain kinds of life experiences.

But, when in the past angels have spoken in a particular conventional language, it was often believed by religious scholars that this was *the* language of the angels. For instance, Bunson humorously recognizes that, up until the Middle Ages, Jewish angelologists held that the angels spoke only in Hebrew; Christian theologians, until Aquinas, authoritatively insisted that angels spoke only Latin; and Islamic lore taught that the angels communicated exclusively in Arabic.[21] St. Thomas Aquinas, however, in his medieval "Treatise on the Angels" (*Summa Theologica* (1267-1273)) brought common sense to bear upon the issue by propounding that angels communicated with humans through a mental process called "illumination"—a notion very similar to the contemporary notion of telepathy. A few hundred years later, Swedenborg corroborated Aquinas' description, noting that through an angel's indwelling of a particular human mind, it could immediately assume and speak in the language of that person. (Swedenborg, through personal experience, offered extraordinary insights in his writings on this subject, many of which are discussed in detail in Section 9 of this book.)

7. Some unusual but important references to angels

Angels are powerful, extraordinary and otherwise strange creatures. We can sense this even from the relatively few descriptions of them in Hebrew and Christian sources. In Hebrew, Christian and Islamic lore, many stories and legends about the angels have been elaborated, and we delight in sharing a few of these with the reader. The first four legends are drawn from non-canonical sources, while the remainder of the angelic references here are found in the Bible, i.e., in the canon of the Old and New Testaments.

Azrael, for instance, is recognized as the angel of death and as residing in the Third Heaven, according to Hebrew and Islamic lore. In Muslim teaching, Azrael has 4,000 wings, 20,000 feet and possesses exactly as many eyes and tongues as there are people in the world.[22] It is believed that every time Azrael blinks an eye, it means that another person on earth has died. In ancient Persian lore, Azrael acquired his mission as the angel of death as a result of meeting a challenge several other illustrious angels had failed in. God had commanded Michael, Gabriel and Israfel to travel to earth and bring back seven handfuls of dirt which He needed in order to create Adam. But the earth, insisting that mankind should not be created because such a species would only bring sorrow to God, refused to yield up the dirt. God then chose Azrael who, because he was successful in gaining the seven handfuls of soil, was entrusted by God with the mission of separating the human soul from the body at the moment of death. As Gustave Davidson quotes, in Arabic tradition Azrael is "forever writing in a large book and forever erasing what he writes; what he writes is the birth of a man, what he erases is the name of the man at death."[23]

The angel Penemu is mentioned in the pseudepigraphal First Book of Enoch (69h-o) as a fallen angel who had committed the crime of teaching humanity certain guarded secrets of wisdom. His worst transgression was having taught humanity the use of ink and paper for writing, since "on account of this matter, there are many who have erred from eternity, until this very day. For humans are not created for such purposes to take up their beliefs with pen and ink." 1 Enoch goes on to declare that by exercising this literary ability to progressively document their "knowledge," human beings are continually subject to "death."

In pseudepigraphal 3 Enoch, many lesser and greater, but entirely glorious, angelic princes are referred to by name. For instance, Simsiel is the angel in charge of the day and Laliel is in charge of the night; there are greater angelic princes in charge of the seven heavens—Michael, who oversees the seventh and highest heaven, Gabriel (sixth heaven), Satquiel (fifth heaven), Sahaquiel (fourth heaven), Baradiel (third heaven), Baraquiel (second heaven) and Sidriel (first heaven); and among the greatest angelic princes is Hayliel YHWH, "a prince noble and terrible, . . . a prince who is able to swallow the whole world at one gulp."[24]

However, 3 Enoch is primarily devoted to describing the extraordinary being of the angel *Metatron* (also called Metaetron, Metaraon, Merraton, Mittron, etc.), perhaps the greatest of all the angels—in Jewish lore, oftentimes considered as standing above even Michael, Gabriel and Uriel. He is variously known as the King of the Angels, prince of the divine face, chancellor of heaven, chief of the ministering angels, and the lesser YHWH (or tetragrammaton, which is the name of God).[25]

Metatron was once the mortal being, Enoch, spoken of in the Book of Genesis. According to ancient Jewish lore, Enoch earned profound merit in God's eyes as a scribe and, as a result, he was carried off the earth and transported to heaven: "Enoch walked with God; and he was not for God took him." (Genesis 5:24) After being given a tour of the creation, Enoch was chosen by God for the honor of being transformed into an exceptionally glorious angel, and thereafter called "Metatron." 3 Enoch purports to quote the testimony of Rabbi Ishmael who, in turn, conveys the direct testimony of Metatron regarding his own angelic metamorphosis, a spiritual transmogrification numerically rendered:

> Before the Holy One [God], blessed be he, set me to serve the throne of glory, he opened for me 300,000 gates of understanding, 300,000 gates of prudence, 300,000 gates of life, 300,000 gates of grace and favor, 300,000 gates of love, 300,000 gates of Torah, 300,000 gates of humility, 300,000 gates of sustenance, 300,000 gates of mercy, 300,000 gates of reverence.
>
> . . . In addition to all these qualities, the Holy One, blessed be he, laid his hand on me and blessed me with 1,365,000 blessings. I was enlarged and increased in size till I matched the world in length and breadth. He made to grow on me 72 wings, 36 on one side and 36 on the other, and each single wing covered the entire world. He fixed in me 365,000 eyes and each eye was like the Great Light. There was no splendor, brilliance, brightness or beauty in the luminaries of the world that he failed to fix in me.
>
> . . . All the mysteries of the world and all the orders of nature stand revealed before me as they stand revealed before the Creator. From that time onward I looked and beheld deep secrets and wonderful mysteries. Before a man thinks in secret, I see his thought; before he acts, I see his act. There is nothing in heaven above or deep within the earth concealed from me.[26]

God then placed Metatron at the entrance to the seventh heaven, making his presence all the more formidable by transforming him into a living flame. Metatron is accounted one of the tallest angels in heaven. Metatron's major missions are first, to sustain and protect humanity and second, in heaven, to maintain the eternal archives of the Lord, recording every event in the universe.

Having reviewed a sampling of non-canonical references to angels, let us now turn to a few of the more remarkable references in the Bible. For instance, the Old Testament records the terrifying retributive power of angels: in II Samuel 24:16, an angel of the Lord waves a plague across the land from Dan to Beersheba, killing 70,000 people to punish the pride of King David; and in II Kings 19:35, at King Hezekiah's prayerful request, an angel of the Lord overnight destroyed the Assyrian army of 185,000 soldiers.

But the greatest and most prominent story of the angels in scripture is that in which a fallen angel promotes the fall of humankind away from God, forever thereafter holding humanity in thralldom. This is of course reference to the machinations of Satan (Hebrew for "adversary"), also known as the devil (e.g., Matthew 4:1-11), father of lies (John 8:44), Beelzebub, the prince of demons (Mark 3:22), prince of the power of the air (Ephesians 2:2), the adversary (I Peter 5:8), and as disguised as an angel of light (II Corinthians 11:14)—nicely summed up for us in Rev. 12:9: "And that great dragon was thrown down, that ancient serpent, who is called the Devil and Satan, the deceiver of the whole world—he was thrown down to the earth, and his angels were thrown down with him."

Many of the Christian church fathers held that Satan was originally the archangel Lucifer ("Light-bearer"), a glorious angel of cosmic intelligence and knowledge. As such, many of the church fathers believed that Lucifer, before his demise, was not only chief minister to the Lord, but also head of the highest angelic choirs of the Seraphim and Cherubim, whose glory lies in their almost infinite knowledge. Lucifer, as explained by medieval theologians, eventually became subject to the great sin of pride and refused to bow down to humanity, which had been newly created by God. Thus, Lucifer fell through pride into disobedience. Unable to repent, Lucifer and a third of the angels were cast out of heaven (some claim they left voluntarily with Lucifer), coming to reside in the nether realms of Hell. In spite against God, Satan (the serpent) came to Adam and Eve in the Garden of Eden and succeeded in deceiving them into violating God's direction to them—thereby multiplying Satan's own original sin of disobedience. Hence, according to Genesis, Adam and Eve were cast out of the Garden of Eden and humanity thereafter stood separated from God, and from happiness.

This is the generally traditional interpretation of Lucifer's and humanity's falling out with God. But there is a second and very important interpretation of how the Fall took place, which has its origins in ancient Hebrew lore and its contemporary expression in the theology of Rev. Sun Myung Moon, i.e., in the theology of the *Divine Principle*. In the understanding of the *Divine Principle*, Love originates in God and belongs first and foremost to God. However, in creating human beings as sons and daughters, God's intention was that they should grow up and fully inherit God's love; i.e., love was the very root and foundation of their humanness, and was the promise that, upon growing to spiritual and physical maturity, Adam and Eve would naturally come to resemble God, inherit divinity and even become, in some sense not presently understood, gods themselves.[27] However, this never happened due to the event in which love itself became compromised and their full development was never achieved.

Divine Principle explains that Lucifer was indeed at the very top of the angelic hierarchy and, as such, God had entrusted Lucifer with the precious responsibility of overseeing the care and growth of Adam and Eve. It was clear, however, that God naturally loved his son and daughter, Adam and

Eve, more than Lucifer, who was created as a helper and servant to God. Lucifer, while feeling honored and blessed to receive this new mission, at the same time began to feel, because he knew God loved Adam and Eve more, that God was now loving *him* (Lucifer) less. This, of course, was not true, but Lucifer allowed this sense of feeling less appreciated to grow in his mind. In order to compensate for the love he felt he was missing, and to move closer to the source of love, Lucifer became more closely drawn to Adam and Eve.

Because Lucifer had been created first and had assisted God with the Creation, he possessed vastly more knowledge than Adam and Eve in their immaturity. We may well imagine that Lucifer was like a very wise teacher who could tutor Adam and Eve. Because Lucifer was masculine in character, he gradually became enamored of and attracted to Eve's developing feminine beauty. Lucifer, while he did not begin with any deliberately negative intentions, allowed himself to enter into a disproportionately intense sharing with Eve, such that their friendship developed into love.

As this love grew, the archangel became jealous of Adam because Lucifer knew that God's intention was for Adam to become Eve's husband once Adam and Eve had fulfilled their growth to maturity. These feelings further compelled Lucifer toward Eve, eventually causing Lucifer to feel that he himself wanted to become Eve's life-partner.

As Lucifer's and Eve's feelings for each other became more intense, their relationship of love grew stronger. Lucifer's desire for *more love* and Eve's desire for *complete love* (which otherwise was to be fulfilled upon her reaching maturity), compelled them into an unprincipled intimacy, beyond the point forbidden by God's commandment.[28] That is to say, Lucifer and Eve entered into an unprincipled sexual relationship[29]—unprincipled for two reasons: first, God had never intended for a sexual relationship to be consummated between a human being and an angel, i.e., a non-human being; second, God intended Eve naturally to enter into her sexuality once she had reached spiritual and physical maturity, but a sexual relationship before maturity would derail the entire growth process as originally conceived by God.

In the moment of their wrongful consummation, Lucifer knew he had violated God's trust in him, and Eve knew she had violated God's commandment. Further, it should be clearly stated that, in any give and take relationship, there is an exchange of elements. In the case of the unprincipled passionate relationship between Lucifer and Eve, Eve inherited three major elements from Lucifer: 1) Eve inherited guilt and fear from Lucifer's guilty conscience; 2) Eve inherited, not the mature and glorious knowledge of God's love, but rather the immature knowing of selfish love; and 3) Eve inherited the understanding of God's original plan of creation, i.e., allowing her to fully realize that Adam was to be her intended, eventual spouse—not Lucifer.

Once Eve understood that Adam was to be her rightful mate, she realized she had made a profound mistake, and felt desperate to somehow return to God. She then turned to Adam, still innocent and beautiful, for comfort. In her desperation, fear and guilt, and with her newfound fallen "knowledge," Eve encouraged Adam to eat the fruit, i.e., she tempted Adam into a premature sexual relationship. Adam, for his part, might conceivably have chosen not to give in to this temptation, but he too allowed himself to move beyond the point of no return and instead experienced a sexual relationship with Eve. Unlike Eve's sexual relationship with Lucifer which was consummated only via their *spiritual bodies,* Eve's sexual relationship with Adam was consummated through both spiritual and physical bodies. Thus, whereas previously Adam and Eve had been living together in sibling friendship as brother and sister in the Garden, Adam had now prematurely behaved toward Eve as her husband. This was yet a further unprincipled act. Hence, the overall devastating results of the Fall of Lucifer, Eve and Adam were: first, God was summarily cut off from humanity, and both God and humanity were simultaneously relegated, spiritually speaking, to sorrowful realms of outer darkness; second, Lucifer became Satan (cast out of heaven with a group of angels following him), and stood thereafter in a position to dominate the human race[30] through his domination, misappropriation and poisoning of the original ideal of God's love; and third, human beings, because they became cut off from God before reaching their intended spiritual maturity, have been fated historically to practice, not God's standard of true love, but rather fallen and selfish love that has kept humanity in the thralldom of confusion and suffering. In other words, the misuse of love has always been, and continues to be, the **root** "disobedience" that has multiplied endlessly into all forms of selfishness, violation, crimes and war, and is, in fact, the true root of all human suffering.[31]

In particular, because God's love was meant to become rightfully differentiated into the major forms of love expressed through the nuclear family, i.e., conjugal love between husband and wife, parents' love for children, sibling love between brothers and sisters, and children's love for their parents, all these forms of love were consequently compromised in the Fall. They have become distorted into dysfunctional and destructive manifestations that keep people in spiritual chains and prevent them from ever discovering that they are, not only spiritual beings, but in fact the original sons and daughters of God.[32]

At first hearing, this may seem such an unusual, even far-fetched, story of how human beings became alienated from God. Yet it is also unusually compelling in its capacity to explicate the *root* of divine and human suffering as the misuse or violation of love. Despite the story's contemporary strangeness, it is sobering, for instance, to consider the comment by F.R.

Tennant, a Christian theologian who made an exhaustive study of the rabbinic literature describing the Genesis event of the Fall:

> It is beyond question . . . that various legends concerning the monstrous intercourse of Adam and Eve with demons, and especially of Eve with the serpent or Satan, were both widespread and ancient among the Jews.[33]

Further, this interpretation of the fall via angelic facilitation was not only endorsed by the ancient Jews, but it is still today understood by many people as the context of the later situation in Genesis in which the "sons of God," or angels, had sexual relations with human women, giving rise to offspring who became giants—the Nephilim (Gen. 6:1-4).

For those who might desire a fuller description of this event, and who do not mind referencing non-canonical sources, the pseudepigraphal First Book of Enoch supplies copious, though admittedly speculative, details. Here we learn that these giants were the children of the union of beautiful human women and 200 fallen angels, each of which took one woman as a wife. The offspring apparently grew into giants "three hundred cubits" in height, or about 500 feet tall. These giants ate such huge amounts of the people's produce that the people came to despise them and became reluctant to continue feeding them. At this point, the giants began eating the people instead, eventually devolving into cannibalism of their own kind.[34] Their ongoing violation against the beasts, birds and the whole of the natural environment was finally condemned by the earth, at which point God determined to cleanse Creation with the Flood. Needless to say, one of the salubrious effects of the Great Deluge was that the Nephilim were wiped out.

Beyond this expatiation, one also should take careful note of the Biblical verse in Jude 6-7:

> And the angels that did not keep their own position but left
> their proper dwelling have been kept by him in eternal chains
> in the nether gloom until the judgment of the great day; just as
> Sodom and Gomorrah and the surrounding cities, which like-
> wise acted immorally and indulged in unnatural lust, serve as
> an example by undergoing a punishment of eternal fire.

Here abides further support for the interpretation that fallen angels could and did engage in "unnatural lust."

Numerous references to angels in the New Testament also serve to emphasize their extraordinary yet indubitable reality. In Luke 2:9-15, an angel announces the birth of the baby Jesus to awestruck shepherds tending their flocks at night in the fields: "Be not afraid, for behold, I bring you good news of a great joy which will come to all the people; for to you is born this day in the city of David a Savior, who is Christ the Lord." After this proclamation, a great multitude of angels praising God appears to the shepherds. On the other hand, Jesus himself later clearly speaks about the angels. As Jesus is arrested in the garden of Gethsemane, he cautions against the violence of using swords, explaining that his own defense *could be* far more substantial: "Do you think that I cannot appeal to my Father, and he will at once send me more than twelve legions of angels?" (Mt. 26:53) St. Paul, as well, believed in the very real power of angels. In Ephesians 6:11-13, Paul counsels that the struggle to follow Jesus entails becoming conscious of and fighting against the influence of fallen angels (i.e., "principalities" and "powers"):

> Put on the whole armor of God, that you may be able to stand against the wiles of the devil. For we are not contending against flesh and blood, but against the principalities, against the powers, against the world rulers of this present darkness, against the spiritual hosts of wickedness in the heavenly places.

B. Three Angelologies

1. Dionysius the Pseudo-Areopagite's Angelology

As an introductory biographical note, Dionysius the Pseudo-Areopagite's identity has never been definitely established, but most scholars agree he was probably a Syrian monk writing in the period between 500 and 600 A.D. "Dionysius the Areopagite" is the pseudonym adopted by this writer. The *actual* Dionysius the Areopagite is referred to by St. Paul (Acts 17:33-34) as the Greek who listened to Paul's teaching (atop the Areopagus, a hill in Athens) and who was thereafter converted. In any case, Dionysius the *Pseudo-*Areopagite was apparently a mystical thinker/theologian who wrote a number of Greek treatises and letters that endeavored to elaborate Christian theology from a Neoplatonic perspective. Because Dionysius wrote his works based on teachings otherwise purporting to descend directly from St. Paul, these works were subsequently regarded as authoritative and deeply influenced the ongoing development of Christian theology right on through the Middle Ages. It is important for our purposes here to recognize that, of Dionysius' four major surviving works—*On the Divine Names, The Mystical Theology, The Celestial Hierarchy,* and *The Ecclesiastical Hierarchy*—it was *The Celestial Hierarchy* became definitive for virtually all Christian angelology elaborated over the next 1,500 years.

Dionysius' opening and major thesis in *The Celestial Hierarchy* is the idea that it is quite acceptable that Biblical scripture attempts to reveal the nature of the Deity and the attendant angels by using descriptive imagery seemingly opposite in character to that which it seeks to describe. For instance, while God's nature is often characterized with exalted and glorious descriptions, e.g., "Sun of Righteousness" (Malachi 4:2), "God is light." (I John 1:5), etc., scripture also legitimately characterizes God using lowly and seemingly profane imagery, e.g., likening God to an animal (a lion in Isaiah 31:4, a bear in Hosea 13:8). Further, sometimes the Biblical authors describe dialectically, i.e., depicting God positively by what He *is*, as well as defining God negatively by what He *is not* or, in other words, saying what God *is* by saying what God *is not* (Dionysius' "negative theology")—almighty but invisible; all-knowing yet unknowable.

Dionysius explains that the above-mentioned scriptural device of revealing heavenly things via "dissimilar similarities" is also applied to descriptions of angels in the Bible. Consider, for instance, Ezekiel's awe-inspiring sighting of the four cherubim, each possessing four faces—human in front, lion on the right, ox on the left, and eagle to the back (Ezek. 1:10). As far as Dionysius is concerned, this imagery is quite symbolic. The human image communicates superior intelligence, rational understanding and independence of spirit (among other qualities), all of which characterize the intelligent beings of heaven, whoever they *really are.* The lion face symbolizes powerful, indomitable command; the ox image betokens strength and "great capacity to plough deeply the furrows of knowledge on which the fertile rains of heaven will fall"[35]; and the eagle countenance suggests regal might, winging speed, aerial agility in the realm of thought.

In the middle chapters of *The Celestial Hierarchy,* Dionysius makes clear that he is little more than a Biblical and theological interpreter who has derived the triadic structure of the angelic hierarchies from his own Neoplatonic mentor, Hierotheus. Thus, the division of the angelic world into three hierarchies of three subdivisions each is not actually Biblical. Dionysius proceeds to sketch the nature of the full nine levels of heavenly beings, from highest to lowest: seraphim, cherubim, thrones—dominions, powers, authorities (or virtues)—principalities, archangels, angels. And, before going further, it is important to acknowledge that Dionysius considers the first eight categories of these heavenly beings also to be "angels"—which do not necessarily resemble human beings in appearance—even though it is only the lowest order here that is properly termed "angels" and the members of which *do* resemble human beings in appearance.

The seraphim, whose name in Hebrew means "fire-makers," are the heavenly creatures whose being of flame renders eternal purification through never-diminishing heat and light. The cherubim, named for their "fullness of knowledge," possess the profound power to see and know God, which becomes the endless outpouring of wisdom. The thrones bask in God's perfection, carry God forth and critically mediate God's majesty to those angelic orders beneath them. The dominions have nothing to do with earthly tyranny, but exercise a benevolent lifting up to God. The holy "powers" evince unshakeable, masculine courage to approach God, the source of all power. The authorities are those beings which harmoniously order the universe, precisely indexing God's authority in all matters. The heavenly principalities "possess a godlike and princely hegemony."[36] And while the angels minister specifically to human beings, archangels stand as the mean between two extremes, invoking transcendent principles to unite the angels.[37]

Dionysius continually reminds the reader that, because these heavenly beings are arranged hierarchically, each order stands in a connecting and mediating position. Not only do "all angels bring revelations and tidings of their superiors,"[38] from the top down, but all lower-order angels (as well as human beings and the created universe) participate in God's love and wisdom via the mediation of higher-order angels.[39] A related and important idea here is the notion that, through this hierarchical mediation, the angels also inevitably participate in nature, or the natural world.[40] Theologian Matthew Fox and philosopher of science, Rupert Sheldrake, in *The Physics of Angels,* also agree that this notion is evidenced in Dionysius' writings:

> . . . his [Dionysius'] doctrines imply not only that all things have power or energy organized by fields, but that *they participate in consciousness and intelligence through the angels,* and indeed through the angels participate in the divine nature.[41] (Emphasis added)

That this may be, in fact, how reality is organized is a notion we will explore more substantially in the consideration of Rudolf Steiner's angelology and beyond.

The aforementioned nine orders of angels came to be known later in Christian history as the nine "choirs," doubtlessly denoting the archetypal role of the angels—to sing praises to God. Briefly, let us review these nine orders again, this time considered in the light of how each of them have come to be understood in the centuries after Dionysius.

Angels and archangels, the two lowest orders of angels, continue to be understood specifically as God's messengers to humanity and as the assigned protectors of the human soul. Traditionally, seven archangels were recognized by name: Michael, Gabriel, Raphael, Uriel, Chamuel, Zadkiel and Jophiel, though this list of seven has been sometimes different with different authors. Of these, Christianity has retained recognition of only three archangels—Michael, Raphael and Gabriel. The principalities, or princes, are likewise concerned with human life, but their missions are broader; they serve as caretakers and protectors of each nation, province, county, district, city, town, village and household. In addition, their special expertise includes rendering inspiration to two particular areas of human culture—religion and politics. The principalities foment the development of religion through encouraging humans to pray and think about God. Similarly, these angels guide and uplift toward God the thoughts of political leaders for the good of humankind.[42]

Moving to the second and intermediate hierarchy, the dominions, or dominations, constitute the fourth order of angels, mentioned by St. Paul in Colossians 1:16. Among the Heavenly Host, the dominions' responsibility is to regulate the tasks of the angelic world such that the order of the cosmos is carefully maintained. Traditionally, the dominions are understood to receive their orders from the thrones and the cherubim. Likewise, the virtues, standing directly above the dominions, share the task of maintaining cosmic equilibrium. In particular, they contribute to the preservation of cosmic harmony in all the movements of planets, stars and galaxies, and are otherwise recognized as presiding over elements of the natural world like wind, rain and snow. In this latter regard, the virtues also have the capability of overriding natural law, thereby executing miracles. Further, and very significantly, the virtues have great power to inspire human beings to turn away from evil, and can grant special grace to those who endure suffering in their determination to love and honor God.[43] Thus, the virtues, as might be expected, are those angelic powers who often watch over and encourage the saints. Finally, the powers or "authorities" (dynamis), oversee the dominions' and virtues' administration of the cosmic order. In addition, the powers' unique mission includes guarding the heavenly passages or paths connecting heaven and earth, as well as generally protecting the universe against evil.[44] These "authorities" are also mentioned by St. Paul in Romans 13:1 and in Colossians 1:16.

Finally, the thrones, cherubim and seraphim constitute the first and most transcendent triad of angelic choirs. The thrones are also referred to as "wheels" and as "many-eyed ones," and are described in the prophet Ezekiel's vision:

> Now as I looked at the living creatures, I saw a wheel upon the earth beside the living creatures, one for each of the four of them. As for the appearance of the wheels and their construction: their appearance was like the gleaming of a chrysolite; and the four had the same likeness, their construction being as it were a wheel within a wheel. When they went, they went in any of their four directions without turning as they went. The four wheels had rims and they had spokes; and their rims were full of eyes round about. . . . Wherever the spirit would go, they [the four creatures] went, and the wheels arose along with

them; for the spirit of the living creatures was in the wheels.
(Ezekiel 1:15-20)

Thomas Aquinas, following Dionysius, recognized that the specific mission
of the thrones was to convey God's judgement in order to fulfill divine justice. In ancient Jewish Merkabah mysticism, the thrones are often recognized as the wheels of the chariot of God, while the superior cherubim are
responsible for driving the chariot. The cherubim are understood as extremely
powerful, magnificent and wise angelic beings. One may recall that these
angels are the first to be encountered in the Bible—they were posted with
flaming swords to guard the entrance to the Garden of Eden after Adam and
Eve had been expelled. Ezekiel supplies for us what purports to be an actual
description of the cherubim in Ezekiel 1:4-12. Each of these "living creatures"
has four wings and four faces. In any case, the cherubim are traditionally recognized as angelic creatures of eternal vigilance and vast knowledge and, more
esoterically, they are charged with the enormously difficult responsibility of
maintaining the records of heaven, dutifully recording the infinite details
that facilitate the flawless functioning of the Heavenly Host.[45]

The seraphim, as already mentioned, are identified with fire—not the
punishing heat of hell, but with the redemptive, healing flame of love.
Dionysius clearly depicted the seraphim as living flames who render divine
purification. St. Francis of Assisi, for instance, is one of the few humans ever
to glimpse the seraphim, this occurring at the time he received the stigmata in 1224, when he beheld a crucified Christ being carried toward
heaven by seraphim. The chief mission of the seraphim seems always to have
been that of singing praises to God, a mission which is prominently featured
in Revelation 4:6-9 (though others, somewhat justifiably, interpret this as a
reference to cherubim). Here, the seraphim are described as "living creatures" having six wings, as "full of eyes all round and within," and as
engaged in the perpetual adoration of God, chanting

> Holy, holy, holy is the Lord God Almighty, who was and is and
> is to come!

The seraphim, standing closest to God, partake most completely of God's
perfection and have unquestioned dominion over all the angelic realms.

2.   Emanuel Swedenborg's Angelology

Lest anyone doubt the full extent of Swedenborg's intercourse with the
denizens of the spiritual world, consider the following extraordinary testimony of Swedenborg in this regard:

> . . . The more inward reaches of my spirit have been opened by
> the Lord, and I have in this way been allowed to talk with all

the people I was acquainted with during their physical life,
after they had died. I have talked with some of them for days,
with some for months, with some for a year. I have talked with
other people as well—so many that a hundred thousand would
be an understatement. Many of these were in the heavens, and
many were in the hells.[46]

In addition, throughout the thousands of pages of Swedenborg's descriptions
of the spiritual world, he records many experiences of meeting and talking
with angels, *as he understood them.* Unlike Dionysius' descriptions of the
angelic realm, Swedenborg's experiences with angels are very personalized,
very personally detailed. One immediately recognizes that Swedenborg's
understanding of angels is also very different from Dionysius'. This difference should be carefully noted and, while neither of these two conceptions
of angels may be completely accurate, both decidedly offer useful contexts
and suggest valuable insights for grasping the reality of the angelic world.
Dionysius understood "angels" in the traditionally Christian sense—as special, glorious, non-human creations who, however, resemble human beings.
Swedenborg, on the other hand, declared unorthodoxly that all angels were
at one time human beings who lived on earth,[47] who only after death *became*
angels in the spiritual world:

All individuals arrive after death in the world of spirits, which
is halfway between heaven and hell, where they work through
their times or their states, and according to their lives are prepared for heaven or for hell. As long as they stay in that world,
they are called "spirits." All the people who are raised from
that world into heaven are called "angels," while all who are
thrown down into hell are called "satans" or "devils."[48]

Further, Swedenborg informs us in *Arcana Coelestia* that when young
children die prematurely in their innocence, all are educated and raised by
angels until they eventually become angels themselves.[49] In other words, for
Swedenborg, all angels are really human persons who, after death, have
been spiritually elevated, becoming heavenly persons.[50]

Swedenborg spends considerable effort characterizing the nature of
angels, which is especially concentrated in *Heaven and Hell.* Here and in
Arcana Coelestia abound descriptions of what angels look like, where they live,
what they eat, how they travel, the character of their thinking and speech and
their responsibilities. For instance, he not only describes angels as having
"resplendent bodies" and as being "lucid with light,"[51] but he declares:

On the basis of all my experience, covering to date many years,
I can say, I can insist that angels are completely people in form.

They do have faces, eyes, ears, chests, arms, hands, and feet. They do see each other, hear each other, and talk with each other. In short, nothing proper to man whatever is missing, except that they are not clothed with a material body.[52]

Further, angels live in houses or homes very similar to those on earth— only more beautiful, inasmuch as these brilliant homes and coruscating palaces are the outer reflection of the greater goodness and love in angels' minds. These homes are often adjoined or situated close together, and are formed into cities with avenues, streets and city squares.[53] Swedenborg says also that angels are nourished through ingesting mind-food, i.e., through understanding what is true and good.[54]

Angels apparently have no concept of time or space, as people on earth do.[55] That is, for angels, there is no passage of time as such, nor progression through space, but there exist only "changes of states" for angels. Swedenborg notes, somewhat enigmatically, that angels travel in the spiritual world via *changes of state,* and that this is, in fact, exactly how Swedenborg himself has been enabled by the Lord to visit many "places" in the spirit-world:

All journeys in the spiritual world occur by means of changes of the state of more inward things, to the point that journeys are simply changes of state. This is how I have been brought into the heavens by the Lord; this is how I have been brought to planets in the universe. My spirit has been brought, while my body stayed in one place. This is how all angels travel. So they do not have any spatial intervals, and without spatial intervals, there are no spaces. Instead, there are states and changes of states.[56]

We have already addressed at length Swedenborg's descriptions of thought, speech and communication in Section 9 of this book. But, as a further complement here, we can note Swedenborg's characterization of the extraordinary powers of discernment that angels possess—or, that is, the quality of *wisdom* that angels are capable of when listening to the speech of any person:

More inward angels can know a person's whole life from the tone, from a few spoken words. From the tone, patterned by means of the concepts involved in the words, they perceive his dominant love, which has recorded in it, so to speak, all the details of his life.

This may serve to show what angels' wisdom is like.

The ratio between their wisdom and human wisdom is on the order of ten thousand to one.[57]

The preceding passage also gives us the opportunity to discuss briefly what Swedenborg means by "more inward angels." Whereas Dionysius classifies the nine orders of angelic beings into three ascending hierarchical triads, Swedenborg distinguishes three degrees of angels as belonging, respectively, to three ascending heavenly realms. In various places throughout his writings, Swedenborg describes that there are three levels of heaven, or three heavens (notwithstanding that heaven is *also* in the original form of a person), occupied by three corresponding degrees of angels. The wisdom of the angels in the third heaven is vastly superior to the wisdom of the angels in the intermediate heaven, and the intermediate angelic wisdom greatly surpasses the wisdom of the angels in the lowest heaven.[58] These three heavens are "vertically" positioned; they are not conjoined but strictly separated from each other, and for this reason, Swedenborg describes the angels indwelling these as "gathered by distinct levels, not by continuous levels."[59] In other words, the radical qualitative differences in the wisdom of the angels of these three levels is so profound that "they have nothing in common"[60] and, in fact, angels in a lower heaven cannot understand the discourse of angels in a higher heaven. Swedenborg offers various explanations of this phenomenon, one of which is the following:

> The reason for these distinctions is that the elements present on a higher level are details, while those of a lower level are generalities, the generalities being inclusive of the details. The ratio between the details and the generalities is on the order of thousands to ten thousands to one. Consequently, the ratio of the wisdom of angels of a higher heaven to the wisdom of angels of a lower heaven is the same.[61]

Swedenborg's understanding of the mission of the angels, as we previously mentioned, is traditional in the sense that angels have the responsibility to protect people on earth from the influence of evil spirits. In addition, however, angels perform many other services in hell and in heaven. Angels try to prevent people in the hells from torturing each other "beyond set bounds."[62] In the heavenly realms, angels serve as caretakers for infants, and as teachers of children. Others serve as spiritual teachers for Christians, as well as for non-Christian peoples. Some angels' work is to protect from hellish spirits those newly deceased and arriving in the intermediate realm or, that is, the world of spirits. In general, says Swedenborg, angels perform many varied ecclesiastical, civil and domestic services.[63]

Angels have tremendous power in the spiritual world. Swedenborg avers that if he were to relate all of what he had witnessed of angels' power, it would be unbelievable:

If there is something there [in the spiritual world] that needs to be removed because it is in opposition to Divine design, they [angels] raze and destroy it by sheer force of will, with a look. I have seen mountains, under control of evil people, razed and destroyed, sometimes shaken from boundary to boundary as if by an earthquake, the central peaks parting into a chasm, the evil ones on them engulfed. Also I have seen hundreds of thousands of evil spirits routed by them and hurled into hell. A multitude is powerless against them, as are ploys, stratagems, and factions.[64]

Finally, Swedenborg explains that in ancient times, the human race was in close contact with the angels, and that the angels could talk directly with earthly humans and lead their minds into heaven.[65] But he also notes that "today" (which is still "today" all the more, over 200 years later), it would be dangerous for people to be able to talk with angels, given earthly people's obsession with bodily pleasures and material possessions.[66]

In fact, Swedenborg says:

I can tell you this—that angels are caught in sadness over the darkness on our planet. They tell me that scarcely anywhere do they see light, that people have seized on falsities and confirmed them and so have multiplied falsity on falsity.[67]

3.   Rudolf Steiner's Angelology

Rudolf Steiner, the son of loving Austrian parents, claimed that the spiritual world was open to him from birth and that he was fully clairvoyant and clairaudient from a very early age. In fact, Steiner explained later in life that the spiritual world was always just as real to him as the physical world. At eight years old, for instance, he clearly saw the spirit of a recently deceased relative but, because his many spiritual experiences seemed incredible to most family and friends, he quickly learned to stop trying to explain his supersensible perceptions to other people.

When Steiner was 15, he met a visionary herbalist who taught him to discipline his clairvoyant abilities so as to be able to fathom the life principle, or "etheric" essence, of plants and herbs. He regarded this as an important part of the preparation for him to meet his "Master" at 19, and to receive from him his spiritual life mission. At 25, five years before he received his Ph.D. in philosophy, Steiner took on the ambitious challenge of educating a severely autistic 10-year-old boy of the Specht family. Though everyone else had basically given up on getting through to this child, Steiner, utilizing his supersensing faculties, was able to penetrate the solipsistic darkness of the boy's autism and, within two years, to bring the boy's cognitive abilities up to the level of a normal 12-year-old. Then, in an extraordinary leap forward, Steiner taught the boy Latin and Greek, which enabled him to attend high-school, followed by college. Beyond these achievements, the boy went on to graduate from medical school, finally becoming a doctor.[68]

Through his Master (whom Steiner never named), Steiner came to realize that his life mission was to develop a new and profound synthesis of science and religion—one that would yield a higher form of knowledge that was simultaneously scientific and spiritual. Thus, Steiner's life-work was his development of Anthroposophy, or the study of spiritual science. Steiner's description of the path of esoteric training that an initiate should follow to acquire such higher-dimensional knowledge is contained in his work, *How To Know Higher Worlds.*[69] Herein he carefully instructs how the initiate can develop, via disciplined meditation, contemplation and loving discernment, the clairvoyant/clairaudient abilities necessary to accurately grasp the char-acter of spiritual reality, and thus attain the fuller-dimensioned knowledge.

We are not interested here in trying to render a full-scale exegesis of Steiner's esoteric teachings, nor are we concerned to validate, for instance, his assertion of a "Cosmic Christ." Rather, our purpose is to provide what we might term a substantial thumbnail sketch of Steiner's angelology, demon-strating how Steiner's clairvoyant reinterpretation of Dionysius' angelic hierarchies opens up some new possibilities for comprehending spiritual real-ity. In brief, Steiner accepts Dionysius' classification of angels into the nine choirs, organized into three distinct hierarchies. Steiner also recognizes, as does Dionysius, that these nine choirs interact with human beings in the tra-ditionally recognized ways. One of the *novel* aspects of Steiner's interpre-tation, however, is his expansion upon how the angelic world interacts with the three kingdoms of nature, i.e., with animals, plants and minerals. Steiner believed that it was, in fact, his historical responsibility as the first "spiritual scientist" to newly reveal how the angelic hierarchies entered into the work-ings of nature.[70] As a consequence, Steiner offers the opportunity for sys-tematically understanding "nature spirits," or "elementals"—in regard to both their ontological status as well as their influence in the natural world.

Steiner's angelology employs some different terminology to name Dionysius' nine levels of angels. Further, Steiner carefully proposes in the ten original lectures (1912) summarizing his angelology that progressively ascending levels of clairvoyant vision are required to view the full range of the workings of the angelic world. This range begins here with the clairvoyant consideration of the world of nature, and then proceeds into discussion of the nine progressively subtler angelic realms proper.[71]

The first level of clairvoyant discernment is of the "etheric" world of nature or, that is, of the spiritual dimension directly "behind" or under-girding our material, physical world. This lowest level of clairvoyance is able to view the elemental world. That is, just as nature shows itself as a multi-plicity, so the etheric world reveals itself as containing multiple elementals, or nature spirits, which tend and support the various life forms in nature. Occult vision can clearly distinguish here nature spirits of the earth, water, air and fire. For instance, consider the following passage where Steiner is speaking about earth spirits (*a.k.a.* "gnomes"):

> If, having had an occult training, and having at the same time, a certain love of such things—it is especially important to have this here—we make acquaintance with miners and go down into the mines, and can forget all external impressions when we are down there, we will then feel rising up before our imag-ination the first class, as it were, of beings that create and weave behind all that is earthly, and especially in all that per-tains to metals. I have not yet spoken today of how popular fairy tales and folk legends have made use of all that, in a sense, is actually in existence; I should first like to give you the dry facts that offer themselves to occult vision.[72]

In addition, Steiner goes on to describe nature spirits of water dis-cernible within falling water condensed into mists and cloud formations. Nature spirits of air may become manifest to clairvoyant vision when the air is free from moisture; these spirit beings "drink in the light which perme-ates the air and causes them to flash and shine." Air spirits, in particular, hover over budding plants, and contribute a principle of growth from above that draws forth plants from the ground. Finally, nature spirits of fire, or heat, may be occultly viewed once the plant has borne fruit containing the seeds of the next generation. At this time, fire spirits not only protect the seeds or germs, but work in such a way as to transmute environmental warmth into the life-giving heat that the seed requires in order to grow.

Behind the etheric body in human beings lies a more interior, imma-terial body known as the "astral" body, which Steiner understands to be the repository of human desires and passions. In the same way, behind the etheric body of nature lies the astral body of nature or, most immediately, the astral body of the earth, discernible only to a higher level of clairvoyance, which consciousness Steiner compares with being awake in the sleep state. So, what can one view at this level? One no longer sees nature spirits, but rather a new level of spiritual beings which have command over the nature spirits. These new "beings," which participate in the astral body of the earth, are called "spirits of the cycles of time," to which is allotted the task of regulating everything in nature that is subject to rhythmical cycles.

Again, we note that, for Steiner, the spiritual structure of nature corresponds to the spiritual structure of a human being; the macrocosm is a reflection of the microcosm. Just as the next more advanced level of clairvoyance enables the initiate to discover the integral human "I" underlying the astral body of a human person, so also does the initiate come to recognize that there is an integrative *planetary spirit* of the earth underlying its astral spirits of the cycles of time. That is to say, in summary, the physical world of nature is governed first through a realm of natural forces (the etheric world of the nature spirits), which is itself informed through the more interior realm of the laws of nature (the astral world of the cycles of time), which is further grounded in the inherent meaning of nature (the realm of the planetary spirit of the earth). From here, Steiner says, one proceeds to the realization that the planetary spirit of the earth "lives in fellowship with other planetary spirits, other spirits of the heavenly bodies."[73]

Once the initiate's meditation moves to consider the full nature and meaning of *love*, he or she cannot but come into the realization that there is a world beyond the self, beyond the "I," through which humans receive inspiration, through which we receive internal support and spiritual guidance. The inexorably dawning insight here is that human beings are guided, taught, cared for and loved, and that, in fact, there are beings especially accommodated to this purpose, i.e., *angels* (or *angeloi*). Occult vision now encounters the reality of angels—who tend to each individual human being. Beyond this, the initiate further recognizes that *groups* of human beings, tribes, and nations, are *all* spiritually guided by beings especially purposed to such responsibility—*archangels* (or *archangeloi*). Refined to yet a higher degree, clairvoyance now realizes that there are spiritual beings with missions of guidance, beyond individuals and beyond larger human collectivities—beings who guide and lead the human race in successive epochs. These beings are understood as the principalities, or *spirits of the age* (or *archai*), who are more powerful than the archangels. Many different peoples or nations stand simultaneously under the governance of the archai.

Thus, we arrive at the point where it is possible to understand the origin of the spirits that inform the workings of nature. Each of the preceding categories of angels in the third hierarchy, Steiner teaches, have their own unique *offspring*—angels' offspring are the nature spirits of the air; archangels' offspring are the nature spirits of water; and archai offspring are the nature spirits of the earth. Each of these types of offspring is detached from their respective parent, and directed toward the rendering of service to the natural world.[74]

Whereas the clairvoyant abilities exercised in perceiving the beings of the third hierarchy constitute "first stage" clairvoyance, Steiner now explains that the initiate must undergo a further substantive transformation of consciousness to become able to exercise the "second stage" clairvoyance needed to discern the spiritual beings of the second hierarchy. The initiate at this point develops clairvoyance that enables a kind of spiritual projection into, or indwelling within, the being that is being perceived. For instance, in regard to nature, the initiate, via deep sympathy/empathy, exercises a *loving* projection into, and exploration of, everything that is alive, i.e., plants, animals and especially human beings.

What new spiritual beings can then be seen through this second-stage clairvoyance? First, through the recognition of the manifold forms of plants and animals, including also human form, one perceives from this totality of forms the spiritual beings called "spirits of form" or *exusiae* (the "powers"). As the initiate directs his contemplation to the aspect of change, growth and metamorphosis of these forms in nature, he is led unerringly to recognize the second class of beings in the second hierarchy—the *dynamis* (or "virtues").

The third category of beings in the second hierarchy is decidedly more difficult to discern than the first two. Here, we must move beyond the multiplicity and metamorphoses of forms, to then apprehend *what is expressed* in the forms and all their variations. For instance, in the case of a human being, the bearing, gestures and facial expressions of a particular person are perceived via occult vision as speaking *directly* and *unambiguously* to the initiate. In like manner, if occult perception encounters different species of plants with their multiplicity of features, it is enabled to comprehend directly the meanings of the movements, physiognomy and colors of plants. And in this comprehension is the simultaneous grasp of ubiquitous wisdom informing nature. In other words, as Steiner explains it, the initiate's inner vision rises to the discerning of the highest class of beings in the second hierarchy— the "spirits of wisdom," or *kyriotetes* (the "dominions"). Steiner further asserts that, just as angels, archangels and archai have as their offspring the nature spirits proper, so also the exusiai, dynamis and kyriotetes have unique offspring that also become detached from themselves and sent out to contribute their part to the governance of the natural world.[75]

The most advanced refinement of occult vision is needed to apprehend the elusive angelic beings of the first hierarchy. These are, in ascending order, the thrones, or *spirits of will;* the cherubim, or *spirits of harmony;* and highest of all, the seraphim, or *spirits of love.* Steiner notes at this juncture that it becomes extremely difficult to describe these rarified beings inasmuch as he can no longer use the same kind of concrete examples and terminology from ordinary life as he used in discussing the first and second hierarchies—that is, he will now have to rely greatly upon abstractions to try to communicate the sublimity of these third-hierarchy beings. For instance, Steiner proceeds to describe the spirits of will in this way:

For we then perceive beings we cannot describe otherwise than by saying that they do not consist of flesh and blood, nor even of light and air; but of what we can only observe in ourselves when we are conscious that we have a will.[76]

Nevertheless, in considering the spirits of will, the "will" spoken of here is not like the very limited personal will of a human being; rather, it is more like an ageless, cosmic will of which we might glean some very imprecise idea by introspectively examining our own personal will. Similarly, we may recognize that the perennial cherubim are beings of *great* wisdom, inasmuch as we grasp that human wisdom is itself the blossom and fruit of a truly mature human life. Yet, cherubic wisdom, clairvoyantly experienced, is enormously profound and ageless, as Steiner suggests here:

Wisdom, not acquired in decades, as is the wisdom of eminent men, but wisdom as is gathered in thousands, nay, millions of years of cosmic growth, this streams toward us in sublime power from the beings we call cherubim.[77]

Finally, the clairvoyant encounter with seraphim reveals cosmic wisdom that is primordially rooted in the heart. The wisdom of the seraphim is ultimately loving wisdom; it is universal wisdom engendered through an eternity of suffering and commiseration, a wisdom which has endlessly ripened into loving service to others. Steiner advises that it is exceedingly difficult to convey adequately the profound character of the angelic order of the seraphim. Again, just as the beings of the second and third hierarchies have offspring that serve and support the natural world, so also do the thrones, cherubim and seraphim have special offspring that facilitate the workings of nature.[78]

In order to enable the reader to more readily grasp the larger scope of how the beings of the first and second hierarchies function, Steiner applies their working within a cosmic, or astronomical, context, i.e., shows how their influence enables the formation of a planet and its orientation to other heavenly bodies. In effect, Steiner intends here to demonstrate the spiritual provenance of the heavenly bodies and systems. Consider a planet. From a spiritual standpoint, a planet receives its external form via the intrinsic activity of the spirits of form. The inner life, or inner mobility, of the planet is the result of the activity of the spirits of motion. The lowest form of consciousness for a planet is established through the activity of the spirits of wisdom. The impulse by which the planet, otherwise stationary, changes its position in space, results from the activity of the spirits of will, or thrones. The regulation of the planet's individual movement in harmony with the whole planetary system is carried out through the action of the cherubim. Finally, seraphim activity yields what Steiner considers to be the inner soul-life of the planet, whereby the planet not only comes into relation with other planets but, in fact, whole planetary systems enter into intelligent relationship with each other. What does this mean? Steiner offers that:

> We could compare this with the fact that people do not live only for themselves, or simply in a social connection—this could be compared with the directing of the spirits of will—but rather understand one another by their speech.[79]

Thus, at a cosmic level, through the agency of the seraphim, there is a kind of mutual understanding between one planetary system and another. Again, Steiner remarks:

> The seraphim carry messages from one planetary system to another, and give information of what takes place in one planetary system to the other system. By this means the world of planetary systems is integrated and forms a whole.[80]

II.　Nature Spirits: Their Character and Reality

Some of the earliest references to the existence of elemental beings, or nature spirits, are those of the medieval alchemists and mystics, e.g., Parcelsus and the Rosicrucians. In general, they divide all invisible beings into four classes—angels; demons, or fallen angels; elementals, who were understood as subhuman nature spirits; and souls of dead human beings. The class of elementals included four different types, corresponding to the four major elements of nature—gnomes or elves (or leprechauns), who live in the earth, in rocks and caverns and in mines; sylphs, or aerials, who indwell air; undines or water fairies, who live in and around lakes and rivers; and salamanders or nature spirits of fire who were often recognized as the most primordial and quintessential type of elemental.

Our thesis here is that these nature spirits do, in fact, exist, and that they have "objective" existence which has been historically confirmed by many mystics and psychics right up until the present day. Consider but a few of the relevant testimonies of nineteenth- and twentieth-century poets, clairvoyants and psychic mediums.

The visionary English poet, William Blake, not only held instructive conversations with the ancient Greek philosopher, Plato, but remained continually open to visitations from angels and others living in the spiritual world. An old Baptist minister who had known Blake for some time was once asked if he thought Blake might be "cracked"—to which he replied: "Yes, but it is a crack that lets the light in."[81] In particular, Blake was once invited by a wealthy London socialite, Mrs. Mathews, to an evening party for up-and-coming artists. Blake was not much of a party person, and on this occasion he reacted against the atmosphere of excessive politeness by revealing more of himself than usual. This event, which highlights Blake's familiarity with nature spirits, is humorously rendered by biographer James Daugherty:

> . . . [Blake] had become so bored that he had suddenly turned to the highly respectable lady next to him and asked, "Did you ever see a fairies' funeral?"
>
> "Never, sir!" she replied indignantly.
>
> "I have," he said, in the casual way he spoke of his visions. "I was walking alone in my garden; there was a great stillness among the branches and flowers and a more than common sweetness in the air; I heard a low and pleasant sound, and I knew not whence it came. At last I saw a procession of creatures of the size and color of green and gray grasshoppers, bearing a body laid out on a rose leaf, which they buried with songs, and disappeared. It was a fairy funeral."

> The lady had looked at him and changed the subject, and Blake had smiled dreamily and become silent. He would not explain to her that fairies were rulers of the vegetable world.[82]

The renowned Irish poet, W.B. Yeats, affirmed his recognition of the reality of nature spirits in the following way (notwithstanding his final, odd suggestion that these creatures might represent a preliminary form of the human soul):

> Many poets, and all mystic and occult writers, in all ages and countries, have declared that behind the visible are chains and chains of conscious beings, who are not of heaven but of the earth, who have no inherent form, but change according to their whim, or the mind that sees them. You cannot lift your hand without influencing and being influenced by hordes. The visible world is merely their skin. In dreams we go amongst them, and play with them, and combat with them. They are, perhaps, human souls in the crucible—these creatures of whim.[83]

W.Y. Evans-Wentz, now well recognized for his definitive translation of *The Tibetan Book of the Dead* (1960), wrote an early treatise presented for the degree *Docteur-ès-Lettres* (University of Rennes, Brittany). This remarkable work was readily transformed into the book, *The Fairy-Faith in Celtic Countries* (1911), and has stood now for many decades as a classic in its field. Evan-Wentz's grassroots study of Fairyland and "the little people," based on hundreds of actual testimonies gathered from people living in Ireland, Scotland, the Isle of Man, Wales, Cornwall and Brittany, serves to highlight the fact that many common folk have had undeniable encounters with various kinds of elementals and/or with seemingly "mythological" races of usually invisible spiritual beings. Evans-Wentz offers a summary consideration of such Celtic experience:

> Not only do both educated and uneducated Celtic seers so conceive Fairyland, but they go much further, and say that Fairyland actually exists as an invisible world within which the visible world is immersed like an island in an unexplored ocean, and that it is peopled by more species of living beings than this world, because incomparably more vast and varied in its possibilities.[84]

Contemporary psychic medium, Mary T. Browne, testifies that, from a young age, her spiritual openness allowed her to see clearly that her "invisible playmates" included nature spirits:

> As a small child I loved singing and acting. Performing came very naturally to me. I also possessed the ability to see fairies and elves as well as human spirits, so I never lacked an audience. In the backyard of my Iowa home I performed for my spirit friends on many occasions.[85]

Ted Andrews, contemporary clairvoyant, spiritualist medium and popular author of numerous books in the metaphysical/occult fields, offers an honest and straightforward claim of experience with the elemental world:

> I don't remember a time in my life when I did not see and hear faeries. As a child some of my strongest memories are of meeting those of the faerie realm through reading simple faerie tales.[86]

Theosophist and clairvoyant, Dora van Gelder, published an entire book of her experiences in viewing and interacting with the fairy world. In her book, *The Real World of Fairies* (1977), she details the reality of fairy life and explains that the human and fairy worlds are really much nearer each other than we might suppose:

> Poets like A.E. [i.e., George William Russell, renown mystic and visionary of the twentieth century], James Stevens, Yeats, Tennyson, and Shakespeare have enriched our knowledge of and feeling for the fairy world. They have known and known truly. A much larger number of people than is commonly sup-

posed are in close communion with fairies and angels. The gap between the two groups of beings, fairies and humans, is not nearly so wide as our ignorance assumes. If we could only realize that we live in a world crowded with fairies, angels, and all manner of beings, it would make an immense difference in our attitude and our mode of living.[87]

Finally, we return to Anthroposophist Rudolf Steiner's sensitively clairvoyant appreciation of the elementals who support and nurture the plant world:

> . . . For in every plant there is concealed—under a spell, as it were—an elemental spiritual being; and really only he observes a plant the right way who realizes that this loveliness is the sheath of a spiritual being enchanted in it—a relatively insignificant being, to be sure, in the great scale of cosmic interrelationships. . . . All about us are these elemental spirits begging us, in effect: Do not look at the flowers so abstractly, nor form such abstract mental pictures of them; let your heart and your Gemüt [i.e., the mind warmed by a loving heart and stimulated by the soul's imaginative powers] enter into what lives, as soul and spirit, in the flowers, for it is imploring you to break the spell. Human existence should really be a perpetual releasing of the elemental spirits lying enchanted in minerals, plants and animals.[88]

Again, what makes Steiner's esoteric rendering of Dionysius' angelic hierarchies especially valuable is that it affirms a *systematic* way of understanding the origins of these seemingly unusual spiritual creatures, the nature spirits. In the following discussion, we endeavor to sketch in greater detail this unique genre of spiritual beings. In order to accomplish this in as lucid a manner as possible, the topic here is presented in terms of answering the four following questions:

1. Where do elementals, or nature spirits, come from?

2. What are the characters of the various elementals?

3. In what ways can elementals be perceived by human beings?

4. Why should it be important for human beings to see and interact with nature spirits?

1.   Where do elementals, or nature spirits, come from?

This is one of the most important questions to address in that answering this question will help us to better decide the ontological status of the elementals. There are, in fact, two very different notions regarding the origin of the elementals. We have already encountered the first of these in Steiner's description of how nature spirits become detached from the angels and then sent into nature in a supportive role. Van Gelder concurs with Steiner, adding that, while fairies stand in the same relation to angels that animals do to humanity, fairies cannot reproduce themselves, either as animals do or in any other way.[89] This general understanding seems also echoed in the testimony of an Irish mystic interviewed by Evans-Wentz.[90] This seer described that he had often witnessed the activities of a commonly acknowledged race of spiritual beings, known as the "gentry" or "sidhe" (pronounced "shee"), in the countryside of Rosses Point county, Ireland. In particular, he said that there appeared to be two different orders of the Sidhe—first, the "shining beings," or lower order of the "mid world," exhibiting no authentically individualized life (i.e., functioning in uniformity), and resembling the elementals traditionally described by medieval alchemists, and second, the "opalescent beings," belonging to the "heaven-world," standing 14 feet tall, brilliantly internally radiant, and clearly, regally actuated by their own subjectivity. In considering this mystic's following testimony, we would suggest that it corroborates Steiner's general description of the relationship between angels and elementals:

> The higher kind [i.e., opalescent beings] seem capable of
> breathing forth beings out of themselves, but I do not under-
> stand how they do so. I have seen some of them who contain
> elemental beings within themselves, and these they could send
> out and receive back within themselves again.[91]

And might not this quote simply be a kind of restatement of van Gelder's description when she reports that angels *cogitate* salamanders (nature spirits of fire) into being in accord with a special mental rhythm (or mantram)?[92]

The second major notion of how the elementals originate is articulated, for instance, in the descriptions of the spirit-world channelled in 1896 from Francezzo (a young deceased Italian man) to A. Farnese (a spirit medium in London). In the following passage, Francezzo is explaining what he understands to be, not only the foundational character of "astral elementals" like gnomes, elves, fairies, mermaids, sylphs, etc., but also what eventually becomes of them:

> All these beings possess life, but as yet no souls, for their lives
> are drawn from and sustained by the lives of earthly men and

women, and they are but reflections of the men amongst whom they dwell. Some of these beings are of a very low order of life, almost like the higher orders of plants, except that they possess an independent power of motion. Others are very lively and full of grotesque unmeaning tricks, with the power of very rapid flight from place to place. Some are perfectly harmless, while others again are more malignant in their instincts as the human beings from whom their life is drawn are of a more savage race. These curious earth elementals cannot exist long amongst nations where the more intellectual stage of development has been reached, because then the life germs thrown off by man contain too little of the lower or animal life to sustain them, and they die and their bodies decay into the atmosphere. Thus as nations advance and grow more spiritual, these lower forms of life die out from the astral plane of that earth's sphere, and succeeding generations begin at first to doubt and then to deny that they ever had an existence.[93]

Francezzo says nothing here about angels producing the elementals. Rather, Francezzo avers first, that the elementals exist essentially as mental reflections of human states of mind, and second, that the "life" which elementals appear to possess is really nothing more than the liveliness of the human emotions that the elementals represent. In other words, these elemental beings amount to little more than inconsequential and evanescent representations of human emotions in a spiritual dimension.

In comparing these two major notions of the provenance of the nature spirits—Rudolf Steiner's and Francezzo's—we need to begin by recognizing that the elementals *are* real creatures, and then we need to assess *how real* they are. In a nutshell, Steiner teaches that the elementals are birthed from angels and, as such, they are dependent creatures who have life, but are not ensouled as human beings are. They are, however, important spiritual creatures inasmuch as they support and facilitate life processes in the world of nature. Francezzo, on the other hand, agrees that elementals possess a kind of "life" but no souls. But he maintains that their existence is derivative from and dependent upon the human mind. That is, the more intellectually developed and spiritually evolved human beings become, the less the elementals can exist and the more they simply dissipate and disappear altogether. This, then, would account for why so few people in the modern world have ever seen elementals. Thus, the elementals are simply fantastical and, as such, basically unimportant.

Each of the above explanations of elementals has a certain plausibility. For our part, we are inclined to find the greater truth here in Steiner's exposition, in view of the fact that there are many psychics and clairvoyants in the present day who continue to testify that they see elemental spirits. Further, Steiner appears to do greater justice to the existence of the elementals. That is, these nature spirits have authentic life and oftentimes possess some significant degree of subjectivity and intellectual cognizance, but otherwise remain curious creatures in that they do not possess an eternal spirit as we recognize angels and human beings to possess. At least in this latter regard, these elementals seem to resemble animals—only resident in the spiritual world.

2.   What do the elementals do?

The nature spirits of earth, water, air and fire that Steiner specifically addresses in his works are gnomes, undines, sylphs and salamanders, respectively. Other clairvoyants include in the category of nature spirits of the earth, in addition to gnomes, mention of a number of other fabled astral creatures—e.g., tree and wood elves, flower fairies, dwarfs, tree spirits, wood nymphs, leprechauns (Ireland), brownies (Britain), kobold (Germany) and trolls (Scandinavian "elves").[94] For our purposes here, we will follow Steiner's classification of elementals into the four basic races of fairies. Stewart Easton, a major scholar of Steiner's writings, provides us with the following general summary of the elementals' responsibilities:

> The invisible elemental beings could be perceived until recent times by many people, and they have passed into the folklore of every country. They were given names, which we shall also use here. The *gnomes* or goblins are the beings of the earth who work with the roots of plants and have a special affinity for the metals of the earth. The *undines* are water beings who used to be pictured so often as living near springs; they work with the leafy part of the plants. The *sylphs* live in the airy-warmth element, and it is their task to bring light down into the plants. Lastly, there are *salamanders* or fire-beings who bring warmth to the blossoms and make possible the formation of a seed that is capable of reproducing the plant anew after the period it has spent within the earth—in the realm, once again, of the gnomes.[95]

Gnomes are an ancient race of spiritual creatures who dwell in subterranean habitats like mines and caves. Of all the elementals, they are the most similar to human beings in form and character, and they apparently grow old just as humans do. They are also the most intelligent of the elementals, usually appearing to possess heads too large for their bodies. Marjorie Spock describes them as the great "knowers" among the nature spirits, able to see and work with ideas as we humans see and manipulate objects.[96] This enables them to achieve veritably instantaneous insight into many diverse matters. Further, gnomes are extremely vigilant, never partaking of sleep themselves, yet wielding an ability to put others to sleep, if desired. One of their major roles in the natural world is to move mineral nutrients to the roots of plants and trees. But perhaps a better way to characterize them is to say that, in general, they are profound craftsmen—always helping to build plants, flowers, trees, minerals and crystals.[97] As might be expected, gnomes are very rugged individualists, even anti-social toward their own race. Yet, under certain circumstances, gnomes are attracted to human beings who are cheerful and generous and may impart unique spiritual gifts to those persons with whom they become friendly.

In general, all the races of fairies have special capabilities associated with their astral or spiritual nature. Some of these abilities, which they may also use to protect or disguise themselves, include: the wielding of "glamour" to compel people to see either what the fairy wants them to see, or nothing at all; levitation; invisibility; shape-shifting into human, animal, vegetable, or even mineral forms; ability to bestow "good luck"; craftsmanship; some control over the weather; guarding of secrets of extraordinary healing; and the ability to instill sleep or altered states.[98]

Undines are water spirits that are sometimes also referred to as nymphs and water sprites. Undines indwell and work through the fluidic element in nature. As such, they are free-flowing, characterized in unceasing metamorphosis and thereby sometimes discerned in flowing rivers, or sheets of rain that undulate across landscapes. Unlike the thinking gnomes, undines manifest a mentality of dreaming, where all things freely transmute into other things. The undines' responsibility in the vegetable world is to draw the sap up stems of plants and trunks of trees, facilitating nurturance and growth.[99] As water spirits, undines have special fluidic abilities for permeating boundaries, overcoming separateness and reestablishing wholeness and wholesomeness. In this regard, undines can promote empathy, purification and healing amongst human beings.[100] Further, because water is the creative primordiality, undines can stimulate creativity in human beings, both as creative imagination and as sexual impulse.

Sylphs, as air elementals, are astral creatures of high intelligence, who flicker through light-filled atmosphere. In their profound sensitivity to the vibrational character of light and sound, they inhabit a world where they experience color as music, and sound as color.[101] Working together with undines, sylphs attend to the rhythms of nature with respect to transforming weather. In particular, their mission to the vegetable world entails bringing the creative forces inherent in light-filled air to facilitate the greening and blossoming of plants. Spock notes that sylphs also have a special interest in the activities of birds and bees. Sylphs themselves not only oftentimes manifest through human form but they sometimes work with human beings to stimulate inspiration and assist in humans' development of clairaudience and clairvoyance,[102] as well as serving as "guardian angels" for humans on occasion.[103]

Lastly, fire spirits, or salamanders, are "the fairy race closest to the cosmic source of things."[104] While it may be generally understood that fire spirits have involvement in heating, lighting and explosions in the natural world, their specific responsibility in the plant kingdom is to transform warmth in such a way that it is readily assimilable by seeds for their sprouting and by fruit for their ripening. One of the locations where salamanders reside is volcanoes. Metaphysically, fire is essentially and simultaneously destructive and creative. In relation to human beings, fire spirits can facilitate great spiritual ardor as well as detoxification and healing processes.[105]

3.   **In what ways can elementals be perceived by human beings?**

Briefly, we should recall that Rudolf Steiner taught that elementals, as well as the angelic realm, could only be viewed through progressively refining the human spiritual sense of sight, or clairvoyance. Van Gelder, Spock and numerous others agree with Steiner that the subtlety of the astral dimension can only be fathomed by developing clairvoyant and clairaudient sensing. Andrews, in particular, also endorses the basically Steinerian notion that the altered consciousness required for viewing elementals can be developed by practicing a series of meditative exercises, which utilize concentration, visualization and creative imagination—with the emphasis upon creative imagination.[106] Interestingly, both Steiner and Andrews clearly acknowledge here a truth that is otherwise not widely understood: that human creative imagination is not simply a faculty of random, usually visual, associativity but is a kind of spiritual faculty for sensing and knowing that can be deliberately disciplined and refined.

Also relevant here is consideration of what human occupations provide the best opportunities for the elementals to be seen. Spock, for instance, notes that farmers labor in expansive fields in the open countryside under open skies—an environment where all four fairy races will often dwell. Thus, farmers seemingly have the greatest opportunity to encounter elementals. Similarly, forestry workers are likely to encounter gnomes, undines and elves (i.e., sylphs). Fishermen, for their part, are continually surrounded by blustery oceans with foaming sprays, the realm of undines and sylphs. As aforementioned, miners, who work in mines and caves, have a greater chance of actually seeing gnomes. These four professions in particular offer a greater probability of witnessing elemental activities.

Finally, we would be remiss if we did not somehow address the ques-

tion: Why is it that people in the modern/contemporary world so infre-
quently see the nature spirits we have been describing here? Given that
elementals continue to exist, there are two plausible answers that might be
given. First, it is certainly true that almost all contemporary people are not
only *not* clairvoyant, but that most don't even believe that clairvoyance is a
real possibility. Dorothy MacLean, one of the founders of the Findhorn
Community in Scotland, puts it in these speculative terms:

> The ancients, of course, accepted the kingdom of nature spirits
> without question as a fact of direct vision and experience. The
> organs of perception of the supersensible world have atrophied
> in modern man as part of the price to be paid for the evolving
> of the analytic scientific mind. The nature spirits may be just as
> real as they ever were, though not to be perceived except by
> those who can redevelop the faculty to see and experience
> them.[107]

The second answer we could offer is that people today no longer see
the elementals because they have been driven out of many of their natural
habitats by pollution, generated as a result of the increasing technologiza-
tion of civilization. Air pollution, and environmental pollution from chemical wastes and chemical insecticides have not only ruined the ecology of
many forests, rivers and ocean coastlines, but have forced the fairies into
retreat.[108] Hence, there is less chance that one will encounter them in urban-
ized and suburbanized regions.

4. Why should it be important for human beings to see and interact with nature spirits?

Certainly most people have *not* seen or encountered elementals. Yet,
this majority of the human race does not seem the worse for this lack of experience. So, what really is the value of being able to discern these astral creatures? We suggest here that this kind of experience can be valuable in three
ways. First, becoming awake to the existence and work of elemental spirits
may benefit human beings inasmuch as it may help people to appreciate the
preciousness and subtlety of all living things. Such awareness of elementals,
in other words, may help human beings to recognize that the world of
nature is not just some materialistic display awaiting human manipulation,
but is, rather, wholly alive, spiritually informed, and ultimately grounded in
the reality of God's love.

Second, Andrews provocatively suggests that humans may benefit
from interaction with the fairy races by 1) being able to experience greater
joy, 2) becoming awakened to our own well-springs of creativity, and 3) being
able to inherit fairy wisdom in regard to profound healing and abilities for

communicating with animals (not unlike those abilities exercised by Native American tribes).[109]

Third, as Rudolf Steiner notes, the elementals can reciprocally benefit through their relationship with human beings. That is, by being appreciated and cherished by humans, the elementals are liberated to perform their responsibilities in nature more efficaciously.

Conclusions regarding elementals:

Briefly, let us restate here those ideas regarding elementals that seem most plausible and most correct. First, the elementals have an actual existence, not as a "figment of one's imagination," but as astral creatures, produced by angels, which directly serve the world of nature and indirectly serve the human world. These creatures may exhibit knowledge and "personality" but are not ensouled as human beings are. Thus, whereas human beings, who age and die, continue to exist and can continue as spirit-persons to grow endlessly in their capacity to realize God's love, elementals traverse their life cycle by growing older and, while we cannot say precisely what becomes of them, it seems that they finally evanesce into some form of non-existence. Yet, while this may be the eventual fate of the elementals, it does not in any way diminish their importance as a unique aspect of God's created universe.

III. UFOs and UFO-Beings: The Contemporary Enigma

The topic of the contemporary investigation of the UFO (Unidentified Flying Object) phenomenon is enormous and, for this reason, we need first to carefully acknowledge exactly what part of this larger investigation we will address here. The general and liberal position we take here is, notwithstanding the relatively few UFO reports that are deliberately fraudulent or honestly mistaken, that by-and-large the great majority of reports are authentic, and are of actual UFO sightings/encounters. What we understand this to entail is perhaps best summarized by well-known UFO researcher, Michael Lindemann, who lays out the following five points:

> 1) The alien presence is real. . . . 2) The alien presence is substantial. . . . 3) The alien presence is active and purposeful. . . . 4) The alien presence is diverse. . . . 5) The alien presence is known to elite and secretive groups within the U.S. government, as well as other major governments. . . .[110]

Without expatiating on each one of these points, we can simply note that point 4 is of greatest interest to us here. The diversity of the UFO phenomenon, which Whitley Strieber has otherwise renamed the "visitor phenomenon," is well captured in Strieber's summary listing of the possible origins of the visitors. In the context of accepting that the "visitors" are real and have objective existence outside the human mind, Strieber suggests that the visitors *might be*: a) from other planets or stars, i.e., *bona fide* extraterrestrials, b) from our own earth, perhaps heretofore unknown species, c) from another aspect of space-time, i.e., another dimension, d) from this dimension in space but not in time, i.e., time travelers of some sort (some reported UFO encounters strongly imply the reality of time travel), e) from within ourselves, i.e., according to Strieber, creatures (or gods?) that come to have objective existence because human imagination has somehow imparted that reality to them, and lastly f) the metamorphosis of a human being in the after-death state, i.e., if there is an afterlife, perhaps the visitors are simply human beings in a more advanced state of existence.[111] Of these six foregoing possible ways of interpreting the objective existence of the visitors, we choose here to focus on the *second* suggestion—that the visitors are from another dimension, i.e., these UFO-beings are, at least in part, *interdimensional beings.* This focus does *not* imply that the other five ways of interpreting the visitors' existence are incorrect, but it does seek to highlight what seems to be one of the best and most plausible notions for comprehending the being of the visitors.

Throughout this book, we have held the position, seemingly together with Swedenborg and various others, that the spiritual world is, in fact, an otherdimensional reality, or is otherwise constituted of numerous other dimensions. With this insight as our foundation, the thesis that we want to unfold here has three parts:

> I. At least some of the reported UFOs, and maybe most, are astral/spiritual in nature; that is, they exist as *spiritual phenomena.*

> II. At least some of the UFO-beings, and maybe most, are spiritual beings.

> III. At least some of the UFO-beings seem to resemble the spiritual beings we call *elementals.*

A.   UFOs as Otherdimensional Phenomena

UFO literature tends usually to emphasize one of two major hypotheses concerning UFOs. The first of these, which is the most conventional and which we will not elaborate on, is that UFOs are simply physical craft or vehicles, manned by extraterrestrials from other planets or stars in the physical universe. The second hypothesis, for which we are seeking to supply supporting evidence, is that UFOs are, or can be, *non-material craft,* capable of traveling across dimensions. From this perspective, French physicist Jacques Vallee has proposed that UFOs might be better thought of as dimensional "windows" rather than as objects.[112] In this regard, one might consider, for instance, certain descriptions by psychic Ruth Montgomery. Her sources—both earthly friends as well as spiritually channelled—have informed her that the beings in UFOs travel via beams of light which become manifest, or become transdimensionally visible, as "UFOs" that people report seeing in our own world.[113] This description of light-travel appears to be corroborated in the testimony of the deceased Sri Yukteswar, who describes to his disciple, Paramahansa Yogananda, the nature of transportation in the spiritual world:

> The inhabitants use astral planes, or masses of light, to travel from one planet to another, faster than electricity and radioactive energies.[114]

Along these same lines, it is valuable to note Rev. Sun Myung Moon's rather cryptic and provocative explanation of UFOs. In 1965, when asked if flying saucers were real, he replied as follows: "They look real but they are not. It is a spiritual manifestation. The people in them are spirit beings, not physical."[115] Rev. Moon further offered at this time that UFOs "appear as a sign of the last days." Anyone who has studied Rev. Moon's teachings regarding the "last days" immediately understands the internal meaning here. To say that UFOs are phenomena of the last days is to say that they appear at a messianic, watershed moment in human history—i.e., a time when the "distance" between the physical and spiritual worlds becomes greatly diminished, allowing these worlds to be drawn much "closer together" (so to speak), resulting in an increase of many varied kinds of spiritual visitation phenomena including, not least of all, sightings of or encounters with "UFOs." Thus, from this standpoint, UFOs may be understood as *one means* for spiritual beings to contact and interact with people on earth, the ultimate goal being to bridge the otherwise ignorant separation of physical and spiritual dimensions.

Whitley Strieber, award-winning science fiction writer, has become best known for his book *Communion* (1987), in which he details his real-life 1985 encounters with intelligent non-human UFO-beings at his forest cabin in upstate New York. In the past 15 years, Strieber has written a number of follow-up books, characterizing the nature of the on-going visitations by these creatures that Strieber has continued to experience.[116] All of these books urgently attempt to comprehend the significance of these visitation experiences and have progressively led Strieber, to a great extent, to agree with Vallee—that the UFO phenomenon, or "visitor phenomenon," is interdimensional rather than extraterrestrial.

Throughout his writing it seems that Strieber's experience with the visitor phenomenon is connected at every turn with the experience of parallel realities or dimensions. For instance, in *Breakthrough* (1995), Strieber recounts two particularly extraordinary experiences, one directly following the other. The night before he was to drive his son's friend back to New Jersey was spent at his cabin in upstate New York, the central locus of his continuing experiences with the "visitors." That night, Strieber suddenly found himself in the unprecedented state of floating out of his body, fully conscious, and then apparently visiting and speaking with his son and his son's friend downstairs. In the next moment, he was back lying in his bed and, while trying to make sense out of what had just happened, he went physically downstairs to check on his son and the friend, who were clearly fast asleep. The next day Strieber set out to return his son's friend to his father, which was an otherwise familiar trip they had taken many times. Strieber drove down the New York State Throughway and, having crossed into New Jersey, was traveling amidst midday traffic south down Route 17. Having spotted the diner where they were to meet the boy's father, on the opposite side of Route 17 (a divided highway), they exited off to the right in order to cross over an overpass to get to the other side of the highway. Suddenly Strieber, together with his son's friend as an intelligent, fully conscious, corroborating witness, entered into some kind of undeniable parallel reality. Both he and the boy were shocked to realize that all the traffic had disappeared and that they apparently had entered a neighborhood that neither had ever seen before, in which all the residences were uniformly set back from the street and seemed to be constructed out of a tan stone that was deeply etched with carvings of large serpents. Needless to say, for a brief period both Strieber and the boy, who did discuss their mutual bewilderment, were gripped by a common anxiety in the midst of this strangeness—until they found an exit back on to the highway. But, in returning to the highway, they ended up, not on Route 17, but on Route 80, some 20 miles from the diner—a distance they apparently had traveled in only a few minutes. At a later date, Strieber tried painstakingly to retrace his steps, but he was never again able to locate the strange neighborhood.[117]

Richard Thompson, who has a Ph.D. in mathematics (Cornell University) and is a disciple of the late A. C. Bhaktivedanta Swami Prabhupāda, renders in his book, *Alien Identities*, a unique and compelling study of the UFO phenomenon, inasmuch as he is able to carefully demonstrate how this phenomenon is recorded in the Vedas, i.e., the ancient spiritual scriptures of India. For instance, he documents that in major Vedic

works—the *Bhagavata Purana,* the *Mahabharata,* and the *Ramayana*—
there are many references to different humanoid races that are described as
living in parallel, higher-dimensional realms within the earth, on its surface
and in its immediate vicinity.[118] Further, there are many descriptions of flying machines, called *vimanas,* piloted by such humanoid races (e.g., *Devas,
Gandharvas* and *Danavas*) and these descriptions closely resemble contemporary descriptions of UFOs. In particular, the *vimanas* are described as
capable of flying through higher-dimensional realms, including traveling
from one dimensional frame of reference to another.[119] In other words,
Vedic depictions suggest that the UFO phenomenon, even in ancient times,
has had strong otherdimensional components. Thompson is circumspect
regarding contemporary UFO claims. Even if one allows that UFO-beings
were simply extraterrestrials, Thompson notes that it seems most plausible
to suppose UFOs travel *interdimensionally* rather than, say, intergalacti-
cally, inasmuch as the latter form of travel would undoubtedly impose great
burdens on extraterrestrials otherwise limited by the speed of light. And, even
if extraterrestrials were not limited by the speed of light, that would, in
effect, make other star systems into parallel worlds that would be directly
connected to our own world.[120] In any case, whether UFO-beings are otherdimensional or extraterrestrial, interdimensional transport of some sort
would seem to make the best sense.

B.   UFO-Beings as Spiritual Beings: Who Are They?

The speculative position we have taken here is that, in many cases,
UFO-beings appear to be *from* other dimensions and that these other dimensions are best understood as non-physical or, that is, as essentially men-
tal/astral/spiritual in character. A "non-physical" dimension is one that
would not have the substantiality of physical matter, but which would in any
case be very substantial for the non-physical beings residing in it, e.g., a non-
physical dimension would be a world essentially composed of thought or
mentality and, as such, would have very different properties than our world
of physical matter. Yet, it also seems to be the case that these otherdimensional UFO-beings have developed what might be termed "spiritual tech-
nology" which not only allows them to travel between physical and
non-physical dimensions but enables them to masterfully manipulate the
world of thought. Admittedly, this sounds like science fiction—but, in fact,
it may not be too far from the truth of the situation.

What can be said with reasonable certainty about the identity of these
UFO-beings? From all the reported experiences of UFO encounters and
UFO abductions, the human persons involved have said over and over again
that these beings are 1) highly intelligent, 2) non-human, in the vast majority of cases, 3) to a great extent, uncomprehending of human feelings and

4) that they appear to have some kind of long-range agenda that seems to involve relating to the human race for mutual benefit (though, in fairness, there are some who perceive these beings' actions as quite negative and parasitic, as we will soon see). When questioned regarding the identity of the beings in the UFOs seen in the 1985 Hudson Valley (NY) sightings, Rev. Moon carefully noted that these beings (i.e., spiritual beings) desire to help human beings learn how to environmentally protect and preserve planet earth, but they find this to be a difficult task because they do not understand human emotions.[121] UFO abductee Betty Andreasson, who has had literally dozens of extraordinary, albeit excruciating, experiences with these UFO-beings, explained to researcher Raymond Fowler, "They are curious about the emotions of mankind."[122] Fowler, who has painstakingly labored for thirty years in search of the truth of the UFO phenomenon, avers that one of his major findings after all this time—a finding which he only reluctantly has been compelled to accept—is that the UFO experience has a "paraphysical" nature.[123] What Fowler means by "paraphysical" is that the experience takes place in a realm beyond the physical, where the physical and psychic are apparently interfused in a manner not familiar to most human beings—i.e., what we have otherwise here termed "otherdimensional." Strieber, who has also discussed the fact that the "visitors" do not seem to grasp human emotions, provides additional evidence that these UFO-beings appear to possess a spiritual character/orientation:

> I have letters from people who have seen dead friends and relatives with the visitors, and Lorie was the third to have such an encounter at my cabin. One thing that is interesting about this is that it is so completely unremarked in the popular literature on the subject that it must be getting reported for the most straightforward of all reasons: it is happening to people.[124]

UFO-beings, which are oftentimes reported to suddenly appear and suddenly disappear, might also be explained, for instance, by the speculative hypothesis of Prof. Roger Wescott. As referenced in an earlier Section of this book, Dr. Wescott has suggested that, if reality is discovered to possess more than three spatial dimensions and/or unique time dimensions, human beings may eventually discover themselves at the "hyperspherical" intersection of an "interdimensional traffic" of a multiplicity of unusual, perhaps folklore-like, beings.[125] This suggestion is important because it lends support to the idea that at least some of the UFO-beings (perhaps many) may turn out to be fantastical otherdimensional creatures like elementals. Thompson's description of Vedic otherdimensional humanoid races explains that these races are traditionally characterized as possessing a variety of *siddhis*, or extraordinary powers, basically identical to those powers exercised by elementals. For instance, Vedic humanoids have abilities for telepathic communication, thought-reading, levitation (*laghimā-siddhi*), invisibility (*antardhāna*), shape-shifting or the ability to assume different bodily forms, and certain "possession" capabilities, i.e., abilities for entering into another person and controlling his/her behavior.[126]

Jacques Vallee is very direct in pointing out that, while many of the UFOnauts witnessed by humans can be said to be of a variety of biological types, the so-called pilots of the UFOs are very often described as dwarfs who answer the traditional folk descriptions of elementals. These dwarf-pilots apparently fall into two main groups. The first group consists of hairy dwarfs with bright eyes and deep, rugged, "old" voices—closely resembling the gnomes of the Middle Ages.[127] The second group consists of dwarf-beings who might otherwise be described exactly like sylphs from medieval times or like elves of the Celtic fairy-faith—i.e., as possessing human physiognomy, heads disproportionately large for their bodies, and silvery voices.[128] Psychic Ted Andrews goes so far as to affirm that the UFO abduction phenomenon is *directly* related to visitations by elementals:

> Many tales exist about the experiences of humans kidnapped
> and taken into UFOs and spaceships. They are then subject to
> strange sights and experiences. When returned, they behave
> and are treated just as those who claimed to have slipped into
> the faerie realms. Because the general public today assumes that
> faeries and fiction are one and the same, the *trooping faeries*
> use their glamour to create UFO encounters. After all, in this
> modern day of sophisticated technology and rational thinking,
> this illusion is more likely to be accepted. It is more probable
> than "a kidnapping to faerieland."[129] (Emphasis added)

We are not here taking the position that all UFO-beings are elementals; rather, our suggestion is that *some* UFO-beings, and maybe many, are *elemental-like* creatures. For instance, many of the UFOnauts have been described as "greys," i.e., as humanoid, dwarfish, and grey in color with large, dark black, slanted football-shaped eyes positioned in a triangular face with a pointed chin. It is these alien "greys" that Betty Andreasson has described as living in other "planes" or dimensions.[130] Similarly, Filberto Cardenas, an invitee of UFOnauts to visit the interior of their ship, testified that these beings assured him they were not gods, but rather simply from other dimensions, and able to travel interdimensionally.[131]

Finally, it is relevant to mention some of the most recent and most enlightening research into the nature of the UFO abduction phenomenon, published in *Passport to the Cosmos* (1999) by John E. Mack, professor of psychiatry at Harvard Medical School. What is especially fascinating about

John Mack's study is that it includes detailed discussions with a Native American, a South American shaman and an African shaman, regarding their UFO abduction experiences. Such a study is extremely valuable in that it contributes needed crosscultural perspectives on the meaning of this very enigmatic phenomenon.

Sequoyah Trublood, descended from Choctaw, Cherokee and Chickasaw tribes, is 60 years old and has dedicated his life to the healing and spiritual awakening of people of all races. He is partially Harvard-educated and, as of 1997, he served on the International Council of Elders without Borders and on the Native American Sports Council.[132] Sequoyah not only related his own very substantial yet otherdimensional encounter with the "greys"—who transported him to another planet where the inhabitants wore "white robes"—but, as Mack notes later, "told me that all of the more than a hundred medicine men and women with whom he [Sequoyah] has talked have had such [i.e., otherdimensional] encounters."[133]

Bernardo Peixoto and Credo Mutwa are both trained shamans. Bernardo Peixoto, the son of a Portuguese Catholic father and a native Brazilian mother (of the Uru-ê Wau-Wau tribe), also has a Ph.D. from Bélem de Pará University and works at the Smithsonian Institution in Washington, D.C.[134] Credo Mutwa's father was a Catholic catechism instructor, later converting to Christian Science, while his mother was the daughter of a Zulu shaman. Credo himself was baptized a Catholic, acquiring the equivalent of a 9th grade education in mission schools. However, Credo later renounced Christianity, and his life work has carried him into the position of spiritual leader of the *sangomas* (medicine men) of South Africa.[135] Both of these shamans have had remarkable and considerably traumatic experiences of being "taken" by the grey aliens, which are reported by virtually all abductees. Peixoto refers to these creatures as similar to, though distinct from, the *ikuyas,* or spirits who take human form in order to be seen, whereas Mutwa disparagingly refers to the grey humanoids as the *mantindane,* or "sky monkeys."[136] Both shamans find these creatures rather fearful and, in Mutwa's opinion, selfish, parasitic and domineering. As Mack notes, both consider these creatures to be from the spirit-world, yet with the ability to be present in the material world or, that is, as somehow simultaneously otherdimensional/extraterrestrial. However, the character most outstanding to the shamans is that these beings are not like the other spirits they encounter, e.g., ancestor spirits:

> While we in the West would emphasize that, if indeed these entities come from the spirit world, they seem to be unique in their capacity to manifest in or "cross over" into our physical world, this is not what the shamans emphasize. For them, this

crossover is not so important, as they are already able to perceive other entities from the unseen realms in the physical world. Rather these beings are distinguished by the fact that they are not manageable through the spiritual skills that shamans have learned; by the intense, sometimes overwhelming, energies that the humanoid beings possess and transmit to the experiencer; by the transtribal universalism that they represent; and finally by the direct linkage they seem to have to a divine intelligence that exists beyond symbolism and form itself.[137]

In summary, Dr. Mack's careful examination of many UFO-abduction testimonies has led him to a number of important conclusions, all of which we concur with, and two that we find especially compelling. The first is that the alien abduction phenomenon is one of a number of contemporary manifestations that suggest that we live in a multiply-dimensioned universe:

> Whatever words we may use to describe this realm or realms, it appears ever more likely that we exist in a multidimensional cosmos or multiverse, within which space and time appear to be constructs of the mind that order or simplify the chaos of energy and vibration in which we are immersed.[138]

The second concluding observation which we find noteworthy is Dr. Mack's admission that, in many cases, it seems unclear whether the abductee is reporting an actual event that happened in the physical world (which is how the abductee most often *thinks* he's reporting it), or is describing an event which has in fact occurred in some kind of subtle or astral dimension. This is a pregnant recognition inasmuch as it points, again, toward the continually recurring insight that, *in the last analysis,* the mind *is* the body, the body *is* the mind, and that the physical and the spiritual are inseparably united, i.e., they are really, finally, the same "thing."[139]

In conclusion, the foregoing discussion is clearly speculative but at least serves to suggest that both mind and reality are naturally multidimensional. Such recognition of other dimensions, we believe, will inevitably lead humankind both toward constructive interaction with the otherdimensional spiritual world and toward authentic spiritual self-understanding rooted finally in Divinity.

IV.   The Status of Animals in the Spiritual World

In our continuing effort to understand the different kinds of beings that have existence in the spirit-world, we come now to consideration of yet a fourth category of non-human denizens—i.e., animals. Many mystics, religious visionaries and psychic mediums have confidently described that animals—in particular, personal pets—*do* exist in the spiritual world, as part of the human societies resident there, just as here on earth. As a result of this, many people have likewise concluded that animals have independent, eternal spirits, or souls, just as human beings do. Part of the reason why this notion seems plausible is the apparent evidence that animals alive on earth exhibit remarkable behaviors that strongly suggest they should be regarded, for instance, as rightfully altruistic, ethical and artistic creatures. That is to say, many people today feel that we should not doubt that, along with human beings, animals have their own unique and autonomous souls.

Briefly consider the ideas of a well-known proponent of animal rights, Gary Kowalski—a graduate of Harvard Divinity School and a minister in the Unitarian Universalist Church. In his book *The Souls of Animals* (1991), Kowalski insists that, while we can never know definitively whether or not animals actually have souls, the evidence available to us strongly suggests that this *is* the reality. In order to make his case in this regard, he attempts to show that many different kinds of animals—e.g., gorillas, elephants, dogs, cats, birds, etc.—exhibit qualities of emotion and intellectual discrimination that we normally attribute to human beings and that many otherwise generally accept as evidencing the spiritual character of human beings. These qualities include: (1) grieving recognition of the death of those close to us; (2) possession of a sense of the mysterious; (3) the expression of joy through making music; (4) having an aesthetic sense or a desire to express oneself artistically; (5) having an ethical sense of right and wrong; (6) the ability to experience love, both as giver and receiver; (7) the need to express oneself through play; and (8) a clear sense of self-consciousness. Let us examine three of these areas in more detail.

In the course of Western civilization, theologians and philosophers have long held that two of the hallmarks distinguishing human beings from animals are the human person's abilities to be his/her brother's keeper as well as to know right from wrong. Kowalski, however, insists that many animals exhibit such an ethical sense, especially with regard to sacrificing themselves for the benefit of others—i.e., altruism. He points out, for instance, that a mother bird will act as a living decoy to distract predators in order to protect her young, and that African wild dogs will, at great risk to themselves, attack a cheetah to protect their young pups.[140] Further, Kowalski is not only convinced that his own dog expresses remorse when scolded, but notes that the great naturalist Charles Darwin also believed that dogs seem to possess a kind of conscience through which they feel shame and modesty (though Darwin, he notes, hesitated to affirm that dogs exhibit genuinely moral conduct). Kowalski's special empathy for animals and his keen appreciation of the sacredness of animal life clearly have been deeply offended by those human beings who have ruthlessly mistreated animals:

By denying that animals possess a moral sense we tell ourselves that human beings are of a fundamentally higher order. We can therefore colonize and enslave with impunity those who are "lower."[141]

Yet, the question we are left with here might be: Even if we decisively attribute a subjective moral sense to animals, which is admittedly questionable, would that mean that human beings would then never enslave or mistreat them? Clearly, human beings have done that to each other throughout history anyway. Is it then necessary (and/or correct) to affirm that animals are "ethical" creatures in order to insist that they should be loved and respected and to otherwise legitimate them as sacred?

Kowalski also sides with Konrad Lorenz who affirms that love is widespread throughout the animal kingdom. Kowalski references Lorenz's descriptions of jackdaws, a bird species that mates for life. Lorenz observed jackdaws to undergo a full year of courtship between the "betrothal," when pair-bonds are formed, and the "wedding," when their relationship is consummated.[142] During their lifetime together, jackdaw pair-bonds are unmistakably strong, mutually supportive partnerships. Thus Kowalski avers: "To call the mating behavior of jackdaws "love" is not a case of projecting human characteristics onto animals, therefore, but of recognizing animal characteristics in human beings."[143] Yet, doesn't this suggest the same notion promoted by those philosophers (e.g., Nietzsche, Marx and Freud) utilizing a destructive "hermeneutics of suspicion"—that love is not something that originates in "God," but instead is little more than an animal impulse that has been deliberately and spuriously divinized in order to index humans as uniquely "spiritual" creatures standing above animals?

Finally, Kowalski affirms that just as human persons can discover and acknowledge each other's selfhood, or soulful interiority, via looking into each other's eyes, so a person may have a very similar experience looking into the eyes of an animal. For Kowalski, such eye-contact can yield the realization that animals *do* possess a "self" that is undeniably engaged in "self-consciousness":

Just because I've never had a sense of making eye-contact with a fish or a snake is no proof that these simpler creatures lack self-awareness. On the other hand, the fact that I have been able to establish eye-contact with dogs, apes, and other mammals constitutes fairly good evidence (in a region where no evidence can be absolutely convincing) that these animals share with human beings a certain degree of self-consciousness.[144]

Kowalski compassionately suggests that any human person may become edified through such eye-contact with an animal, thereby entering into an "interspecies meditation":

> And as you look into this being's eyes, pay attention also to
> what you cannot see, the inwardness, the selfhood, the "I" that
> is as singular as its outward expression.
>   What you look upon is a living spirit.[145]

Yet, even if we grant that there is some sense in which an animal seems to have interiority which it is aware of, it seems extremely doubtful that this is in any way comparable to the complexities of human self-consciousness and self-reflection. The main philosophical problem that Kowalski's analysis brings to the fore seems to be this: Notwithstanding his wonderful sensitivity to the animal kingdom, in his effort to show how much like human beings animals are, doesn't he end up suggesting that human beings are really no better than animals? Isn't he intimating throughout that animals are just as "spiritual" as humans? While we agree that Kowalski's ideas have a certain plausibility and are usefully thought-provoking, in the last analysis, we feel that such notions are really only poetic speculations about the "soulfulness" of animals and do not clarify anything about whether animals *have* souls or spirits.

Nevertheless, even if we cannot decisively determine, from their earthly behavior, whether animals have independent souls, there are quite a few testimonies from contemporary psychics and near-death experiencers that would seem to confirm this. Francezzo, speaking from the spirit-world through his earthly scribe, A. Farnese, offers the following representative statement:

> Whenever you see the power to reason and to act upon such
> reasoning manifested either in man, the highest type, or in ani-
> mals, the lower type, you may know that a soul exists, and it is
> only a question of degree of purity of soul essence. We see in
> man and in the brute creation alike a power of reasoning intel-
> ligence differing only in degree, and from this fact the school
> of thought to which I belong draws the inference that both
> alike have a conscious individual immortality, differing, how-
> ever, in the type and degree of soul essence, animals as well as
> men having an immortal future for development before them.
> What are the limits of the action of this law we cannot pretend
> to say, but we draw our conclusions from the existence in the
> spirit world of animals as well as men who have alike lived on
> earth, and both of whom are found in a more advanced state of
> development than they were in their earthly existences.[146]

Jan Price, having revived after being clinically dead for four minutes following a heart attack in 1993, testified that, in the course of her astonishing near-death experience, she was greeted by her beloved dog in the after-life. She confidently comments:

> . . . and yes, dogs have souls—Plato knew it and so did Saint
> Augustine, along with most other true saints and sages.[147]

A third description, which typifies those related by psychics, is given by renown psychic medium George Anderson in *Lessons from the Light* (1999). Such a statement would seem especially convincing inasmuch as it suggests that personal pets in the spirit-world can have an independent "personality" which is otherwise indistinguishable from personalities of beloved deceased persons also trying to communicate through Anderson:

> I sometimes don't know that a soul is a pet until they tell me.
> This is their insurance that I won't just discount their communi-
> cation by saying, "The pet says hello," and leave it at that.[148]

Thus far, we have indicated that there are many people, perhaps a majority, who have chosen to believe, not only that animals have their own independent souls or spirits, but that these spirits continue to exist indefinitely in the spiritual world after the death of such animals—exactly as do the spirits of human beings. However, we submit that this constitutes a naive viewpoint inasmuch as animals, by their very nature, are not designed to be able to exercise the higher cognitive and empathic faculties that human beings exercise. This point has to do with grasping that, while animals are not just "dumb" creatures, animal behaviors are inevitably and inexorably circumscribed by their *instinctual* nature. Human behavior is certainly instinctual in part, but it is not limited to, or circumscribed by, instinct; human instinctual behavior may be profoundly moderated, for instance, by intellectual discernment, rational choice and/or complex emotional sensitivities. That animals are singularly distinguished by not having any choice but to follow the habituality of their instincts is eloquently rendered by Emanuel Swedenborg. In the following passage, "discernment" refers to the principal intellectual faculty in a human being, while "intentionality" refers to the sense of purposefulness rooted in the emotional self of a person:

> If people pass judgement on the basis of the way things
> look to their physical senses, they will reach the conclusion that
> animals have intentionality and discernment just the way people
> do, the only difference being that people can talk and can there-
> fore express what they are thinking and intending, while ani-
> mals can only make noises about these things. However,

animals do not have intentionality and discernment, *but only some image of each, which scholars call an analogue. . . .*

The life of an animal can be compared to that of a sleep-walker who moves around and does things as a result of an intentionality whose discernment is asleep, or to a blind person who follows paths with a dog leading him. So, too, it is like the life of a retarded person who does his task according to set standards as a result of practice and consequent habit. Or it is like the life of an amnesiac who has thereby lost his intellect. He still knows—or learns—how to get dressed, eat fine foods, make love, walk the streets from his house and back again, and to do the sorts of things that gratify his senses and make his body comfortable, and is guided by these enticements even though he is not thinking and therefore cannot talk.

We can see from this how wrong people are when they believe that animals enjoy rationality and are distinguished from man only by their outward form and their inability to express rational things that lie within. These errors lead many people to conclude that if man lives after death, so will animals, or, conversely, that if animals do not live after death, neither will humans. And then there are other dreams that arise out of ignorance about intentionality and discernment . . . .[149] (Emphasis added)

In other words, Swedenborg wants to clarify here, not only that animals are instinctual creatures, but that the "intentionality" and "discernment" they *seem* to exercise is really only a kind of *image* or *reflection* of authentic human intentionality and discernment. One way to exemplify this understanding might be to point to an instance where a personal pet, perhaps a cat that you have loved and cared for for 10 years, appears to deliberately return your affection by rubbing up against your leg and purring. Is this cat subjectively expressing affection and appreciation towards you, or is it, on the other hand, simply *responding instinctually* to the many times you have lovingly cared for the cat? We suggest that the latter explanation best describes what is really happening in this situation. The cat's response is, finally, a *reflection of the human affection* it has received.

This basic principle of reflection undergoes an ingenious transformation when carried into the spiritual world. Here, as a general rule, the things one has loved deeply during one's earthly life may be made to manifest, sometimes instantaneously, through the power of thought which is desire. This rule applies, not only to manifesting an imaged form of material things one once loved, but also to producing an image of plants and animals one has loved. Such images, generated out of deep love, are not, however, weak or faded; rather, they are profoundly exact, *substantial* and fulfilling in the spiritual world. What does this phenomenon imply with regard to a beloved personal pet who has died? Sun Myung Moon, Emanuel Swedenborg and various others explain that a personal pet or, for that matter, any other animal, can exist in the spiritual world, not because it has its own subjective spirit, but because deceased human persons *desire* it to exist. Just as in the above-mentioned example the cat's response is best understood as a *reflection* of the affection it has received from a human person, so also in the spirit-world, the existence of a personally beloved pet is in reality, again, a *thought-reflection* of a person's love for their pet. In the following question and answer, Rev. Moon once gave just this sort of reasoned explanation:

Q: I'm afraid of having my love for animals, and not having any animals on which to lavish the love. Will I be able to have animals in the spirit world?

A: If you love animals, you will have them in the spirit world. Your love toward Sheba [Questioner's dog] will be created there as Sheba for yourself. It will be a reflection of your attachment. It will not be Sheba herself, but a reflection of your mind. But it will still please you.[150]

Finally, then, the question of whether animals actually have their own independent and immortal souls is most definitively resolved, we feel, in the following quote from *Apocalypse Explained.* Herein Swedenborg clarifies that we can rightfully regard animals as possessing "souls." But these souls are, in reality, *corporeal*—a fact that can be known with certainty when animals are seen in the environment of the spiritual world. That is, in the spirit-world, animals exist only as the manifestation of human and angelic desire, and only as long as that desire persists:

... That every animal has a soul is known, for they live, and life is a soul, wherefore also they are called in the Word 'living souls.' [That] that soul in its ultimate form, which is corporeal, such as appears before the sight, is animal, cannot be better known than from the Spiritual World. Every kind of beast, bird, and fish is as plainly seen in that World as in the Natural World, and in so similar a form that they cannot be distinguished from those in our World; but the difference is that in the Spiritual World they exist apparently from the affections of Angels and Spirits, so that they are appearances of affections; wherefore they vanish as soon as the Angel or Spirit goes away, or his affection ceases. Hence it is evident that their soul is just that.[151]

The central meaning of this quote, which is also most relevant to the present discussion, lies in its final sentence—i.e., that animal souls, as experienced from the perspective of the spiritual world, are nothing else than the quality of the human or angelic affections that have generated them. In his continuing statement, Swedenborg emphasizes this reality by describing that different kinds of animals naturally manifest as part of different societies in the spirit-world, according to the quality of character of the members composing those societies:

> Since the animals there are appearances of affections, therefore one genus of animal with its species appears in one Society, and another in another, and all the genera of animals with their species in the whole together. In the Societies of Heaven there appear gentle and clean animals, in the Societies of Hell ungentle and unclean beasts, and in the World of Spirits [i.e., the realm intermediate between Heaven and Hell] beasts of an intermediate kind. . . .
>
> Since there is such a likeness of the animals that appear in that World with the animals in this World that no difference can be discerned, and since the former derive their existence from the affections of the Angels in Heaven and the cupidities of the Spirits in Hell, it follows that natural affections and cupidities are their [i.e., animals'] souls . . . .[152]

In bringing this Part IV to a close, we would finally observe a key understanding to emerge in this discussion about animal souls: that reality, and the universe itself, are structured in accordance with the principles of true love. Beyond the notions of a simplistic anthropomorphism, we note that human love for an animal on earth will magnetically summon the animal to that person, thereby transforming its responsivity into an expression of affection and thus investing the animal with seeming ensoulment. True love, like God, is eternal, unchanging, yet absolutely and infinitely creative. To the extent that one's love in the spiritual world for an animal or pet approximates true love, that animal can be created—and will continue to exist and bring one great joy in the life after death.

V.   Summary Conclusions

This Section has been devoted to the examination of four categories of non-human beings that exist in the spiritual world, the first three of which we understand to evince subjective intelligence in varying degrees. Animals, constituting the fourth category, exist in the spiritual world essentially as reflections of human affection and desire.

Angels, we have seen, exist with the general purpose of serving as messengers for God, maintainers of cosmic harmony and as supporters and nurturers of humanity. The offspring of angels, which we have herein discovered to be nature spirits, are spiritual beings whose specific mission addresses the nurturance of the world of nature. While angels are highly intelligent, their offspring in the fairy worlds possess a more moderate intelligence adequate for fulfilling their responsibilities in the natural world. Noteworthy also is the fact that, while the angels have been historically understood both as the Heavenly Host praising God as well as fallen beings, like Satan, who maintain the existence of evil, so also nature spirits thereby have both good and evil provenance. (We have, however, limited our discussion here only to the character of those nature spirits whose efforts are *constructive*.)

UFO-beings, the third category of intelligent spiritual creatures, are admittedly more difficult to understand and classify, and our efforts to do this here have been the most speculative of all. But, having recognized that there are *at least* three distinct kinds of intelligent beings existing in the spiritual world, *in addition to human beings,* we are led finally to suggest that there may well be still other different kinds of intelligent beings existing in the spiritual world than we are presently aware of. In this regard, humanity may be in for many surprises in the centuries to come. After all, God may have only one Image after which the created universe has been fashioned, but there may also exist as-yet untold variations on that Theme.

Section 12

How does spiritual growth, i.e., soul evolution, take place after
the death of the physical body?

I died as mineral and became a plant,
I died as plant and rose to animal,
I died as animal and I was Man.
Why should I fear? When was I less by dying?
Yet once more I shall die as Man, to soar with angels blest;
but even from angelhood
I must pass on . . .[1]
　　　　—Jalalu' L-Din Rumi

The Body of B. Franklin
Printer,
Like the Cover of an Old Book
Its Contents Torn Out
And
Stripped of its Lettering and Gilding
Lies Here
Food for Worms
But the Work shall not be Lost
For it Will as he Believed
Appear Once More
In a New and more Elegant Edition
Revised and Corrected
By the Author.[2]

—Benjamin Franklin

According to a well-known story, Pythagoras stopped someone from beating a dog, because he had recognized the voice of a friend in the yelping of the dog. The late Austrian conductor Herbert von Karajan did not claim to have been an animal in a previous life, but he was sure that he would return as an eagle. In the Brihadaranyaka Upanishad, it is taught that some wicked human beings are reborn as insects—wasps, gnats and mosquitoes. The Harvard anthropologist Oscar Lewis, who studied the behavior and beliefs of peasants in an Indian village, was told that people guilty of serious crimes may in the future sink so low as to become jars. . . . According to *The Tomorrow of Death*, a book published in Boston in 1888, "the soul of a musically inclined child" may not have come from a human being at all but from "the nightingale, the sweet singer of our woods." . . . The author of this charming work does not express any opinion about how some New York City landlords acquired their blackmailing proclivities. My own opinion is that they were once sharks. It is widely believed that the poet Edith Sitwell was a flamingo in an earlier life and there cannot be any serious doubt that Winston Churchill had once been a bulldog. Bull terriers, the lovable little dogs whose noses look as though they had been bashed in, were probably prize fighters in a previous life. . . .[3]

—Paul Edwards

The theory of reincarnation probably came into being during the early stages of mankind when departed spirits took possession of the bodies of susceptible individuals and acted through them, thus seemingly indicating reincarnation. In reality this was only spirit obsession or possession. The idea of reincarnation is, therefore, a misunderstanding and a misinterpretation of the phenomenon demonstrated by the temporary residence of an alien spirit in the body of an earthly being. In actuality, there are neither previous lives for man on earth nor endless individual, bodily reincarnations. The only way of return to this earth after the death of man's physical body is to descend in spirit form.[4]

—Young Oon Kim

discussion

I.   Introduction

The question, "How does the spirit grow?," which is also the question, "How does the soul evolve?," is a question of paramount importance. Everything in the living universe goes through a process of growth to reach maturity, including the human spirit. Since there is a great deal at stake in correctly understanding how the process of spiritual growth takes place, we undertake in this Section to carefully examine and critique the most widely acknowledged theory of soul development, that is, the theory of reincarnation. However, as profound and as metaphysically superior as the theory of reincarnation may seem to many spiritually concerned people in our time, we will finally propose that there is, in fact, a far better way to explain the same phenomena that the theory of reincarnation seems to explain, i.e., we will propose the Theory of Spiritual Cooperation and Returning Resurrection.

Reincarnation, as a commonly held belief, is that every human soul or spirit gradually evolves toward spiritual perfection through the means of assuming a new physical body after the death of its previous physical body, in an indeterminate series, sometimes extending through even millions of such re-embodiments. Thus, reincarnation entails the conviction that one physical lifetime is impossibly too scant an opportunity to completely grow our character to become fully realized human beings, and this belief is endorsed by vast numbers of people today as by far the most plausible notion of how humans achieve spiritual maturity.

The Persian poet, Rumi, and Benjamin Franklin (in the Opening Quotes to this Section) together epitomize the polar extremes of belief in reincarnation—encompassing a vast spectrum from East to West, and from acceptance of a notion of progressive rebirth in seemingly inanimate form through the fully human, to the more limited notion of rebirth *only* in human bodies. It is sobering to realize that, as Steven Rosen has noted, after all poll statistics are tabulated, it can be reasonably estimated that more than half of the world's population, i.e., more that 3,000,000,000 souls on earth today, subscribe to some form of belief in reincarnation.[5]

It is well-known that the notion of karmic reincarnation figures prominently in Hinduism, Buddhism and Jainism. But it is also true that belief in reincarnation is openly endorsed by the mystical or esoteric branches of those world religions acknowledging the God of Abraham, Isaac and Jacob, i.e., Judaism, Christianity and Islam. Hence, esoteric Judaism, rooted in the medieval mystical interpretation of Torah known as the Kabbalah, acknowledges *gilgul neshamot* (i.e., the "turning" or "rolling" of souls) as the primary form of reincarnation, in which a soul, seeking atonement through rebirth, enters the fetus during pregnancy. Mainstream Christianity has always disavowed belief in reincarnation, having declared as heretical at the Fifth Ecumenical Council (553 A.D.) Origen's original and later popular notion of the soul's pre-existence and transmigration. But it is worth noting that, in addition to Origen, a number of the other early Church Fathers, including Clement of Alexandria, Justin Martyr, St. Gregory of Nyssa, St. Jerome and even briefly, Augustine (as an early Manichean), all advocated reincarnationist ideas. In the Middle Ages, the Bogomils and Cathars, gnostic Christian sects that were viciously exterminated by the Catholic popes, also held distinctive beliefs in reincarnation. Prominent Christian reincarnationists today, who interpret numerous of Jesus' sayings as affirmations of reincarnation, include Christian theologian and philosopher, Geddes MacGregor, the well-known professor of theology at Fordham University, John J. Hearney, as well as Dr. George Ritchie, whose near-death encounter and journey with Jesus has become legendary. Again, while mainstream Islam rejects any notion of reincarnation, the Sufis, or mystical branch of Islam, affirm *Tanasukh,* the ordinary process of transmigration that all souls must endure to attain ethical perfection.

As a way of highlighting in particular the fact that many eminent statesmen, philosophers, scientists, artists and others in the history of Western culture have embraced reincarnationist thinking, we may marvel at the following list of such luminaries: Benjamin Franklin, David Lloyd George, Pythagoras, Plato, Plotinus, Voltaire, Immanuel Kant, Friedrich Nietzsche, Pierre Curie, Thomas Edison, Goethe, Balzac, Tolstoy, Victor Hugo, Emerson, E.A. Poe, Herman Melville, H.G. Wells, W.B. Yeats, Walt Whitman, Henry Miller, Wagner, Mahler, Gauguin, Salvador Dali, Sylvester Stallone, Peter Sellers, Shirley MacLaine, Henry Ford, Albert Schweitzer, George Patton, C.G. Jung, Henry David Thoreau, Thomas Carlyle, etc.[6]

II. Reincarnation: Definition and Significance

The word *reincarnation*, generally connoting the consecutive rebirth of souls in new physical bodies, is often used interchangeably with several other notable terms: *transmigration* (the migration of souls across a series of physical lifetimes), *metempsychosis* (the process through which souls are changed, after death, into new bodies), and *palingenesis* (meaning "generated again" or rebirth). Reincarnationists generally hold that souls are eternal and uncreated, existing before and after the death of each physical body, up until the omega point of perfection. But all souls, as *incorporeal* entities, in order to mature into their rightful fruition, need to inhabit *corporeal* bodies, in fact a whole series of bodies in succession. The realization here is, interestingly enough, that spiritual growth depends upon, and is primarily accomplished through, physical-body experience—an insight which is fundamentally correct. But, beyond this, reincarnation theory insists that one physical lifetime could never be enough to enable us to complete our soul development; hence, it seems logical to infer that numerous physical lifetimes must be required for this achievement. As Rosen notes, ". . . reincarnation speaks directly to the logic of God's compassion, as it provides repeated opportunity for conditioned (embodied) souls to correct themselves."[7]

In effect, this notion is the above-mentioned notion of karmic reincarnation embraced in Hinduism. The Law of Karma is basically the law of spiritual/ethical cause and effect. For example, if a man spent one lifetime callously abusing his wife, he may perhaps in the next life be reincarnated as a woman who becomes the spouse of a wife-beater. Only in this way is it plausible that justice will be done, i.e., that this soul can *atone* for its transgression while becoming constructively educated about why such abusive behavior is never acceptable. Let us take a second example. Suppose that a man has lived his life as a sociopath and has been a serial murderer for much of his life. Karmic reincarnation could very well ordain that this person deserves devolution from a human being into an animal or plant of some sort in his next incarnation. As Geoff Viney explains in regard to Hindu notions of transmigration:

> Each individual's destiny is their own responsibility and severe transgressions can result in a future incarnation in the body of a beast. . . . No soul may count itself unlucky to be inhabiting a particular body, even that of a cripple, for each incarnation has been chosen according to that soul's level of spiritual understanding. We get our just deserts, no more, no less.[8]

Similarly, taking the first example again—if the woman, who was battered by her husband, somehow continued through her long-suffering to love and serve her husband, out of her love for God and without succumbing to resentment and hatred of her husband, then perhaps in the next life she would have the spiritual credentials to become a spiritual teacher to hundreds or thousands of people. This sort of example serves to further highlight the idea that reincarnation enables soul purification through suffering, which is the primary means of spiritual growth.

In the Western world, it is safe to say that the most prevalent conception of reincarnation is one that retains this notion of rebirth for karmic atonement and purification, but usually dispenses with the idea that rebirth occurs in sub-human bodies. Additionally, unlike the Eastern notion, the

Western notion often emphasizes that each soul, while in the disembodied interim state before reincarnation, *personally* determines or chooses what sort of body and what probable kind of life one should have in order to learn the lessons one needs to learn in his/her continuing evolution.

III.   Evidence for Reincarnation

It is probably best to begin here by explaining that, while the spiritual/ethical consequences from life to life generally are not easy to ascertain, the *fact* that some people have lived through a series of lives is allegedly well-evidenced. In this section, we will first summarize three rather famous cases that strongly suggest the validity of reincarnation. Beyond this, a second kind of evidence that will be presented here, especially important to Christian reincarnationists, is that corroboration of reincarnation that seems to come from the sayings of Jesus.

The first two of the three well-known cases exemplify a common conviction of most reincarnation researchers: that the most convincing past-life recollections come from toddlers and young children who do not otherwise have the necessary sophistication to perpetrate any kind of fraud. One of the most remarkable of these toddler cases might be that of Romy Crees, a two-year-old girl living in Des Moines, Iowa.[9] In 1981, Romy started telling her parents that she was a married man named Joe Williams, who was completely unknown to Romy or her parents. Romy insisted that she, that is, Joe, had died in a motorcycle accident and that her family, i.e., Joe's wife, Sheila, and his two daughters, lived in Charles City, 140 miles from Romy's home. Romy pleaded with her parents to take her to visit her (Joe's) family.

These pleadings fell on somewhat deaf ears, as Romy's parents remained deeply alarmed and puzzled by these events. Romy's parents, who were strong Catholics, completely rejected the possibility of reincarnation and felt instead that their daughter's behavior might indicate some kind of possession by the Devil. An exorcism was performed to no avail, and thereafter the Crees resorted to consultation with a child psychologist named Dr. Hermendra Bannerjee. Dr. Bannerjee, after considerable skepticism, became steadily convinced that Romy's descriptions and protestations were uncannily accurate and eventually arranged for himself and Romy and her parents to travel to Charles City. Here, Romy spontaneously and correctly identified many locations, including the home of Joe Williams. Williams' widow, Sheila, who still resided in the home, confirmed not only that her husband, Joe, had died in a motorcycle accident, but many other details of their relationship that had been narrated by Romy. Even Romy's parents at this point could not but acknowledge that some kind of rebirth or transmigration was the most likely explanation to account for their daughter's knowledge of Joe Williams' wife.

The second case was originally researched by Peter and Mary Harrison and published in their book, *Life Before Birth* (1983) which details numerous cases of children apparently reincarnated in the United Kingdom. Carl Edon, a three-year-old boy living in Middlebrough, described to his parents his vivid past-life recollections of being a Luftwaffe pilot in WWII, and then finally dying in a plane crash.[10] In this case, there was considerable, astonishing and later, carefully verified, supporting evidence. First, Carl produced uncannily accurate drawings of the badges and insignias of the flight command. Second, Carl provided descriptions of the internal operations, levers, controls, dials, etc. of his Heinkel aircraft's cockpit. Third, Carl's knowledge of the dimensions, performance and bomb payload of his aircraft were confirmed by his stunned parents to be correct to the last detail. Needless to say, that a three-year-old could possess such knowledge, while claiming it to be natural since he was a WWII pilot, certainly seems suggestive of reincarnation.

Finally, the third noteworthy case was first published in *More Lives Than One* (1978), by Arnall Bloxham, an English doctor who used hypnosis to regress friends and volunteers in the early 1970s. This case differs from the first two specifically in that (a) it deals with the past-life memories of an *adult woman* instead of a child, and (b) the past-life memories are *hypnotically recovered,* rather then directly consciously recalled. "Jane Evans" is the pseudonym of a woman who recalled seven past lives.[11] Jane, in her thirties, was an intelligent woman who finished high school and had studied history, French and Latin, but not to advanced levels. Under hypnosis, Bloxham discovered that Jane could describe distinctive memories of having been: a Roman living in first century A.D. Britain; a Jewess murdered in a medieval pogrom in York; a prostitute in Paris, France; a maid servant in the Loire Valley; a serving girl under Queen Anne; a lady-in-waiting at the Spanish Court; and an American nun who had lived and died in a convent in Des Moines, Iowa. While each of these past lives yielded a great deal of accurate historical information, Jane's most impressive incarnation was as a Jewess named Rebecca who was murdered in an antisemitic riot in 1190. Professor Barrie Dobson of the University of York, an expert on this historical period, was amazed by the accuracy of Rebecca's descriptions of this pogrom.

However, an important weakness in her story became apparent. Rebecca claimed that just before she had died, she and her family had hidden in the crypt of St. Mary's Castlegate church which, as far as Prof. Dobson or any of Jane's contemporaries then knew, did not in fact have a crypt. But six months later, workmen renovating the floor of St. Mary's discovered a long-hidden room with vaults and arches, i.e., a crypt. Bloxham later pointed out that, since no living person had known about the existence of the crypt, this fact could not have been known through any conventional means to Jane Evans. He concluded that the only plausible explanation for Jane's knowledge must be that Jane really had lived past lives on earth.

As mentioned earlier, the doctrine of reincarnation is widely featured throughout the spiritual texts of Hinduism and Buddhism and, as such, it is commonly accepted in these religions and is unproblematic. However, it is unusual to find Christians who insist that the Bible supports reincarnation. Philosopher Geddes MacGregor and George Ritchie, M.D., are two well-known Christian writers who find unmistakable evidence that Jesus endorsed transmigrational thinking in several critical scriptures.

The seeming foundation of Biblical reincarnation begins with the conclusion of the Old Testament. The Old Testament ends with Malachi's promise of the second coming of Elijah (Mal. 4:5) which, in itself, seems an obvious declaration of a further incarnation of this prophet. Beyond this, Jesus, speaking to his disciples' inquiry in Mt. 17:10-13, directly informs them that, indeed, Elijah has returned, just as the scripturally educated Jews of Jesus' time were expecting, and that, further, Elijah has returned in the person of John the Baptist. The only problem here, unfortunately, is that the Israelites just don't understand that John the Baptist is Elijah and, as a consequence, have been prevented from recognizing that Jesus is the Messiah, who was otherwise expected *after* the re-appearance of Elijah. Jesus, of course, knew that it would be difficult for the Israelites to grasp what seems only rightfully classifiable as the reincarnation of Elijah in John the Baptist, a situation that Jesus *first* addresses in Mt. 11:13-15:

> For all the prophets and the law prophesied until John. And if
> you are willing to receive it, he is Elijah who is to come. He
> who has ears to hear, let him hear!

Furthermore, two other New Testament passages seem to suggest that reincarnationist thinking was well-rooted in the popular mind. In Mt. 16:13-14, when Jesus asks his disciples who the people say that he is, they reply that some say he is John the Baptist, some say Elijah, while yet others say that he is Jeremiah or one of the prophets. Accordingly, it seems that one might reasonably infer that many first century Jews believed in the possibility of the soul's return. Similarly, in John 9:2, the disciples ask Jesus: "Rabbi, who sinned, this man or his parents, that he was born blind?" Here, the unmistakable implication is that there seems to be the possibility that the man has been born blind as atonement for sins he committed before birth, i.e., in a previous existence. In summary, then, though there are relatively few Biblical verses that seem to merit a transmigrationist interpretation, these few are so striking that it is difficult to imagine a more plausible interpretation.

IV. Critique of the Theory of Reincarnation

While some evidence for reincarnation seems very compelling, it is important to acknowledge that disbelievers, and sometimes even sympathetic observers, have leveled a variety of critiques against the theory of reincarnation. In this section, we can consider a number of the major critiques which might conveniently be classified in the following categories: critiques from implausibility/ludicrousness, empirical critiques, philosophical critiques and theological critiques. Also, the ordering of these critiques seems to this writer to reflect their corresponding significance, from least important to most cogent.

1. Critique from implausibility/ludicrousness

The critique from implausibility/ludicrousness consists in the objection that the notion of reincarnation inevitably generates results that are, *prima facie,* not only implausible, but even ludicrous. The third Opening Quote from philosopher Paul Edwards is a good example of this species of critique. Another humorous example would be the following passage from Peter Washington's recent book, *Madame Blavatsky's Baboon:*

> For it turned out that in each of these previous lives everyone else known to Leadbeater also figured, but with different identities and sometimes different sexes. Some had been famous historical characters. Others had lived on the moon and Venus.
>
> Thus in 40000 BC Leadbeater had been Annie's [Annie Besant's] wife and Krishna [Krishnamurti] their child, while in 12000 BC Leadbeater married Francesca Arundale in Peru and produced Bertrand Keightly and A.P. Sinnett as offspring. In other ages Mrs. Besant acquired twelve husbands for whom she roasted rats, and Julius Caesar married Jesus Christ. The final charts are a triumph of cosmic soap opera, including over two hundred characters. Inevitably in such a large undertaking there were occasioned contradictions or discrepancies. Whenever Leadbeater's assistants found one they would tell their master, who immediately went into a brief trance and rectified the errors.[12]

2. Empirical critique

Empirically speaking, there seem to be six major objections against reincarnation. First, there exist no undisputed and generally acknowledged data establishing reincarnation. This is as true today as it was back in the 1960s when Professor Ian Stevenson published what has come to be regarded as *the* definitive study promoting the plausibility of reincarnation, in which he openly admits that his 20 studied cases only *suggest* the possibility of rein-carnation.[13] Second, and somewhat related to the first critique is, for instance, C.T.K. Chari's pointed, specific critique of Stevenson's original data. Chari, along with many other detractors generally, criticize that, due to a lack of ade-quate screening, most of Stevenson's findings in his 20 cases amount to little more than cultural artifacts. He otherwise characterized Stevenson as a naive researcher who had not adequately appreciated how the rein-carnation stories of Asian children could be generated out of childhood fantasy elaborated in a certain cultural context.[14]

Third, while some isolated individuals apparently experience past-life memories evidencing reincarnation, either consciously or via hypnosis, *most people* have no recall of a past life. Prof. Mark Woodhouse, however, does not feel that this objection need be taken too seriously and offers the fol-lowing rebuttal: a) Most people don't recall past lives because, simply, they probably could not psychologically handle such undoubtedly traumatic recall; b) Past-life recall is not common inasmuch as it would tend to under-mine the very purpose of reincarnation, i.e., to catalyze authentic growth of human character through spontaneous natural responses to current dilem-mas—a kind of responsiveness that would otherwise be daunted by obses-sive recall of many failures in many past lives; and c) It is no wonder most people can't recall *past lives* when, for that matter, most people can't even accurately recall their early childhood years.

Fourth, and relevant also to the third critique, past-life memories recovered specifically through hypnotic regression are notoriously unreliable. Whereas Stevenson's experience with hypnosis yielded what he felt were ambiguous results, Paul Edwards together with many contemporaries are so suspicious of hypnotically recovered memories as to consider them practi-cally worthless.[15] Woodhouse at least tries to explain *why* such memories are unreliable, noting that hypnotic regression techniques tap into unconscious reservoirs of information:

> This reservoir *may* be our own subconscious, our collective
> unconscious, our past lives, or some combination of these that
> is perpetually in flux. From a scientific standpoint, much of the
> data from regressions can be made to fit any of the models of
> consciousness. (From a paranormal standpoint, there is the
> additional possibility that some of the past-life personalities are
> faked or distorted by discarnate spirits taking advantage of a
> subject's vulnerability.)[16]

Fifth, many debunkers raise the objection that population mathemat-ics give the lie to reincarnation theory. That is, given that reincarnationists typically maintain that souls are never created and otherwise always existed, how can reincarnation theory account for the steadily increasing population of earth, i.e., where have all the additional souls come from to inhabit the increasing numbers of bodies? Morey Bernstein, author of the most well-known reincarnation study entitled *The Search for Bridey Murphy,* has offered the solution to this enigma that "The total number of entities both in this and the afterworld can remain the same while the balance shifts between the number of entities on earth and the number of entities in the unseen world."[17] Woodhouse echoes Bernstein and suggests further ways to account for the apparent shortfall of souls:

> One might, for example, suppose that . . . we began with an excess number of souls. Or possibly that there is an evolution-ary migration from, say, whales and dolphins to humans. The clearest explanation requires merely that we abandon the assumption that we are the only populated planet in the uni-verse. In Vedic traditions, for instance, there are believed to be many other civilized worlds in the universe from which sen-tient beings may "transcarnate."[18]

While these above suggestions for resolving the "population problem" retain much plausibility for reincarnationists, they are not convincing to most skeptics who regard them, as Edwards does, as little more than "noxious *ad hoc* assumptions."[19]

A sixth empirical critique concerns the issue of heredity. As Viney notes:

> Heredity is rarely a factor in reincarnation, it seems, for, according to [Dr. Helen] Wambach's sample, eighty percent of [her 750] subjects felt certain they had chosen their previous incarnations as well as their present one.[20]

The objection here is that believers in reincarnation do not take seriously the issue of heredity. Christian theologian Hans Küng has elaborated this objec-tion in the following argument. The doctrines of karma and rebirth together explain individual differences in moral make-up and in social and economic circumstances, without calling God's justice into question. One might regard this as a positive aspect of reincarnation theory. Yet, from a long view, doesn't this translate into a kind of "ahistorical individualism," which does not adequately comprehend and appreciate how genetic-hereditary, early childhood developmental and otherwise social-natural factors have made each person into who they are?[21] That is, doesn't reincarnation fail to take into account, for instance, that individual human uniqueness comprises a reality critically determined by specific human lineage? If a pre-existent soul rather *arbitrarily* chooses a particular mother or family to be born through, as reincarnationists claim, doesn't this completely overlook the genetic continuity necessary to create and experience authentic lineage? In other words, biological heredity and ancestral lineage undoubtedly have a deep relevance for the creation of human personality that reincarnation theory simply disregards.

3.   Philosophical critique

A contemporary philosophical rebuttal to reincarnation theory has been elaborated by analytical philosopher, Professor Paul Edwards. Edwards considers that there are two primary ways in which reincarnation theory can be shown to be false: first, through recognizing that reincarnation theory violates the requirements for authentic personal identity, and second, that it endorses survival of physical death which, he maintains, is in fact not possible, given that the existence of our mind (or "soul") necessarily depends upon the existence of a physical brain.

Edwards begins by noting that many people have pondered the question that if, as reincarnationists claim, we have all lived many lives, why is it that only a minuscule few claim to have memories of such past lives, i.e., why is it that the great majority of human beings *cannot remember* their past lives? Doesn't this fact in itself suggest that reincarnation is invalid? While reincarnationists plausibly explain such forgetfulness as not much different than our commonplace inability to recall many childhood experiences, etc., Edwards insists that such a lack of past-life memory in almost all people shows that there is really no singular personal identity that endures through many lifetimes, i.e., that reincarnation is a myth. It is perhaps best to allow Edwards to make his own case here:

> Bodily continuity and memory seem to be the two major constituents of personal identity. If a later person, B, whose body is obviously not identical with that of an earlier individual, A, also fails to remember experiencing or doing anything as A, B cannot be said to be the same person as A. The total absence of memories, even of the possibility of bringing any memories back by means of hypnosis or free association, does not destroy identity if the individual has the same body. However, if we do not have the same body, and of course in putative reincarnation cases we do not, the absence of memory does destroy personal identity: nothing that could constitute identity is left. Suppose I assert that I am the same person as Julius Caesar, but I do not remember any of my experiences as Julius Caesar. What could this possibly mean?[22]

Edwards does make an important point in this passage. Memory must stand as *the* critical ingredient in all definitions of personal identity; thus, the fact that the vast majority of people have no memory of past lives may reasonably suggest that it was not *they* who were living such past lives. Of course, even Edwards is quick to admit that the philosophical discussion of what constitutes personal identity is an ongoing debate.

With regard to Edwards' second major critique of reincarnation, he starts out by defining the three following ways of understanding the relationship between the mind and the brain (or, that is, between the mind and the body):

(1) mental states are identical with brain states (materialism);

(2) mental states are distinct from brain states, but they are causally ineffective—they are mere by-products of brain states (epiphenomenalism);

(3) a living brain is a *necessary* condition for all mental states (I will call this the "brain-dependence thesis").[23]

Edwards rejects (1) and (2), proposing that (3) describes the true state of affairs. But accepting (3), while it does endorse a form of dualism, entails rejection of the idea that the physical brain (as well as the physical body) is an *instrument* of the mind, i.e., the idea that the mind (mental states), as immaterial, is *mediated* through the instrument of the brain such that, if the brain dies, the mind or soul continues to exist in some way. The brain-dependence thesis would maintain that if the brain dies, the mind or soul also ceases to exist, which means of course that this thesis not only invalidates reincarnation theory but also dispenses with any type of belief in survival beyond physical death. Similarly, as a way of illustrating the implausibility of the "instrument theory," Edwards poses the example of the brain disorder, Alzheimer's disease. In one particular case, a well-to-do older woman, who was known for being a considerate and compassionate person before developing Alzheimer's disease, became hostile and abusive after eight years of the illness, even beating up the paralyzed lady she had been rooming with. She also lost all recognition of her daughter and other relatives. Edwards points out, given acceptance of the instrument theory, one would have to believe that a) the Alzheimer's lady's mind really *was* intact; b) she really did recognize her daughter but was incapable of expressing such recognition; and c) she continued to be considerate and compassionate but that the brain disease prevented her from acting in accord with her true emotions. Edwards considers these implications to be absurd and even fatuous,[24] insisting that we are far better off and far closer to the truth if we acknowledge the brain-dependence thesis, i.e., that, as a result of the brain becoming diseased, the mind (or soul or self) has also necessarily become diseased. Further, if the brain degeneration continued into total brain dysfunction, so also the mind would have to decline irretrievably into total dysfunction or death. But, as Ian Stevenson and others have suggested, why must we suppose that the memories of those with Alzheimer's are *necessarily* destroyed? Why, for instance, could we not interpret the amnesia, even irreversible amnesia, of Alzheimer's as manifesting a condition in which the memories continue to exist but are inaccessible due to brain damage? As to the abovementioned emotional aberrations, why is it so hard to entertain the idea that, while chemical/electrical imbalances in the brain *can* facilitate mental imbalance, mental balance itself does not necessarily or solely depend on chemical balance, or on an undiseased brain? For Edwards, these questions seem absurdly speculative and barely deserve to be taken seriously.

Yet, despite all of Edwards' "reasonable" protestations, it does not seem to us that he succeeds in presenting a convincing rebuttal to the survivalist contention that the personality/behavioral aberrations observed in those with brain disease are, indeed, due to the mind being mediated through a damaged instrument. Hence, Edwards' critique in this regard does not seem sufficiently cogent for the purpose of showing reincarnation, or life after death generally, to be false.

4. Theological critique

The theological critique of reincarnation that seems useful to mention here comes from sources acknowledging the God of Abraham, Isaac and Jacob—in particular, Judaism and Christianity. With regard to Judaism, belief in reincarnation seems to have emerged definitively in the Middle Ages, articulated by those Jews who accepted and followed the mystical teachings of the Kabbalah. Even today, the Hasidic Jews, who cherish Kabbalah teaching, continue to honor the notion of successive rebirth enabling full atonement for sin. But it is important to understand that most non-mystical Jewish religious thinkers, from medieval times to the present, reject reincarnation and further, that most contemporary Jews generally reject reincarnation. Among the noteworthy disbelieving non-mystical Jewish philosophers was Abraham ibn Daud (b. 1110), who offered a very simple, yet very relevant, criticism of reincarnation theory. He proposed that the human soul is not designed, or suited, for inhabiting many different bodies, but that a person's soul is uniquely matched to its own physical body: "One cannot have the soul of another unless the two bodies are identical."[25] The relevant implication here seems to be that numerous physical bodies cannot be arbitrarily inhabited by the same soul, but that the soul is linked exclusively to a *particular* physical body during a *particular* period of life on earth. Daud's suggestion here is well-taken. Realizing that the body and soul of a particular person are profoundly and uniquely interdependent throws serious suspicion upon the notion of reincarnation.

A second area of preliminary theological critique stems from certain scriptures in the New Testament. While reincarnationists point out that Jesus affirms the return, or rebirth, of Elijah as John the Baptist (Mt. 17:10-13), Hans Küng supplies an opposing, historically informed Christian perspective on this scripture:

> As far as the New Testament is concerned, passages such as the one about the return of Elijah are at best popular traditions marginal to the gospel. But even so, what they have in mind is not the rebirth of the dead Elijah in another body, but the return of Elijah in his own body, after being carried off into heaven. And this much is historically certain: All the fathers of the Church, beginning with Hippolytus and Irenaeus in the second century—including Origen, who is often misquoted in this connection—just like the later Councils, criticized the doctrine of reincarnation as advanced by the Pythagoreans and Platonists.[26]

Furthermore, traditional Christians referring, for instance, to Hebrews 9:27, which confirms that "it is appointed for all men to die once . . . ," insist that reincarnation is contrary to the scriptures. Notwithstanding Edgar Cayce's claim that the messianic Jesus was the result of numerous reincarnations and that Jesus believed deeply in such, traditional Christians insist that Jesus had no notion of reincarnation.

Finally, Hans Küng has rendered what we consider to be a substantial and thought-provoking critique of the doctrine of reincarnation. This is a general critique from a Christian perspective, given in six major points which deserve to be summarized here.

First, Küng points out that reincarnation theory does not solve the problem of theodicy, as it has claimed, but has in fact only postponed the problem. The problem of theodicy might be posed as this question: *How can there be divine justice in the face of the existence of evil?* Reincarnationists often believe that their rebirth philosophy solves this problem of divine justice "because we could explain why the good so often do badly (on account of earlier guilt) and why the evil so often do well (on account of earlier good deeds)."[27] But the problem of theodicy finally entails answering the question: Why were human beings, as part of their original design, free to do evil? Thus, neither Christianity *nor* reincarnationism succeeds in resolving this mystery.

Second, reincarnation's "karmic justice" across numerous lives is not a better way of conceiving of cosmic justice than through the merciful justice of the Christian God. That is, reincarnation theory claims that all human beings are given an equal chance to gain perfection, inasmuch as the totality of lives, with its sum total of requisite suffering, guarantees that eventually all people will evolve into the highest possible human realization. But, Küng asks, are we perhaps not better off believing in an "equality of human beings before God, created not by their actions but by the merciful justice of God, which embraces both good and evil deeds"?[28] Thus, God's definitive justice is efficacious, not via innumerable finite lives in time, but through one eternal life.

Küng's third critique here has already been presented earlier as the last *empirical* critique, in which he points out that reincarnation promotes a kind of "ahistorical individualism" that does not comprehend the full integrity of human personhood. Are not one's ancestral lineage and early childhood development, factors that are almost never acknowledged by reincarnation theory, absolutely essential in constituting our spiritual identity as a son or daughter of God?

Fourth, reincarnation theory is, again, premised upon the notion of karmic justice, or expiatory compensation, carried out through many physical lifetimes. But this notion fails to grasp the *seriousness* of history, which is by nature singular and unrepeatable. As such, shouldn't we rightfully understand reality in the context that a missed opportunity can never really return? Küng notes that, against this Western notion of history, Hinduism for instance generally holds to a cyclical understanding of history which denies any notion of uniqueness or nonrecurrency. Nevertheless,

> The Judeo-Christian approach to history would emphasize that God has given man this portion of time and history as a task for which he must in the end give an "account." In this way, and only in this way, unrepeatable history gets its seriousness, as the place where the individual person is put to the test in the presence of God, his merciful judge.[29]

Fifth, the doctrine of reincarnation, which is culturally ingrained, has demonstrated that it lends itself to the legitimizing of the status quo, which may be deeply corrupt and/or oppressive of basic human rights, e.g., as in its legitimation of the caste system in India, complete with all of its grotesque social injustices. If the general expectation of further lives promises the inevitable fulfillment of moral justice, then what is the urgency for social reform in the present life?

Lastly, reincarnation's notion of karmic justice cannot acknowledge, as Christian tradition does, that there are certain debts that can never be "paid back," that can only otherwise be *forgiven*. That is, it is not implausible to recognize that there exist certain personal or historical injustices (e.g., the Jewish Holocaust, the Rape of Nanking, etc.) so heinous in their character that they could never be expiated by any human action. As such, the expiatory compensation of reincarnation, which seems to be primarily built on the ethics of "an eye for an eye," does not adequately acknowledge the human need for forgiveness, which is, in the end, only that forgiveness that can come through God's grace.[30]

V. Alternative Explanations to Reincarnation Theory

In addition to the abovementioned critiques of reincarnation, we need to give some honest consideration to plausible alternative ways of explaining the same phenomena that are otherwise taken to evidence reincarnation. In this regard, the major evidence for reincarnation is the *memories of past lives.* Thus, the guiding question here is this: What, besides reincarnation theory, could plausibly account for the memories of past lives?

The speculative alternatives fall into four basic categories: 1) those explanations that do not acknowledge life after death but which do recognize the human mind as possessing extraordinary multidimensional potentials for knowing; 2) theories emphasizing genetic transmission of memories; 3) a theory that recognizes that memory is inherent in all of nature and that the human mind has special capabilities for accessing such memory; and 4) those explanations that acknowledge that human beings continue to exist after death in the spirit-world and that past-life memories arise as the result of the interaction between persons in the spirit-world and persons living physically on earth.

1.   Memory potentials of the mind

The first set of alternative explanations might be thought of simply as variations on a theme. All of them seek to recognize that the human mind is much more profound than most of us normally experience it to be. Ian Stevenson, as well as various parapsychologists, have pointed to *cryptomnesia* as one way of understanding how memories of past lives arise. Cryptomnesia, meaning "hidden memory," refers to the relatively well-documented phenomenon of how the human brain/mind seems to have an unlimited capacity to store every sense impression ever received over the course of a person's life. These memories are hidden away, only becoming conscious under certain conditions, e.g., as recovered under hypnotic regression therapy. But Stevenson notes that cryptomnesia may also serve to explain past-life memories that arise *naturally and spontaneously*:

According to this theory, the child would somehow have known a person or other source having the information he later "remembered" about the alleged previous family. The child would somehow come in contact with this person or information and would later forget both the source of his information and the fact that he had ever obtained it, although he would remember the information and later present it dramatically as derived from a previous life.[31]

Interestingly, while Stevenson is willing to admit that cryptomnesia might acceptably account for past-life memories, he points out that it does not account for two other aspects of cases of the reincarnation-type, i.e., the behavioral aspect and the aspect of telltale birthmarks corresponding to previous-life injuries of the "reincarnating" soul.[32]

Some parapsychologists have suggested that memories of "past lives" are gained through some process of "psychic osmosis" in which the receiver, for whatever reason, gains explicit and accurate information about other persons' lives by dipping into the vast reservoir of knowledge that is the (Jungian) collective unconscious. The acquisition of "memories" here, though, takes place as an act of unconscious extrasensory perception. This seems to be exactly the same thing that Woodhouse describes as "retroclairvoyance" plus the subconscious identification with the person whose identity is recalled.[33] Retroclairvoyance occurs as supernormal intuitive insight into the life of a deceased person and is similar to Stevenson's mention of "retrocognition," or extrasensory perception that transcends time. Woodhouse, for his part, remains unconvinced that retroclairvoyance plus impersonation can adequately account for (1) the great specificity of past-life memories and (2) the extraordinary transmission of learned skills (e.g., speaking a language one has never learned or been exposed to) evident in reincarnation-type cases.

Similar to Woodhouse, Stevenson rather thoroughly explores the possibility that a kind of subconscious extrasensory perception plus "personation" might account, not only for past-life memories, but also for critical behavioral expressions occurring in cases suggestive of reincarnation. "Personation" basically refers to the process of the identification with another person that becomes impersonation, but Stevenson's precision here is instructive—"personation" is

> dramatization of the information into a personality sufficiently plausible to impress others with the appropriateness of behavioral and emotional responses expected of the previous personality.[34]

This is to say, extrasensory perception operates first as a kind of telepathy. The telepathic connection, which operates mostly subconsciously, enables transmission of information from relatives and friends of the deceased person to the telepathic subject. The subject, having appropriated these memories as well as the sense of the deceased's personality, then effectively impersonates the deceased, claiming rebirth. There is no fraud here, no intention to deceive—only a kind of misidentification of oneself due to the misunderstanding of psychic processes.

A substantial percentage of past-life recall occurs under hypnosis, that is, through hypnotic regression. Needless to say, because hypnosis is generally recognized to yield unreliable results in many different areas, it is not difficult to propose alternative explanations for the past-life memories recovered under hypnosis. On the one hand, these memories are thought to be the product of ego-gratification. Many psychiatrists and psychologists acknowledge that one of the ever-present liabilities of hypnosis is that a person who is placed in such a suggestible state will respond by allowing his imagination to take over and spontaneously generate fantasies of more glamorous selves. That is, there is no guarantee at all that "past-life recall" is a remembering of actual events. On the other hand, a second major liability of hypnotically retrieved information is that it may have been generated, facilitated or "confabulated" in response to the directions of the hypnotist himself. Nicholas Spanos (1991), in researching the legitimacy of hypnotic past-life regression therapy, conducted controlled experiments with 175 subjects at Carlton University in Ottawa, Canada. In short, his study demonstrated that subjects confabulated, or made up stories, with progressively greater intensity as the hypnotherapist provided more and more information to the subject; that is, the subject's past-life regressions became correspondingly more and more detailed. As the study developed, it became very clear that many of the subjects had fantasized their "previous lives' histories from books they had read, plays they had seen, newspapers they had read, or travels they had taken."[35] In sum, "past-life recall" under hypnosis, to a large extent, seems to consist in creative fantasizing.

2.   Genetic memory

A second type of theory put forward to account for past-life recall generally is the theory of "genetic" memory. This theory proposes that memories of past lives do not indicate reincarnation, but are, rather, records of ancestors' personalities and experiences that are passed down genetically in a particular lineage and which are finally known by a descendant in the form of memories. In other words, these records (or possibly, ancestors' own specific memories) of ancestors' lives are perhaps transmitted in a way similar to how DNA patterns, determining physical traits, are transmitted from parent to child. This is basically the same understanding that Betty Eadie acquired during her near-death experience. In the following passage, Eadie makes reference to "new bodies" because she is explaining how spirits, in their pristine "pre-mortal existence," eagerly anticipate their one and only physical embodiment:

> We understood that memories would be contained in the cells of our new bodies. This was an idea that was completely new to me. I learned that all thoughts and experiences are recorded in our subconscious minds. They are also recorded in our cells, so that, not only is each cell imprinted with a genetic coding, it is also imprinted with every experience we have ever had. Further, I understood that these memories are passed down through the genetic coding to our children. These memories then account for many of the passed on traits in families, such as addictive tendencies, fears, strengths, and so on. I also learned that we do not have repeated lives on earth; when we seem to remember a past life, we are actually recalling memories contained in our cells.[36]

This hypothesis of "ancestral" memory has some merit. Stevenson, for instance, correctly notes that this explanation is only plausible for a minor class of cases of the reincarnation-type in which the physical body of the subject descends from the same ancestral line as the physical body of the previous personality, i.e., in those cases where the genetic link is either to parents or across numerous generations. However, in most of the cases involving children studied by Stevenson, the subject's personality and the previous personality lived 1) only a few years apart and 2) in genetic lines that were clearly unrelated.[37] So these reincarnation-type cases point to the physical impossibility of the genetic memory hypothesis. In other words, there was no way in which the subject's personality could possibly manifest itself in a body genetically descended from the previous personality's body (i.e., the body in which the previous personality's life memories would be stored).[38] Thus, the genetic memory hypothesis by itself, while it can explain *some* "past-life memories," does not and cannot completely eliminate the possibility of reincarnation.

3.   Sheldrake's theory of universal memory

A third way of accounting for memories of past lives, without invoking reincarnation, might be through Rupert Sheldrake's scientific hypothesis of "formative causation" via "morphic resonance." This intriguing thesis proposes that all things existing in the present, e.g., societies, persons, shrimp, trees, cells, atoms, etc., are what they are because they have inherent, cumulative and general *memory* of all the past instances of what they were. Critical to understanding Sheldrakes's theory is his notion of a *morphic field*, which determines the character or uniqueness of each different kind of natural system: "There is an insulin field, a beech [tree] field, a swallow [i.e., particular bird] field, and so on. Such fields shape all the different kinds of atoms, molecules, crystals, living organisms, societies, customs and habits of mind."[39] Sheldrake suggests that such morphic fields are similar to the fields described in contemporary physics. Morphic fields should be thought of 1) as non-material and 2) as spontaneously localized within and around natural systems, but 3) as also persisting indefinitely as potential organizing patterns of influence, unlimited by time or space. In other words, the way in which the aforementioned *cumulative memory* in nature operates is through the process of "morphic resonance," which enables *formative causal patterns of influence* from past instances to be transmitted into or, i.e., remembered by, the present instance. Or again, the present existence of a human heart tissue cell is, in reality, a kind of "habitual" manifestation determined, via morphic resonance, by all previous existences of human heart tissue cells (that is, by all previous formative causal patterns of influence pertaining to human heart tissue cells). Thus, morphic resonance describes the key process through which the past is enabled to become present on the basis of similarity.

Clearly, then, morphic resonance operates through *similarity*. The greater the degree of similarity, the more potent the influence of morphic resonance. As Sheldrake points out, not only do we have the greatest similarity to ourselves in the past, enabling us to have our *own memory,* but we can acknowledge our similarity to "members of our own family, to members of social groups to which we belong, to people who share our language and culture, and indeed, to some extent we are similar to all other human beings, past and present."[40] Such similarity provides a possible way of explaining certain psychic phenomena. Telepathy, for instance, might be conceived as facilitated through morphic resonance between our own mental functioning and that of someone to whom we are in some way connected or linked, i.e., to whom we bear a special mental similitude that enables us to access their thoughts, impressions, feelings, etc. In addition, Sheldrake's hypothesis provides a novel and plausible way of understanding the phenomenon of "past-life" memories:

> . . . in such cases a person may for some reason tune in by morphic resonance to a person who lived in the past. This might help to account for the transfer of memories without having to suppose that the present person *is* the other person whose memories he or she can pick up.[41]

Sheldrake emphasizes that the *primary* way in which we are influenced by other people in the past is through a kind of *pooled memory* or, that is, a collective memory of progressively generalized (i.e., de-individualized) human habit patterns. Such memory (i.e., morphic resonance) of these habit patterns serves to facilitate, for instance, the learning of languages by persons in the future. But Sheldrake also recognizes that morphic resonance can operate between *individual* persons, yielding memories of *particular* past lives of deceased others. So, morphic resonance, to the extent that it *can* explain "past-life memories," disposes of the need to believe in reincarnation. On balance, however, most reincarnationists would probably not find Sheldrake's hypothesis compelling inasmuch as it cannot/does not explain *the karmic process of soul development,* which is, after all, one of the most attractive aspects of reincarnation theory.

4. Possession theory: memories from spirit-persons

The fourth major alternative that deserves to be considered is some kind of "possession" theory. That is to say, it is conceivable that a person on earth may experience memories of previous lives as one consequence of the "possessing" influence of a discarnate personality, i.e., a spirit-person in the spirit-world. Even a ferocious skeptic like philosopher Paul Edwards, agreeing with C.T.K. Chari's critique, is willing to admit that such a possession theory is at least as consistent with the data as the reincarnation hypothesis.[42] What is especially noteworthy, however, is that reincarnation advocate, Ian Stevenson himself, after detailing four objections to the possession theory, fails to find any of these really compelling—i.e., the theory of possession very adequately accounts for the memories of past lives. Overall, Stevenson admits:

> It may turn out that cases of the reincarnation type are in fact instances . . . in which (a) the deceased personality died before the birth of the "possessed" personality, and (b) the possessing influence . . . [is such] that there occurs a complete and sustained sense of continuity with the previous personality. This hypothesis will explain nearly all the facts and it jumps over all the difficulties which the theory of extrasensory perception plus personation encounters in trying to account for features of personation in cases suggestive of rebirth.[43]

In the end, Stevenson finds only one notable deficiency to the theory of possession. Such a theory does not seem to have any way to account for the correlative birthmarks manifest in some cases suggestive of reincarnation. He points out that, while a "possessing" influence would operate *after* birth, a correlative birthmark would have to be due to some influence operating *before* birth. But he then *also* recognizes (1) "birthmark" cases make up a very small percentage of reincarnation-type cases; (2) most cases suggestive of reincarnation could be accounted for by a theory of possession; and (3) that "birthmark" cases, in order to be seriously addressed, would have to be "well authenticated," but that the 20 cases presented in his book do not include any well-authenticated birthmark cases.[44]

In this way, the possession theory, premised as it is upon the understanding of life after death, seems to be the most plausible alternative to reincarnation theory that we have encountered so far. What is especially important to understand here, though, is that the possession theory itself is really a subclass of, or subsumed under, a much more universal category of interaction between the physical world and the spirit-world, i.e., the category of *spiritual cooperation,* or *Spirit Return,* as first mentioned by Prof. Young Oon Kim in the Opening Quotes to this Section. In Part VI of this Section, we will discuss the full significance of the idea of spiritual cooperation as the authentic phenomenon which has been otherwise systematically misinterpreted to be reincarnation.

VI. The Theory of Spiritual Cooperation and Returning Resurrection

A.   The Nature of Spirit Return: Spiritual Cooperation

The following exposition of the nature of Spirit Return is critical for comprehending the dynamics of continuing spiritual growth for those persons who are deceased, i.e., for those persons who no longer have a physical body and who thereby dwell in the spirit-world in a spirit-body. At the outset, we should realize that, out of all those people who acknowledge that spiritual growth is ongoing, the great majority have chosen to believe in reincarnation, with only a small percentage ever suspecting that there might be a more correct explanation than reincarnation, and with an even smaller percentage understanding that the *actual* phenomenon was not one of reincarnation at all but, rather, one of Spirit Return. Hence, it is somewhat difficult to discover sources that deny reincarnation to affirm Spirit Return, but some of these valuable sources, who do have a voice in what follows, are Carl Wickland, M.D., Emanuel Swedenborg, esoteric Judaism, Prof. Y.O. Kim and Rev. Sun Myung Moon.

Carl Wickland was a medical doctor of fine reputation. He and his wife, Anna, as followers of the Spiritualist Movement in the 1920s, conducted their own mediumistic investigations of some of the lower and darker realms of the spirit-world. In particular, Wickland's wife was a spiritual medium through whom "earth-bound" spirits were allowed to speak and describe their oftentimes miserable, confused and desperate existences. While his wife was in a trance state, Wickland would question and converse with these spirits, often trying to educate and reorient them. The transcripts of these remarkable sessions are presented in his classic work, *Thirty Years Among the Dead*. One of Wickland's most strongly stated, unambiguous findings was that reincarnation was not only false, but conviction in such was terribly disorienting in the life after death. In the following quote, Wickland notes that spirits who tenaciously hold to such a conviction 1) often end up becoming a detrimental "obsessing" influence to children on earth and 2) thereby cause themselves to become trapped in the "magnetic aura," or basic substance, of the child's spirit:

> That belief in reincarnation on earth is a fallacious one and
> prevents progression to higher realms after transition, has been
> frequently declared by advanced spirits, while numerous cases
> of obsession which have come under our care, have been due
> to spirits who, in endeavoring to "reincarnate" in children,
> have found themselves imprisoned in the magnetic aura, caus-
> ing great suffering to both their victims and themselves.[45]

One of the earth-bound spirits channeled by Wickland's wife was, notably, Madame Blavatsky, founder of the Theosophical Movement (1875) who, as apparent in an earlier quote in this Section, was a foremost promulgator of reincarnationism. But in the following transcript, Blavatsky acknowledges her error while explaining the devious subtlety through which false beliefs, such as reincarnation, originate:

> I felt that I remembered far back in my past, . . . but I
> was mistaken.
> Memories of "past lives" are caused by spirits that bring
> such thoughts and represent the lives they lived. A spirit
> impresses you with the experiences of its life and these are
> implanted in your mind as your own. You then think you
> remember your past.
> When you study, especially when you study Theosophy,
> you develop your mind and live in an atmosphere of mind. You
> remove yourself as much as possible from the physical.
> Naturally you become sensitive, and naturally you feel the spir-
> its around you.
> They speak to you by impressions and their past will be
> like a panorama. You feel it, and you live over the past of spir-
> its and you make the mistake of taking this for the memory of
> former incarnations.
> I did not know this when I lived. I took for granted that
> these memories were true, but when I came to the spirit side of

life, I learned differently. . . .

No, reincarnation is not true. I believed it, I taught it, and I was sure that I should come back and be somebody else. But I will not.[46]

It is especially stunning here to realize that almost 200 years earlier, Emanuel Swedenborg, also disavowing reincarnation, described the source of "past-life" memories in almost exactly the same way as Blavatsky:

No spirit or angel may talk with a person from his own memory. Angels and spirits do have a memory just as men do. If a spirit were from his own memory to talk with someone, then it would seem to that person as though the things he was thinking were his own, yet they would still belong to the spirit. It is like recollecting something he has never heard or seen. I have been granted knowledge of the truth of this by experience.

This phenomenon gave rise to the belief among some early people that after several thousand years they would return to their former life and all its events, also that they had already made such a return. They based this on the fact that occasionally a sort of recollection would occur to them of things they have never seen or heard. This happened because spirits had from their own memories flowed into their [the early people's] thought concepts.[47]

In this way, Wickland and Swedenborg both point out that the belief in reincarnation is a kind of misunderstanding that arises as a consequence of the subtlety and complexity of the communicative relationship between people in the spirit world and people on earth. Even though such a misunderstanding may have *originated* unintentionally, it has continued to be deliberately multiplied by those in the spirit-world who, in their ignorance, expect to reincarnate.

In addition, Wickland recorded the testimony of another channeled Theosophist, Ella Wheeler Cox, who directly replaces reincarnation with Spirit Return:

We cannot return and be babies again, but we step down to earth life to help our loved ones and friends. . . .

Churches will be empty, but it will only be for a short time, because a new religion will spring up, a religion which will be founded on the truth of spirit return, and not on dogma. People will live for others and not grasp all for themselves. . . . There will be churches which will have open doors for the spirits as well as the mortals.[48]

In esoteric Judaism, the phenomenon of Spirit Return is acknowledged as *ibbur* or "impregnation." Ibbur occurs through a process in which the soul of a deceased person "enters" the body of another individual on earth, for the purpose of guiding and supporting that individual during some limited period.[49] Rabbi Gedaliah Fleer, speaking at a 1986 Boston workshop on the Kaballah, made this point explicitly: "The sparks of the soul of someone deceased join the soul of someone living in order to strengthen that person in ways he couldn't come to on his own. . . . "[50]

While esoteric Judaism does not further clarify *how* it is that a soul in the spirit-world *enters* the body of someone on earth, except to suggest that it takes place as a kind of partial and temporary "reincarnation," Unificationist theologian Young Oon Kim recognizes this as a clear exemplification of the dynamics of Spirit Return. In the following passage, she notes the amazing similarity between Isaac Luria's understanding of "ibbur" and Sun Myung Moon's understanding (in *Divine Principle*) of Spirit Return:

> Luria taught that man must initiate his restoration to the original spiritual state of harmony with God. If a soul does not complete its task on earth, it must return and work with the soul of another living person so that it can receive support from it in its own striving to overcome its shortcomings. Or conversely, a stronger soul may come to the earth to work with a weaker one, nourishing it with its own substance as a mother nurses a child in the womb. In this process, the soul in the spiritual world "impregnates" the soul of the person on earth. For *Divine Principle* great men are assisted by great souls. However, on the other side wicked men can be in league with pawns of evil spirits. Thus, the struggle of good and evil on earth is a reflection of the struggle of good and evil in the spiritual world and vice versa. The concept of "impregnation" suggests a partial explanation at least for various spiritual phenomena, from speaking in tongues, healing and precognition to unfortunate cases of multiple personality, schizophrenia and other psychic aberrations.[51]

We arrive at the point where it is appropriate first, to carefully explain the full dynamic of Spirit Return or spiritual cooperation, and second, to provide clear examples of the operation of this dynamic. In fact, whereas "Spirit Return" mostly pictures the action of spirits in coming back to work with persons on earth, "spiritual cooperation" describes the actual dynamic of relationship that develops between the returning spirit-person and a person on earth.

Let us begin by asking: *Why is spiritual cooperation necessary?* It is necessary because, when human beings die, they invariably have not attained spiritual maturity, and there has to be some dynamic through which they can continue to grow spiritually in the life after death. Spiritual cooperation is that dynamic, and it is just a variation of how one grows spiritually during his/her life on earth. So, how do people on earth grow spiritually? The physical self requires certain physically-based nutriments for its growth—things like food, water, sunshine, air, etc. In a parallel manner, the spirit-person or spirit-self requires non-physical, and otherwise spiritual, nutriments for its growth. Such spiritual nutriments must come through two sources—first, through our experiences of love with God, and second, through our experiences of love with other persons and with nature during our life on earth. If either of these is lacking or is somehow distorted, through one's selfishness, such a person cannot complete his/her spiritual growth into spiritual maturity.

It is important to grasp here that all of one's life experiences on earth are actually transformed into a kind of energy called "vitality elements" and these elements are fed spontaneously into the substance of the spirit-self. *In other words, vitality elements are generated in virtue of possessing a physical body.* Thus, if a person's life has been characterized by unselfish love and service to others, then these life-experiences will generate very *constructive* vitality elements, and the spirit-self will be nourished, becoming brighter and brighter. On the other hand, if a person has lived most of his life, say, as a serial rapist, the vitality elements generated will actually be poisonous and *destructive*, causing a spirit-self to devolve, becoming darker and darker, and more and more shapeless. Having said this, however, it is critical to point out that the reason physical life on earth is so vastly significant is because (A) the physical body, enabling life-experience on earth, is the soil for the growth of the spirit-self, and (B) the physical body and life-experience on earth are not the only way, but the *primary* way that the spirit-self can undergo a corrective, regenerative or atoning experience.

With the exception of Jesus Christ, inevitably all human beings have failed to achieve spiritual maturity. Hence, the means for continuing their spiritual growth, i.e., continuing to receive the vitality elements necessary for spiritual growth, is realized as the dynamic of *spiritual cooperation.* This is to say that, as spirits in the spirit-world return and render guidance and support to particular individuals on earth, these spirits qualify to receive some of the vitality elements from the earthly person's physical body; on this basis, these spirits can continue to grow spiritually in the spirit-world.

Spiritual cooperation itself operates on the basis of the principle of "like attracts like," entailing that there be a fundamental similarity between the spirit of the person in the spirit-world and the spirit of the person on earth. What is the nature of this similarity? On the one hand, we can say this is a similarity of *character* or *heart* (i.e., basic attitude or motivation). On the other hand, Prof. Kim describes the operation of this similarity as follows:

> In keeping with the law of attraction, these descending spirits, however, cannot arbitrarily influence nor work with just any human being at random. They must seek out people who have the same spiritual status or level of growth as themselves, otherwise they cannot establish rapport with the individual.[52]

If this similarity does exist, then a *sympathetic vibrational relationship* can be established between these two persons. This vibrational relationship consists in a developing give-and-take relationship through which the two persons enter into a kind of spiritual unity or unification. Such a relational unity is then the basis of spontaneous exchange of thoughts, memories and feelings between the two persons and this is, for instance, how a person on earth comes to possess memories of lives of persons now deceased.

But this sympathetic relationship has certain aspects to it that are not apparent to common-sense understanding. First, the subtlety of this relationship renders it mostly undiscoverable to a person on earth. The person in the spirt-world, of course, will have *some sense* of being consciously in touch with a person on earth though, again, the subtlety of the vibrational relationship often does not permit the spirit-person to *know exactly* how he/she is influencing the person on earth. But the person on earth almost never consciously realizes that he or she is connected to persons in the spirit-world. While this is not the original, or ideal, dynamic of relationship, it is the practical situation existing at the present time in human history. Second, because of the profound limitations inherent in this sympathetic *non-physical* relationship, spiritual growth of spirit-persons, via cooperating with earthly persons, is a very difficult and very time-consuming process. Consider the following representative passage from one of Rev. Moon's speeches:

> Going this path [i.e., the path of struggle in learning to love others] is homework you should do before going to the spirit world. If your homework is not done, you are not qualified to go to class the next morning. The spirit world is your school, so you have to prepare the homework. If you don't do the work then you have to come back and work through people on earth, which is much more tedious and discouraging. The only way you can come back to earth is spiritually, so how can you do the homework? It is millions of times more difficult because you have to go back and forth constantly. You really have to understand how precious it is to have a physical body.[53]

In summary, the point here is this: It is *because* human beings are granted only one physical body of their own that, when they die and shed this body, they can only continue their spiritual growth by returning and working with people on earth who still have their own physical bodies. Again, while spirit-persons do change and develop in certain ways just within the environment of the spirit-world itself, their core development as *beings of heart*, i.e., as beings who need to learn the foundational fullness of love, constitutes the primary spiritual growth that can only take place in conjunction with a physical body; hence, the on-going necessity of spiritual cooperation. Metaphysically speaking, what this state of affairs suggests to us is that human beings were *ideally* intended to experience the full dimensionality of God's love *during their life on earth* and, once their physical bodies became quite naturally worn out, all persons would transition into their next natural environment in the spirit-world. At this point, it would not be necessary for spirit-persons to engage in Spirit Return, since neither they nor the people on earth would be driven by any deficiency in the experience of authentic love. Such spirit-persons would naturally enter into a higher stage of life and a correspondingly more profound phase of development.

Having explained the basic dynamics of relationship between people in the spirit-world and people on earth, we need now to turn to actual exemplifications of Spirit Return. The first set of examples demonstrates how the three specific reincarnation-type cases detailed earlier in this chapter are in fact better understood as instances of Spirit Return. The second set of examples serves to highlight the ways in which Spirit Return can efficiently account for several different types of psychic/spiritual phenomena.

While the following three reincarnation-type cases do not illustrate the dynamic of spiritual cooperation specifically, they do show how the phenomenon of Spirit Return can result in different kinds of spiritual connections to, or relationships with, people on earth. The first of these cases was that of Romy Crees, the two-year-old girl who declared that she was Joe Williams, a family man who had died several years earlier in a motorcycle accident. In a different perspective, what had happened here was that the spirit of Joe Williams, which may well have been confused as a result of sudden death, became attracted to the manifest brightness of the spirit of a child, i.e., Romy Crees, in the spirit-world. Joe Williams, in his ignorance of what had happened to himself in the accident, had become a kind of disoriented, possibly earthbound, spirit who happened to contact Romy's spirit somewhat at random. His subsequent attachment to Romy's spirit became the connection through which his thoughts and memories could be transmitted to Romy. Romy, for her part, in receiving these psychic elements as her own thoughts and memories, simply declared herself to be Joe Williams. In this way, Romy had no trouble further identifying the location of Joe's home in another city, and otherwise correctly narrating many other details of Joe's life together with his family. All of this information would be easily transmittable through the vibrational linkage established via Spirit Return.

A similar explanation would apply in the case of three-year-old Carl Edon, who vividly recalled his career and death as a WWII Luftwaffe pilot. A certain, perhaps innate, psychic receptivity on Carl's part became transformed by the deceased Luftwaffe pilot into a spiritual connection. This connection could then readily serve as a channel through which a great deal of accurate information, e.g., about the Heinkel aircraft and the pilot's flight command, could be communicated.

The third case, that of "Jane Evans" who recalled seven past lives under hypnosis, is interesting primarily inasmuch as Jane, as the medieval Jewess Rebecca, possessed certain knowledge of a hidden church crypt long before this fact could be verified. On this basis it was concluded that Jane's claims of past lives had to be true. But, consider here that Jane's remarkable knowledge of the hidden crypt could easily have been communicated to her from Rebecca in the spirit-world. In this case at least, we could speculate a unique affinity existing between Jane's spirit and Rebecca's spirit, permitting communication.

Spirit Return also provides clear explanations for numerous psychic/spiritual phenomena, including the three we will address here—deja vu, xenoglossia and obsession/possession. The first two of these, which are often used to suggest the reality of reincarnation, can easily be accounted for as residual effects of the spiritual relationship established via Spirit Return. Deja vu, for instance, is the common experience of almost everyone in which we seem to remember that we have visited a certain person or place before when, ostensibly, we are visiting that person or place for the first time; or otherwise, the vague sense of having been through a certain situation before when we consciously know that we have not. To understand the context of this kind of experience, you need first to realize that there are, at any given time, many people in the spirit-world who are connected to you and relating to you, for one reason or another. Some spirits may be loving relatives/ancestors who are trying to aid and protect you in your life on earth. Other spirits may have other commonalities (e.g., similar personality, motivations, addictions, etc.) with you that attract them to you and allow them to develop a give-and-take relationship with you.

Deja vu occurs as a residual effect of being in touch with many spirits and their memories of life on earth. Hence, your vague, eerie sense of having done something before is oftentimes your experiencing of the memories of a spirit who actually did that thing and who may be working with you or who is otherwise connected to you in some way.

Xenoglossia, or the enigmatic capacity for speaking almost extinct languages, or existing languages unknown to the speaker, bears some similarity to *glossolalia*, or the Christian experience of speaking in foreign and/or ancient tongues, inspired by the Holy Spirit. Both of these manifestations result from a particular kind of interaction between the minds of people on earth and the minds of spirit-persons living in the spirit-world. Viney mentions a noteworthy case of xenoglossia investigated by Ian Stevenson in 1958. While under hypnosis, a Philadelphia housewife (37 years old) was able to converse in fluent Swedish, verified on numerous occasions by native speakers. Yet she had never studied Swedish, had never visited Sweden, had no Swedish acquaintances and had never otherwise had any exposure to the language. In addition, not only could she speak Swedish very well, but she was able to identify artifacts in a Swedish museum using the precise dialect and terminology of someone living in Sweden several hundred years earlier.[54] Such xenoglossia, rather than being taken as evidence of reincarnation, should be rightfully understood as one of the residual effects of the sympathetic vibrational relationship between a spirit-person in the spirit-world and a person living on earth. The fact that the above-mentioned housewife could speak in a historically dated form of Swedish in itself indicates that a person from that historical time period, now deceased and living in the spirit-world, had become sympathetically conjoined with the housewife.

Spirit possession, including *spirit obsession,* exemplifies yet another species of Spirit Return. Unlike the mild spiritual linkage sensed in deja vu, and the more assertive spiritual linkage evident in a phenomenon like xenoglossia, the spiritual linkage present in obsession and possession is very heavy-handed, and is such that it attempts to selfishly overwhelm the personality of the person living on earth. Obsession and possession, by definition, entail disorienting and harmful spiritual influences.

Again, the case of Romy Crees well illustrates Wickland's statement that oftentimes spirits intent upon reincarnating in children create instead only a disturbing obsessive complex in the child. Spirit possession is well-documented, for instance, in *Hostage to the Devil* by Malachi Martin. From this book as well as from many other sources, one can see that spirit-possession takes place when extremely selfish (and often cruel) spirits locate someone on earth with whom they have some kind of common base and, mostly unbeknownst to this earthly person, they deliberately and gradually develop a give-and-take interaction with him or her. Since relationship deepens and compounds into unification, the spirit or spirits will eventually come to have free reign to ruthlessly exert its or their powerful will, often completely overwhelming the will and dominating the body of the possessed person.

Of course, one thing that should be kept in mind here is that spirits who *obsessively* or *possessively* engage people on earth are lower spirits or, that is, earth-bound spirits who are typically ignorant and/or uncaring, or otherwise resentful and deliberately destructive. Thus, such earth-bound spirits *generally* do not enter into these relationships because they realize that spiritual cooperation is necessary to continue their spiritual growth, but only because, in their ignorance, they feel driven to try to relate to that which is familiar and which has always held the greatest reality for them, i.e., earthly life.

B.   Returning Resurrection: A Providential Opportunity

Though we have given above a few assorted examples of how the dynamic of spiritual cooperation functions, one cannot really begin to grasp the larger significance of this dynamic unless it is rightfully placed in the context of God's providence. For this purpose, it is probably best to begin by explaining the concept of "God's providence." "God" is here the God of Abraham, Isaac and Jacob, the God of the Bible, and the God who sent Jesus as the Son of God and as the Messiah. "Providence" refers to a plan, or revealed historical strategy, through which God has been working to bring salvation to the human race. The *providential* understanding of spiritual cooperation is given in the teaching of Rev. Sun Myung Moon, who explains it as the providential phenomenon of "Returning Resurrection." Hence, the following is a brief summary of the background and process of Returning Resurrection, which is otherwise elaborated more fully in the main text of Rev. Moon's teaching, *Divine Principle.*[55]

From an original standpoint, the human person is designed to emulate God's capacity for the giving and receiving of love, i.e., the human spirit is designed to attain its maturity in God's love. This process of development was intended to be fulfilled in three orderly, archetypal stages—a formation stage, a growth stage and a completion stage—within the duration of one physical lifetime. At a certain point, however, human beings experienced a devastating separation from God—a Fall—which drastically fixated their spiritual development, preventing them from ripening into maturity. The resulting situation was that virtually all human beings throughout history lived their lives on earth and then entered the spirit-world in a spiritually maldeveloped and/or spiritually underdeveloped state. Since these multitudes of spirit-persons no longer possessed physical bodies through which to receive vitality elements for the healing and/or growth of their spirits, they have been compelled to "descend" and work in conjunction with persons on earth who do have physical bodies. This process of spiritual cooperation is *normally* an extraordinarily painstaking process, requiring vast amounts of time and effort. But, due to the progressive enactment of God's earthly providence to heal and restore human beings, a certain *grace* also becomes available to spirit-persons, through Returning Resurrection.

Again, the healing and restoring of the human capacity for love is understood, from a Unificationist standpoint, as the process of "resurrection"—or, that is, as the process of being lifted out of the fallen realm of spiritual "death" back into the realm of spiritual "life" wherein humans are revived through reconnection to God's love. Thus, God's plan for the restoration of the human heart, or God's *providence of resurrection*, necessarily applies both to people living on earth as well as to people living in the spirit-world. Since our primary purpose here is to gain insight into the providence of resurrection as it primarily concerns people in the spirit-world, we will specifically focus discussion on the phenomenon of Returning Resurrection. Before rendering this discussion, however, we need to briefly draw the broad historical outline of the development of God's *overall* providence of resurrection.

From a macrocosmic perspective, God's providence across 6,000 years, as revealed in the Bible up until the present day, has unfolded progressively in three distinctive stages of approximately 2,000 years each. The first stage, running from Adam's family through Abraham's family, was the era in which divine and human efforts together succeeded in laying the *foundation* for resurrection. The 2,000-year period from Abraham to Jesus is referred to as the *Old Testament Age,* during which faithful persons honoring God through their adherence to the Mosaic Law (i.e., the core truth of the Old Testament) could qualify to participate in a corresponding degree of spiritual resurrection. That is to say, providentially speaking, these persons could participate in *formation-stage resurrection,* by virtue of the merit of the providential age in which they lived on earth. The 2,000-year period from Jesus up to the present age, which imminently expects the Lord of the Second Advent, is known as the *New Testament Age* in which faithful Christians, loving God through loving Jesus and adhering to the higher truth of the Gospel, are able to receive *growth-stage resurrection.* Again, this degree of resurrection is available to good Christians in virtue of the merit of the age in which they live. Growth-stage resurrection, in other words, affords sincere Christians the opportunity for spiritual advancement, an advancement which, after death, translates into the opportunity to dwell together with Jesus in the growth-stage level of the spirit-world called *Paradise.* The era inaugurated with the arrival of the Lord of the Second Advent, who brings forth a consummate expression of truth in the *Completed Testament,* is understood to be the *Completed Testament Age,* or the period in which *completion-stage resurrection* will become available. Those persons able to faithfully apprentice themselves to Christ at this time through their willingness to follow and disseminate the Completed Testament, will thereby be able to complete their growth to spiritual maturity, in accordance with the merit of the age. On this basis, such persons who have merited full resurrection may choose, after death, to reside in the most advanced realm of the spirit-world, the *Kingdom of Heaven.*

Given the foregoing explanation, we are now able to consider the corresponding historical providence for the resurrection of *spirits,* i.e., the providence of Returning Resurrection. Formation-stage resurrection enabled faithful followers of the Mosaic Law, once they had left their physical bodies behind, to enter the *form-spirit stage of the spirit-world.* They dwelt here as form-spirits for 2,000 years until the time of Jesus, through whom the merit of *growth-stage Returning Resurrection* became available. These form-spirit persons then had the providential opportunity to "descend" (i.e., return) and enter into spiritual cooperation with the faithful followers of Jesus on earth. By assisting and guiding these followers to fulfill God's will, thereby helping them to achieve growth-stage resurrection (as *life spirits*), such form-spirits could merit the same benefit—that is, they too could participate in the higher-level resurrection, becoming life spirits and finally entering into Paradise at the same time when those earthly followers of Jesus died and entered Paradise.

Some examples from the New Testament illustrate well the symbiotic dynamic involved in this phenomenon of growth-stage Returning Resurrection. Consider first Jesus' encounter with the spirits of Elijah and Moses at the event of the Transfiguration. This indicated unmistakably that the prophet Elijah was very much alive in the spirit-world. But, in Mt. 11:13-15 and Mt. 17:10-13, Jesus directly proclaims that John the Baptist is Elijah, whose return was prophesied in the *Tanakh* as necessarily preceding the advent of the Messiah. Far from John the Baptist being the rebirth of Elijah, as reincarnationists claim, John the Baptist could be *called* Elijah by virtue of growth-stage Returning Resurrection. That is to say, because Elijah and John the Baptist had similar providential missions, Elijah could return to spiritually cooperate with John the Baptist, in this way fulfilling dual purposes—first, to help John the Baptist fulfill his mission in regard to Jesus, and second, to enable Elijah to vicariously accomplish, through John the Baptist, certain aspects of Elijah's own mission that he could not accomplish while he lived on earth. This became possible because a *relational unity* was established between Elijah and John the Baptist. From this perspective, we are then able to understand that Elijah sought to experience Returning Resurrection through the person of John the Baptist, and Jesus, who understood these spiritual dynamics, could very legitimately claim that John the Baptist *was* Elijah, in virtue of their relational unity.

A second example of Returning Resurrection is the dramatic description, given in Mt. 27:52-53, of the bodies of the saints rising out of their tombs after Jesus' expiration on the cross.

> And the graves were opened; and many bodies of the saints
> who had fallen asleep were raised; and coming out of the
> graves after His resurrection, they went into the holy city and
> appeared to many.

This passage does not refer to the saints' decayed bodies being biologically regenerated, then arising and walking around. Rather, this is a metaphorical description, by those who had their spiritual sight opened, of an instance in which the spirits of long-deceased Jewish saints descended to earth to encourage and assist the followers of Jesus. Clearly, if these saints had been able *literally* to rise from their tombs and roam about in their physical bodies, they surely would have testified directly that Jesus was the Messiah, and otherwise would have done remarkable deeds. But there is no further mention whatsoever in scripture of these risen saints. However, from the perspective of Returning Resurrection, this passage makes a great deal of sense.

A third notable depiction of growth-stage Returning Resurrection is given in Hebrews 11:39-40:

> And all these, though well attested by their faith, did not
> receive what was promised, since God had foreseen something
> better for us, that apart from us they should not be made per-
> fect.[56]

In this passage the writer of Hebrews has just concluded an extensive exhortatory illustration of the meaning of faith practiced by the great Fathers of Faith in Jewish history. We might render a cogent exegesis as follows: "These" who were "well attested by their faith" refers, in context, to all those faithful and saintly individuals in the Old Testament Age who had sincerely struggled to realize God's will. But as righteous as their efforts were, these saints were never able to receive their messiah and to enter into the heavenly kingdom. Rather, God's providence has afforded *us* (followers of Jesus) this opportunity to receive Jesus, and *through us*, those saintly spirits from the Old Testament Age are enabled to attain the long-sought-after perfection of the heavenly kingdom (which, as Jesus indicated, turned out to be Paradise).

Similarly, a dispensation of *completion-stage Returning Resurrection* occurs at the time of the Second Coming of Christ. At this time, faithful Christians who have been dwelling as *life spirits* in Paradise will return to earth to assist those who are following and attending the Lord of the Second Advent. Then, in virtue of the merit of the age, and via the dynamic of spiritual cooperation, these life spirits may become qualified to enter "piggyback" with the spirits of the disciples of the Lord into the completion-stage level of the spirit-world, i.e., the Kingdom of Heaven.

Some fundamental questions naturally arise at this point: What about those spirit-persons in the spirit-world who are not Jewish or Christian? Or, that is: Do spirit-persons from other religions participate in Returning Resurrection? What about non-religious spirits? Or even evil spirits? The answer is that all of these other classes of spirit-persons do, in fact, have the chance to participate in Returning Resurrection in the following ways.

Given the providential context of Returning Resurrection, spiritual cooperation will take place between *religious* persons by means of establishing a *religious* common base. For example, when the Lord of the Second Advent is working on earth, certain Hindu spirit-persons who, from their vantage point in the spirit-world, can more readily recognize the Lord, will return to work with particular Hindus on earth, guiding them to recognize the Lord on earth. This same dynamic would occur for the adherents of Islam, Buddhism, Jainism, etc.

In a parallel manner, those spirit-persons who had lived conscientious lives on earth, but who were otherwise non-religious, would return to inspire and cooperate with other essentially conscientious persons presently living on earth. If this cooperation proves to be fruitful, the conscientious person on earth can be spiritually led to assist in various ways the fulfillment of God's providence, thereby achieving a certain level of spiritual growth or a certain spiritual merit. This same spiritual growth or merit then accrues to the cooperating spirit-persons.

Finally, even evil spirits are able to receive the providential merit of the age by returning to earth. But this kind of relationship is only fruitful if, in accordance with precise spiritual laws, their tormenting of a person on earth occasions an opportunity for the earthly person to overcome or atone for certain past sins (either his or his ancestors') which have heretofore blocked his further spiritual development.

If this dynamic is successful, the evil spirit may be able to inherit the same spiritual benefit realized by the tormented person who has overcome these trials. It is further useful at this point to recognize that returning spirit-persons, of whatever class, gain only the merit or benefit that is finally realized by the person on earth that they are cooperating with. In Matthew 18:18, Jesus addresses this law quite clearly: "Truly, I say to you, whatever you bind on earth shall be bound in heaven, and whatever you loose on earth shall be loosed in heaven."[57] With regard to Returning Resurrection, this verse explains that, unless believers on earth *first* loose what is bound, spirits also cannot loose what is bound in them.

C. Restoration through Indemnity: A Providential Imperative

Thus far in Section VI we have shown that the theory of reincarnation is false and that it is really a misinterpretation of the phenomenon of Spirit Return. Consequently, Spirit Return, upon fuller elaboration, provides a more systematic and more plausible means of understanding the process of spiritual development than that given in the theory of reincarnation. Further, by placing Spirit Return in a larger providential context, we have been able to grasp this phenomenon in historical perspective as one of Returning Resurrection.

But there is a final piece of the puzzle that must now be put in place, the piece that is needed to account for the "karmic" aspect of reincarnation-type cases. The theology of *Divine Principle* makes clear that God has conducted a *lawful* providence across thousands of years in the effort to restore a relationship of heart and love with human beings.[58] This, however, is not a one-sided effort on God's part. In order that God's providence of restoration, or providence of salvation, can be fruitful, human effort is required. If it is God's salvific responsibility to *send* the Messiah, it is the responsibility of human beings to do whatever it takes to *receive* the Messiah. If we transpose this recognition to its most fundamental level, we understand that, even *before* God can send the Messiah, human beings have an undeniable responsibility to fulfill certain providential conditions that, in their symbolic and lawful import, convince God and even allow God to send the Messiah.

What does human responsibility entail in this regard? To answer this question, we first need to recall that human persons experienced a "Fall" at a certain stage of their growth, becoming thereby spiritually alienated from God through an act of their own will. Thus, in the course of God's providence of restoration, human beings, through an act of their own will, must make efforts to reverse the direction of the Fall in order to symbolically regain their own original position. This reversal effort represents a *symbolic process of indemnification,* which is accomplished through an acting out of behavior opposite to the behavior that caused the Fall. However, this indemnification does not allow human beings to cleanse their own sin or to save themselves. Instead, if it is successfully accomplished, it becomes the *condition* upon which they have the opportunity to receive the Messiah, who then makes salvation available to all. This is a very brief theological elaboration of the principled providential strategy implemented by God, and otherwise carried out historically in the Bible through such central figures as Adam, Noah, Abraham, Isaac, Jacob, Moses and numerous others, all of whom cumulatively contributed to the spiritual and physical foundations upon which Jesus could finally be born.

Thus "restoration" refers simply to restoring the original position or original spiritual status before the event of the Fall. "Restoration through Indemnity" means making the effort, or *paying the price* to accomplish such restoration. "Indemnification," as a legal term, refers to making compensation for some loss or damage. In the present theological context, the process of indemnification is the process of symbolically restoring what was lost (in the Fall). So, again, restoration through indemnity refers to this process of indemnification. Further, in multiple perspectives, the providence of restoration through indemnity may also be understood as the providence of resurrection, involving restitution, and which, finally, is realized as God's providence of salvation.

In summary, God's providence of salvation has, in fact, progressed on the basis of human persons being willing and able to fulfill their responsible part or, that is, to pay the price involved in fulfilling indemnity conditions that enable them eventually to receive the Messiah. However, due to humans continuously *failing* in their responsible part, this indemnification process could not be fulfilled in one generation, and the result has been that God's providence has been painfully prolonged over thousands of years. Since the providence of salvation thereby came to be vertically prolonged down through hundreds of generations, the *scope* of the indemnification process likewise expanded horizontally from the individual level to the family level, through tribal, national, world-wide and cosmic levels. For example, because Adam was unable to resist the temptation from Eve and, since Adam and Eve in their fallen state went on to have their own family, the providence necessarily had to expand from the individual level to the family level. However, because Cain killed Abel, the family-level indemnity conditions were not successful in Adam's family and the family-level providence became prolonged, through numerous twists and turns, through Noah's family and Abraham's family, eventually expanding (defaulting) to become a national-level providence under Moses, etc.

We have, so far, moved from the understanding of spiritual cooperation, to its providential context as Returning Resurrection, to the notion of providential indemnification which informs, not only the providence of resurrection *generally*, but specifically the providence of Returning Resurrection. In the following passage, Rev. Moon carefully explains how, in the course of God's providence, returning spirits have always been in the situation of fulfilling indemnity (or karmic-like) conditions, and that this has been misunderstood to be reincarnation:

> The value of human beings before the fall is such that they can dominate the angelic world and cosmos. They fell down a few stages because of the fall, and thus they must go back up to the original place. In going up, however, they cannot go all at once but through . . . stages; through the stages, they should restore individual, family, tribe, nation, country, world and cosmos. . . . Going through each stage inevitably requires indemnity . . . .
>
> For instance, [speaking via blackboard illustration] if this spirit is [St.] Paul, in an attempt to go up through each stage,

if the first man he returns to [i.e., spiritually cooperates with] fails to complete the indemnity condition within the given time period and dies, he returns to another man and helps him. Indemnity is necessary. According to the [*Divine*] *Principle,* indemnity is not completed in a short time. For this reason, if the second man does not fulfill the indemnity, a third man is chosen for a returning resurrection. So finally, Paul returns to a third man. The second man will say he is working with Paul's assistance. Likewise the third man in the next age will also say he is working with Paul's assistance and even that he is himself Paul. This way, it looks as if Paul's spirit appeared in the second man and again in the third man. Looking at such a phenomenon, they come up with the theory of reincarnation; *it is because they do not see the whole.*[59] (Emphasis added)

Rev. Moon's point here is well-taken. People who can see only the *external manifestation* of the phenomenon of Returning Resurrection are very prone to interpreting, or misinterpreting, such as reincarnation. After all, in the above-quoted example, the spirit of Paul *is* present in numerous individuals and, in each instance, there *is* the sense that the past has to be compensated for (i.e., indemnification is required)—on the surface, karmic reincarnation seems quite plausible. But, once the *whole* is grasped, reincarnation is immediately recognized as a mistaken conception.

Let us, however, give added clarification to what is at stake here. Consider the following quote, which typifies reincarnationist thinking:

The baby born blind has done nothing in this life to attract that situation. It's a challenge for the soul. The only rational explanation for this seeming injustice lies in reincarnation, where the test is attributed to experiences in a past life or lives.[60]

Again, this sounds plausible enough—but it is certainly *not* the "only rational explanation," nor is it the best explanation. Let us contrast this quote with the following questions and answers in which Rev. Moon addressed this same topic of spiritual justice in a broader perspective:

Q: There are some unanswerable questions which reincarnation answered, such as how little children can die at a very early age, before they really have a chance. It doesn't seem fair.

A: It is all restitution. In the case of a child dying, some of his ancestors must have caused something which called for his young death. If not, the child's death is indemnity for any blessing the family may receive in the future. Either the child paid restitution for the evil caused by the ancestors, or he paid indemnity for the blessing his family was to receive in the future.

Q: Are "karma" and restitution the same? Do they have the same meaning?

A: Yes. For every result, there is a cause. But this is the difference: The reincarnationist thinks that his present life has its cause in his previous life, whereas we say that our ancestors' lives can have some effect on our present lives. Then, what we do today can result in the quality of our future life. It can also affect the lives of our offspring. The law of karma is correct, but not as it concerns lives on earth of the same individual.[61]

We can see from the foregoing that the theory of reincarnation recognizes that there must be atonement (e.g., being born blind) for one's past negative karma and that this enables progressive soul development in future eras. By contrast, comprehending a baby's blindness or death in more macrocosmic perspective, *Divine Principle* recognizes that what has taken place is part of the process of indemnification of sin, and that this atonement may serve the higher or larger purpose of the ongoing spiritual healing of *one's own blood lineage,* thereby progressively liberating future generations. What is particularly thought-provoking here is the realization that lineage is a corporate entity with unique spiritual status, ontologically speaking. Or, again, each differentiated human lineage is rightfully conceived as an interconnected ontological whole, standing as a unique spiritual entity. Thus, indemnification may be fulfilled by persons in the present generation as atonement for past negative karma (either ancestors' sin or past personal sin, or both). But, as Rev. Moon points out in the quote above, paying indemnity may also be interpreted *positively,* as a spiritual price paid in earlier generations for a blessing to be received in later generations.

This major contrast between karmic reincarnation and indemnificatory restoration also brings into focus yet another profound contrast. Whereas karmic reincarnation is, in almost all instances, premised upon the notion of (or in terms of) *individual karma,* the process of indemnification is conceived systematically to apply, not only to the individual, but to larger corporate entities, i.e., family, tribe, nation, world and cosmos (as well as lineage). In this way, corporate atonement applies, not only to the family, but also to the tribe, nation, world and cosmos, each of which is also conceived as a spiritual entity in its own right.

It is true that the notion of corporate atonement, let alone *multidimensional* corporate atonement, is difficult for many people to accept. But, as part of a larger, more systematic, providential understanding of human soul development, we maintain that it far surpasses the weakly expedient and much less plausible interpretations offered by the theory of reincarnation.

VII. Conclusion

In summary, let us review the significant overall weaknesses of reincarnation theory, followed by a brief restatement of its overall strengths. After each of these points, we will indicate how the theory of spiritual cooperation/Returning Resurrection provides a more comprehensive perspective.

First, reincarnation theory is particularly vulnerable to being criticized as implausible (and even ludicrous) in that it has no way to establish a coherent sense of familial lineage, and consequently, no way to affirm the absolute uniqueness of personal identity. For instance, in *popular* reference, reincarnationists often loosely speculate that they might have been, or probably were, any number of other people who lived in the past. As a corollary to this, we also need to seriously consider that the soul is not originally designed, or suited, to inhabit many different physical bodies, but that a person's soul is uniquely matched to its singular physical body. In the context of a particular lineage, it is this match which otherwise constitutes personal identity. — By contrast, spiritual cooperation is premised first, upon the recognition that, not only is human lineage an honored spiritual entity, each human person has a unique individual identity. Second, all spiritual growth or soul development takes place in the context of each human person having *one* physical incarnation, *during* which one's spirit-self develops in relation to one's own physical body, and *after* which one's spirit-self is compelled to evolve in the spirit-world primarily in symbiotic relationship to persons on earth with physical bodies.

Second, reincarnation theory, where it is culturally ingrained, tends to promote complacency even towards an oppressive status quo, discouraging the impetus for constructive social reform. Thus, we would suggest that the conception of reincarnation does not lend itself to healthy social organization, primarily because it is inherently false. On the other hand, we would suggest that spiritual cooperation/Returning Resurrection is a relational dynamic that can, and most often does, promote an honest and constructive solidarity amongst human beings both on earth and in the spirit-world.

Third, reincarnation theory is founded upon a notion of karmic justice via expiatory compensation, which tends to emphasize the atavistic ethic of "an eye for an eye." To the extent to which this is true, karmic justice does not comprehend forgiveness through God's grace. Returning Resurrection, however, is itself a providential manifestation of God's grace, which grants spirit-persons the opportunity to cooperate with the followers of Christ, and thereby to participate in the greater fullness of God's love.

A fourth weakness of reincarnation theory appears in its reliance upon "past-life memories" as the primary evidence for its validity. As already shown above, there are several theories that can just as plausibly account for past-life memories as reincarnation theory, e.g., Sheldrake's theory of "morphic resonance," and possession-theory, otherwise fully acknowledged by Ian Stevenson. However, it is the theory of spiritual cooperation which provides the broadest compass of understanding here. Spiritual cooperation/Returning Resurrection not only embraces possession-theory, but also goes beyond "morphic resonance" in that it provides a way to make sense of the indemnification (karmic) process involved in soul development.

These four preceding weaknesses already constitute very significant reasons for impeaching the doctrine of reincarnation. In addition, the theory of reincarnation should be recognized for its strengths, both of which are again more fully realized in the theory of spiritual cooperation. First, karmic reincarnation offers an attractive theory of how a soul can atone for all wrongs, sins, offenses, etc. it has committed in the past. Since such atonement occurs across numerous lifetimes, instead of just one lifetime, the theory imparts a sense of freedom in that there is no pressure or particular urgency for the soul to evolve. Second, reincarnation theory offers a convenient way to explain, overall, the process of soul growth to maturity, or into liberated perfection. Spiritual cooperation/Returning Resurrection, however, makes clear that, while atonement usually *does* require more than a single lifetime, it is carried out, not via further lifetimes of the same individual, but rather through the lifetimes of many different individuals in the same lineage, across numerous generations. Thus, the indemnification process is not just the one-dimensional atonement of the individual; rather, it is a multidimensional phenomenon that includes the individual, but also expands *horizontally* to further encompass corporate entities of family, tribe, nation, etc., and expands *vertically* down through numerous generations. In addition, this historical indemnification process simply takes as long as it takes, until it finally assumes a special sense of urgency with the arrival of the Messiah.

In the end, we must regard the theory of reincarnation to be an unfortunate and procrustean misunderstanding of the much more finely articulated phenomenon of spiritual cooperation/Returning Resurrection, otherwise carried out in accordance with precise spiritual laws. For the benefit of those who tend stubbornly to embrace reincarnation, we could suggest that a version of *Ockham's Razor* applies in assessing the contrast between the theory of reincarnation versus the theory of spiritual cooperation/Returning Resurrection. That is to say, if the notion of *one* physical lifetime, followed by *one* ongoing, unbroken life in the spirit-world—inherent in the theory of spiritual cooperation—is sufficient to explain the growth of the human spirit, then why would we want to assume *multiple physical lifetimes,* alternating with *multiple intervals of interim dwelling in the spirit-world,* proposed in the theory of reincarnation, to accomplish spiritual growth?

Further, we should understand that the overarching *purpose* of human life is the realization of true love as participation in God's love. Unificationist teaching makes clear that such authentic love is meant to originate in the nuclear family, differentiated through God-centered relationships amongst distinctly unique persons standing in the positions of grandparents, parents and children. Thus, we can see that God's love, fulfilled in this way, is also meant to become tradition informing and grounding society—which is otherwise to say that true love, by its very nature, is necessarily realized on a generational basis, through lineage. Reincarnation does not and cannot comprehend this wholeness of authentic love.

Finally, the fact of the matter is that, in pinning our hopes on reincarnation, we are not only gravely misled but we are also distracted from appreciating the meaning of *authentic* rebirth—that is, the general understanding that our singular physical lifetime on earth is indeed a very special opportunity, given to each human being, to learn how to give and receive true love, or of becoming continuously reborn through bringing God's love to its rightful fruition in our everyday lives.

Section 13

question

What are the spiritual consequences of committing suicide?

answer

For your lifeblood I will surely require a reckoning . . . .
        —Genesis 9:5

I say, "Thou art my God."
My times are in thy hand.
                —Psalms 31:14-15

Do you not know that your body is a temple of the Holy Spirit
within you, which you have from God?
You are not your own. . . .
                —I Corinthians 6:19

A great number of unaccountable suicides are due to the
obsessing or possessing influence of earthbound spirits. Some
of these spirits are activated by a desire to torment their vic-
tims; others, who have ended their physical existence as suicides, find themselves still alive, and, having no knowledge of
a spirit world, labor under the delusion that their self-destruc-
tive attempts have failed and continue their suicidal efforts.

When these intelligences come into contact with mortal
sensitives, they mistake the physical bodies for their own, and
impress the sensitives with morbid thoughts and instigate them
to deeds of self destruction.

The fate of a suicide is invariably one of deepest misery,
his rash act holding him in the earth sphere until such time as
his physical life would have had a natural ending.[1]
                —Carl A. Wickland, M.D.

Then I was shown how I would harm other people close to me, such as my husband and my sister, by taking my life; and by extension, countless others. There were people on earth whom I would never meet who would be affected by my suicide. Because of the anger and pain I would cause them, my loved ones would be unable to store up the goodness that they were meant to pass on to others. I would be held responsible for the damages—or the lack of good—they would do while immersed in the pain of my selfish death. And I would pay dearly for it, since spiritual law dictates that all of the harm, including lack of good, stemming from my death be punished by a measure of suffering. *Even though I couldn't foresee the ripple effect my death would cause, I would be held accountable.* God Himself is bound by spiritual law, and so there could be no escape for me.[2] (Emphasis added)

—Angie Fenimore

discussion

In effect, the several passages quoted above definitively answer the question regarding the spiritual consequences of suicide: *These spiritual consequences are terribly devastating and cannot be overstated.* Yet, though this be the case, curiously enough, suicide is rarely specifically mentioned in the Bible (e.g., at I Sam. 31:4; II Sam. 17:23; I Kings 16:18; Mt. 27:5; Acts 1:18 and in Job 3:21, where Job briefly contemplates the possibility of suicide), and these few references do not discuss or even hint at the point that there might be considerable "hell-to-pay" for the act of suicide.[3] Suicide is a profoundly widespread malaise, especially of contemporary civilization and especially among young people, e.g., suicide today is the third leading cause of death among teenagers in America, with one attempt every 80 seconds.[4] Because it is a fashionable contemporary mindset to "deconstruct" or "demythologize" the traditional stigma of suicide and to otherwise materialistically suppose that suicide is simply another efficacious option that should be available (even legally sanctioned) for the emotionally troubled man-in-the-street, it is critical to present the following discussion of what *actually* becomes of the suicide in the spiritual world. Only then can we substantially appreciate the absolute caveat: "We must never consider suicide."[5] In order to gain a full perspective on the ramifications of suicide, we will consider first how the person who has committed suicide is affected in the spirit-world, and second, how those whom the suicide has connection to on earth are affected.

It is oftentimes the case that young people who take their own lives have no conception whatsoever that there could be any other kind of existence lying beyond the death of the physical body. Their ill-conceived desire is simply to escape their present emotionally painful circumstances, little realizing that their self-centered feelings will carry them "from the frying pan into the fire." This phenomenon is graphically illustrated in the following passage from psychic medium James Van Praagh's recent book, *Talking to Heaven*, where he recounts his contact with a disturbed young man, Andrew, who committed suicide. James Van Praagh describes to Andrew's parents what Andrew is communicating to him from the spirit-world:

> Your son hanged himself from an oak tree in the backyard. He climbed up a ladder to one of its branches. Does that sound right to you?
>
> Andrew's mother began to weep. She took a tissue out of her bag, wiped her eyes, and acknowledged the information as correct.
>
> Andy shows himself floating above his body. "He can't believe he is dead because he feels so alive. He thinks he screwed something up and is trying very hard to get back into his body through his head. He can't do it, and he is getting very frustrated. He begins to cry!"[6]

Clearly, this boy, like all suicides, discovers almost immediately that he has made a mistake, that he didn't die after all and, further, that there are no second chances with which to reconsider one's actions or, that is, that things are now actually much worse than *before* he committed suicide, because he has destroyed his most precious key for growing out of and beyond his emotional problems, i.e., his physical body. Now, in addition to all of his *other* problems, the person has managed to *murder* himself or herself. In one sense, the issue of suicide almost always in the end reduces to the question of how one overcomes emotional suffering in one's life. Given the emotional/spiritual make-up of human beings, there can never be a quick fix; emotional suffering is only resolved through gradual emotional development, which occurs through spiritual growth or the maturation of character. Spiritual growth itself can only take place, as we have established in numerous previous Sections of this book, upon the foundation of the physical body. Once the physical body is gone, spiritual growth, while not impossible to fulfill, is inevitably excruciatingly difficult (for reasons mentioned previously), and this is all the more true if one has directly violated spiritual law by taking his/her own life.

A singular question, then, that is relevant here is: What does a person feel as a spirit-person in the spirit-world, after having committed suicide? From the immediately above-quoted passage, while the spirit-person, for openers, is beset with feelings of fear, frustration and disorientation, this is *not nearly* the worst of it. The spirit-person, because he or she is overwhelmed by the sense of guilt at having killed oneself and having caused so much grief and anger for others on earth, is often incapable of forgiving himself or herself. This inability to forgive oneself, a recalcitrant syndrome of endless self-recrimination specifically described by numerous psychics such as James Anderson, James Van Praagh, etc., immobilizes the spirit-person and traps him or her in the lower spiritual world, usually for great lengths of time. As James Van Praagh notes:

> To this day I have not had one spirit come through and tell me it is happy with its decision. . . . The suicide act slowed their spiritual progress, and they had a very difficult time forgiving themselves.
> . . . Many times I have been unable to reach a suicide simply because he or she was unaware or in a limbo state.[7]

Oftentimes, suicides in the spirit-world, in pursuing self-forgiveness, will seek forgiveness from relatives and friends on earth. George Ritchie, in narrating his near-death experience, describes his visitation, accompanied by the "Light" he understands to be Jesus, in witnessing spirit-persons (suicides) frantically begging relatives on earth to forgive them. But, sadly, no one on earth is able to see or hear these distraught spirit-persons, who are thereby unceasingly reminded of their own futility. Given this scenario, the Light tells Ritchie: "They are suicides, chained to every consequence of their act."[8]

In addition to guilt being transformed into the inability to forgive oneself, it is also reflected or manifested as the obsessive *sense of regret*. And like the absence of forgiveness, regret also functions as a ball-and-chain to incarcerate the spirit-person in darkness. This sense of regret carried by suicides in the spirit-world is well explained by psychic George Anderson:

> And—I've probably heard this from spirits a thousand times by now—you will suffer terribly over there when you see the grief and pain your death caused. Most times, spirits of suicides come through and, ironically, because of the outpouring of sympathy at their wakes and funerals, see that many more people cared about them than they realized. Also, virtually every spirit who has taken his or her own life has told me that now they see that they could have worked out their problems if they

had given it more time here, and they are sorry they did not choose that option. For them, the most painful part is knowing that they chose to end their lives, and that now, as much as they may wish to, they cannot turn back time. It's too late.[9]

Clearly, if one is bereft of his or her physical body, and is otherwise left only with an interminable feeling of regret at having killed oneself, then regret is a devastatingly potent experience or, perhaps more directly, as Rev. Moon has pointed out, "According to the amount of regret you feel, by that much you are distant from God and in hell."[10] An even more dramatic depiction of the suicide's fate is related in the following passage from the testimony of a recently divorced, severely depressed woman named Karen, whose near-death experience was precipitated by a deliberate overdose of tranquilizers. During her NDE, Karen recalls:

The voice said: "You have a choice. You can stay here, or you can go back. If you stay here, your punishment will be just as it is, right now. You will not have a body, you will not be able to see, touch, or have other sensations. You will have only this darkness and your thoughts for eternity."[11]

As if it were not bad enough to be continually tormented by frustration, guilt, inability to forgive oneself and regret, the suicide's obsessional agony is also one which condemns the suicide to witness over and over the act of taking his own life and the resultant condition of his physical body. This phenomenon, which has been reported by numerous psychics and mediums, is here characteristically expressed by James Van Praagh:

When a person kills himself, one of the first things he realizes is that he is not dead. . . . The most unfortunate circumstance is that he finds himself in a limbo state. He is not able to go to the heaven worlds, nor is he able to return to the physical world. He is stuck in a "no-man's land" with the constant memory of his horrific act. He sees his death over and over again, and it plays like a bad movie. He is trapped and there is no way out of the theater.[12]

Carl Wickland records the channelled testimony of an anguished mother (a suicide) of two children in which she reports that she could not escape the vision of her own dead body:

I should not have reached the spirit side of life before my allotted time, and my punishment was to constantly see my body hanging before me for ten years. All that time I could realize that my husband and children were in great need of my help.[13]

This mother's allusion to an "allotted time" is also echoed, for instance, in the following quote from Francezzo. Francezzo, a spirit-person commenting from his observations in the spirit-world, suggests that at least part of the reason that a suicide is beset with such repeating visions of one's murdered physical body is because the soul or spirit has attempted to shed its physical body before the spirit itself has ripened:

> The soul of a suicide is not ready to leave the body, it is like an unripe fruit and does not fall readily from the material tree which is nourishing it. A great shock has cast it forth, but it still remains attached, till the sustaining link wither away.[14]

Finally, in typifying the sad predicament of most suicides, George Anderson describes that a friend of his who had recently killed himself and who otherwise could not forgive himself for this, was inextricably bound to the scene of his death, very much as an *earth-bound spirit*:

> Also, he was having a problem with the fact that after he had taken his life, his spirit obviously lingered around the scene of the act. He could not overcome the memory of his father's discovering him, and that was haunting him emotionally to a tremendous degree in the next dimension. What he and many of us don't understand is that there is judgement there, but it is not done by God on a throne. Judgement rests basically with yourself. And we all know that the greatest enemy we can face is ourselves.[15]

From the foregoing, it is important to glean that there are, indeed, specific spiritual laws governing the act of suicide. Spiritual laws, while not as clearly understood as physical laws, are no more violable than is, for instance, the law of gravity. Just because a person doesn't know or believe that there is a universal law of gravity and stubbornly decides to drive off a cliff, doesn't mean that he will not be subject to the law of gravity, otherwise physically dying in the crash. In the same way, even if a person is not aware of spiritual law, that does not prevent him or her from being fully subject to its consequences. In this context, then, let us examine some of the spiritual laws governing suicide.

First, Wickland and Francezzo, and numerous others, attest to the fact that the suicide has consigned himself to a position wherein he must remain earth-bound *at least* until the time when his physical body would otherwise have deceased in a natural (or possibly accidental) way. James Van Praagh explains that this phenomenon is due to the spirit-person having certain pre-set "magnetic ties" to the earth, that is, via the physical body. Psychic Mary Browne offers this summary:

> Some one who takes their physical life neither lives nor dies; instead, the spirit resides between the earth and the spirit worlds until the time of its normal passing (the time that the spirit would have passed over if death hadn't been self-inflicted).[16]

Having said this, however, we must offer an immediate proviso to such a law, by way of asking the following question: Is there any guarantee, just because a suicide (spirit-person) is anchored to the earth until its normal physical life-time finishes, that this spirit thereafter will become *automatically* liberated? The answer here is "NO!" Psychic mediums inevitably report that suicides, who are able to coherently testify, communicate that they have been trapped in the lower spiritual world for seemingly endless periods of time. James Anderson notes, for instance, "It can take eons of time as we understand it before they [suicides] go into the light."[17] Thus, once a person has taken his/her own life, liberation is never automatic, and is achieved only with great difficulty, and only in accordance with an individual's uncommon desire to pay the price to overcome his/her situation.

The preceding then leads directly into the consideration of a second nasty phenomenon (if not exactly a law), which is aptly described by Carl Wickland in the Opening Quotes to this Section, and is generally corroborated in the Unificationist teaching about the spiritual world. Suicides in the spirit-world are often compelled or impelled to multiply their crime by inciting others on earth to commit suicide, via "obsessing or possessing influence." This occurs in the following way: Often, a spiritually sensitive person on earth does not have any clear sense that an obsessing/possessing spirit may possibly be influencing himself. *And*, oftentimes, the suicide or possessing spirit (as a necessarily earth-bound and uneducated spirit), who has discovered himself to be alive after all, thereby will continue to try to kill himself. The suicide in the spirit-world is in darkness and, in the process of seeking greater light, is often attracted to and becomes attached to, a spiritually sensitive person on earth (which may also mean a person with whom the suicide has its greatest *vibrational affinity*). The ignorance of the earth-bound spirit allows it to mistake the earth person's physical body as its own body and, via the spirit's continuing obsession with suicide, it otherwise impels the earth person to experience destructive and suicidal thoughts. Thus, the spiritually sensitive person on earth may, in this way, be led progressively into depression, becoming finally motivated also to commit suicide. One of the most astonishing aspects of this relational phenomenon is that it is so often perpetuated through **ignorance**, i.e., just as the suicide in the spirit-world is oftentimes ignorant that his ongoing suicidal efforts are being exercised against a physical body that doesn't belong to him, so also the person on earth who owns the physical body and who is becoming predisposed to suicide, is usually ignorant that his predisposition is being facilitated by a spirit-person who previously committed suicide.

In addition, as mentioned earlier, even though a person in the spirit-world holds a natural spiritual affinity with his or her own relatives on earth or, that is, with people on earth in his or her own familial lineage, and vice versa, this genealogical spiritual affinity is not generally comprehended by either people on earth or people in the lower spiritual world. This point, then, together with the aforementioned relational mechanism promoting suicide, helps to shed light on the mystery of why suicide inevitably seems to run in families. In other words, we might suggest here that the human person is not only physiologically predisposed in a genetic sense, but is also spiritually predisposed in a lineal sense. That such is, indeed, the case should be a further reason why suicide must always be rejected, i.e., so that one's lineage is not condemned to bear the heavy spiritual consequences of suicide.

Third, it needs to be grasped that, just as one's free will is a gift from God, so also one's physical body is a gift from God. Just as it would be criminal to brutally suppress the exercise of one's free will, so also it is a crime deliberately to destroy the human physical body which, in a very real sense, is the temple in which the spirit needs to dwell for a critical period. Thus, it is a great mistake for human beings to believe that, because they have free will, they are free to decide to destroy their physical body, that they have a "right" to commit suicide if they so choose. The law here is this: Since we did not create our physical bodies, there is an important sense in which they *do not* "belong" to us, notwithstanding conventional common sense to the contrary, and we therefore do not have the simple option to destroy them. If we choose to commit suicide, we not only do not die, but must pay the penalty for violating spiritual law.

The opening Bible quotes to this Section basically convey this same truth, especially highlighting that we belong first of all to God, not to ourselves; we are *not ever* our own in the matter of destroying ourselves. The following excerpt, offered by NDE researcher Melvin Morse, M.D., recounts part of the near-death testimony from 7-year-old Beverly who, because she had been seriously abused by her parents, tried to commit suicide by sledding down a steep hill head-first into a bench at the bottom. Upon smacking into the bench, she floated out of her body, traversing darkness and encountering a brilliant light:

> Then I heard a voice from the Light: "You have made a mistake. Your life is not yours to take. You must go back." I argued with the voice. "No one cares about me." The answer I

got back was shocking. "You're right. No one on this planet cares about you, including your parents. It's your job to care for yourself."[18]

It seems useful to offer the comment here that if the above is the admonition being given to a 7-year-old girl, we may well imagine that such counsel is relevant for all human beings, no matter how old they are. Ultimately, there are no acceptable excuses for suicide.

Fourth, let us consider the Opening Quote by Angie Fenimore, in which she reports being made aware of the possible spiritual consequences of her suicide, being informed of the penalties in suffering that would have to be paid. We have already discussed the reality of how the suicide himself or herself pays a great price for his or her selfishness through suffering immobilizing guilt and regret for long periods in the spirit-world. Fenimore makes it crystal clear that such intensive guilt and regret are, in fact, especially the result of the suicide being held accountable for the spiritual/emotional damages experienced by relatives, friends and even unknown others on earth; being held accountable even for destroying specific, unforeseen potentials for realizing goodness in the future. In this we are vividly reminded that it is not only the suicide who suffers. All those relatives and friends who were closely connected to the suicide back on earth are compelled to pay a price in suffering as well, through their excruciatingly painful feelings of guilt and anger, through their acute sense of feeling abandoned, their sense of being betrayed.

In view of the foregoing, then, we need to pose a final question: *Is suicide ever acceptable?* In almost every situation and for almost all purposes, the answer is: "NO!" We agree in this regard with Mary Browne that suicide, or even assisted suicide, is never the answer, even in dealing with patients suffering inalleviable pain from incurable diseases like cancer and AIDS.[19] There are too many unknown spiritual variables that undoubtedly are being disregarded so that the "compassionate" (and medically efficacious) alternative of assisted suicide can be administered. For all we know, such a materialistic resolution of physical pain (in assisted suicide) may serve only to generate otherwise needless suffering for the spirit-person in the spirit-world. Assisted suicide is a drastic measure—we would recommend that it is much wiser to adopt a more conservative approach that allows for the cautious consideration of as-yet little-understood spiritual realities.

There is *one* conceivable circumstance in which we can imagine that suicide would be justifiable. As Browne notes, this circumstance necessarily would be devoid of any kind of selfishness:

> Only in cases of *selfless* behavior motivated by the highest
> ideals is suicide acceptable. It's not acceptable to commit this
> act in order to escape life's problems.[20]

(Interestingly, though, we wonder: If someone deliberately sacrifices his or
her life in order to save the lives of others, e.g., if a soldier throws himself
upon a live grenade to save his fellow soldiers, is there anyone who would
seriously describe this act as "suicide"?)

Finally, we need to recognize that, while the plight of the suicide in the
spiritual world is indeed dismal, God's love mandates help for those suicides
who are able to receive it and God's love is always available to those who
seek it. It is good to recall here that God does not judge suicides and does
not consign them to nether gloom; rather, the suicides themselves have created their own dark predicaments in response to their own self-judgement.
But God's love is such that it is unceasingly seeking to embrace these spirits, ever offering forgiveness to them if only they can receive it through forgiving themselves, ever striving to cleanse their hearts of guilt and regret if
only these suicides can relinquish guilt and regret.

Though we have in this Section primarily sketched the devastating
dilemma of those who *succeeded* in committing suicide, we would perhaps
do well to end by recognizing that God's attitude towards one who would
take his own life is always that of urgently discouraging suicide by lovingly
encouraging life. This is, for instance, reflected in the NDE testimony of a
27-year-old woman who, as she committed suicide, offered up a final
thought: "My God, tell me if you forgive me, before I die." She had barely
finished this thought when two giant hands appeared before her in the tun-
nel, and a voice full of compassion and joy communicated to her: "I forgive
you. I forgive you. I offer you a second chance."[21]

Section 14

What is the nature of "earthbound spirits"?

Certain tyrannical demons require for their enjoyment some soul still incarnate; being unable to satisfy their passions in any other way, incite to sedition, lust, wars of conquest, and thus get what they lust for.[1]

—Plutarch

[T]here was an alarming heat breathing out of it [a "great depth"] that was gathered from different hells, stemming from various kinds of craving, like arrogance, lasciviousness, adultery, hatred, vindictiveness, quarrelsomeness and belligerence. These are sources of the heat in the hells that breathes forth from them. When this heat was active in my body, it brought on an instantaneous disease like a burning fever, but when it stopped flowing in, this symptom suddenly stopped.

When someone [on earth] gets this kind of disease because of the way he has lived, then an impure sphere corresponding to the disease immediately attaches itself, and it is present as an aggravating cause.

To let me know for certain that this was how it worked, there were spirits with me from many hells, affording a communication with the sphere of exhalations from them. As these were allowed to be active in the solid parts of my body, I was seized by tension, pain, and even corresponding disease, which suddenly stopped as these spirits were driven out. To leave no room for doubt, this has happened thousands of times.[2]

—Emanuel Swedenborg

From time to time one of the human beings [in the bar] would become totally intoxicated, which caused the electrical field or aura to separate, starting at the head and going to the feet. When this would happen, one of the less dense beings without the aura would try to beat out the other similar beings getting into the human being through the separated electrical field.

To save words, I shall call this realm and the beings who belonged to this realm *astral.* Though the Lord did not make any explanation, I gathered that these astral beings had become alcoholics when they were living on earth and had never been able to rid themselves of their addiction while they were human beings. They were still driven by this addiction and the only way they apparently could enjoy feeling intoxicated again was to enter a human's aura.[3]

—George Ritchie

The spirits that possessed my patients were once people from all walks of life, who—after death—remained in the physical world and became "displaced persons." They had not made the proper transition between the earth plane and the "other side" at death. Sometimes years later, without bodies of their own, they merged accidentally or intentionally with people whose lives thereafter were never the same. For these spirits, there was no worse fate than sentencing themselves to residing in other individuals' bodies, for they thereby postponed their chances to enter the spirit world where they belonged.[4]

—Edith Fiore

discussion

What, in fact, are earthbound spirits? Earthbound spirits are those spirit-persons who, for various reasons, have become bound or stuck close to the earth after death. The implication here is that these spirits, in being stuck, have not been able to accomplish their full transition into the spirit-world proper. This is very much to suggest that these spirits, for reasons we will discuss herein, have not been able to complete their birth into the next higher level of existence.

Earthbound spirits actually fall into two distinct categories. The first type of earthbound spirit, historically acknowledged and presently popularized, is *ghosts* or *poltergeists*—those spirits who remain confused and usually wandering alone. Remarkably enough, these have been the *serious* subject of recent major Hollywood movies, e.g., *The Sixth Sense* and *A Stir of Echoes* (both September 1999), *Ghost* (1990) and *Poltergeist* (1982), to name only a few. The other type of earthbound spirit, much less recognized or understood, constitutes those spirits referred to above in the four Opening Quotes. These disoriented and often desperate spirits eventually become attached to people still alive on earth, usually to the mutual suffering of both the displaced spirit-person and the possessed (or obsessed) earth-person.

How often do spirits end up in an earthbound state? Put another way, we may ask: How widespread or common is the presence of earthbound spirits? Are they relatively few and far between? Or are they profoundly ubiquitous, existing in vast numbers, indwelling a kind of "limbo" space, spiritually speaking? Psychologist Dr. Edith Fiore, who has developed certain healing therapies via hypnosis for dealing with attached earthbound spirits, admits her ignorance on this question in a very thought-provoking way: "Interestingly, I never have conversed with a spiritually evolved possessing entity. Those [spiritually evolved] must go automatically into the spirit world after death."[5] But the many psychics, shamans and assorted clairvoyant others that this writer has referenced agree that, in actuality, there is a huge population of "stuck" discarnates. Psychic medium James Van Praagh avers: "The world is filled with earthbound entities."[6] In the movie, *The Sixth Sense,* the young boy, Cole, finally reveals his secret to Bruce Willis, the child psychologist: "I see dead people—they're everywhere."

Where is it, exactly, that earthbound spirit-persons seem to be trapped? Paramahansa Yogananda, George Ritchie and Edith Fiore, for instance, describe the "limbo space" or realm of these spirits as a kind of lower "astral plane," populated with discarnates who are severely *emotionally* fixated in various ways. On the other hand, Dr. Carl Wickland in *Thirty Years Among the Dead* refers to this generally dark and murky limbo zone as the "earth sphere," where earthbound spirits wander lost, bewildered or transfixed. Dr. Ritchie, recounting his near-death experience, notes that while this heartbreaking realm should not be understood as hell existing in the spirit-world proper, it nevertheless presents a hellish condition, i.e., earthbound spirits occupy some "level of hell . . . remaining on earth but never again able to make contact with it."[7] While the full impact of Ritchie's description will be understood further on, suffice it to say here that both earthbound spirits, as well as those earth-persons they become attached to, often experience deep suffering. Thus, the real importance of appreciating the dismal situation of earthbound spirits lies in understanding what can be done to mitigate their suffering and to eventually facilitate their liberation, along with the corresponding liberation of those earth-persons they are negatively influencing. That is to say, if the dysfunction or disease can be correctly identified, authentic healing can follow.

In the ensuing discussion, the terms "earth-person" and "earth sphere" will be used. "Earth-person" is used simply to refer to a person, physically embodied, living on the earth. "Earth sphere" is used, as Carl Wickland used it, to refer to the realm where earthbound spirits dwell, a realm that is often sensed by earth-persons but is normally invisible except to those rare psychic individuals (and perhaps also, sometimes, young children). Finally, the method of discussion adopted here is via answering four major topical questions:

A. Why do certain spirit-persons become earthbound in the first place?

B. What is the condition of earthbound spirits in the earth sphere?

C. In what ways do earthbound spirits influence earth-persons?

D. How can earthbound spirits become educated and liberated, enabling them to move beyond the earth sphere into the spirit-world proper?

A. Why do certain spirit-persons become earthbound in the first place?

As Swedenborg makes clear[8] and, as virtually all near-death experiencers have reported, when human beings "die" and enter the spiritual world, they are almost always met, consoled, embraced and counseled by loving relatives and friends who are already living there. Newly arrived spirit-persons then go through a process of reorientation through which their proper residence is determined. This describes what may be thought of as a relatively *normal* transition into the spirit-world.

But if (i) a person does not (or cannot) understand that they have "died" and/or (ii) their state of mind at death is deeply troubled, disoriented or preoccupied, then these conditions will often compel a spirit-person to remain in an in-between "earthbound" state. Of course, it is true that even if a person dies, not realizing *at first* that they are "dead," they may well be able to respond to loving appeals and educational counsel from their relatives in the spirit-world, and in that way eventually choose to make the complete transition. Yet, it is the sad case that many spirit-persons become earthbound for long periods of time through ignorance and fixating preoccupation. This phenomenon can be detailed in the following categories:

1.   Ignorance

It is the case, as Swedenborg, Wickland and many others have commented on, that many people go through the experience of death without realizing that they have died. This may happen, for instance, in those cases where a person has lived his whole life stubbornly believing that there is no life after death, and therefore clinging to this expectation of nothing even in death. Radical skepticism and apathy are variations of such ignorance, as Wickland notes here:

> The binding influence of skepticism, of mental apathy and unconcern regarding the higher life is so powerful after transition that many are held in a condition of helpless despair, darkness, bewilderment and rebellion, often clinging to mortals [earth-persons] as their only means of expression.[9]

2.   Confusion and regret

If a person dies in a very traumatic, confused and/or deeply preoccupied state of mind, this oftentimes leads to his or her becoming an earthbound spirit. Fiore points out that many people who died very suddenly and unexpectedly, in car accidents or plane crashes for example, were greatly disoriented after death and often ended up fixed or anchored to the spot of their death for hours, months or even years.[10] As detailed in an earlier Section of this book, suicides are often profoundly confused and regretful after death, inasmuch as they end up discovering that their attempt to escape suffering on earth has, shockingly, only compounded and multiplied their suffering in the spirit-world. People who die, for instance, from drug abuse or drug overdose cannot properly awaken after death, wandering in a stupor for sometimes long periods in the earth sphere. It is important also to point out here that, adding to the confusion experienced by many earthbound spirits, is the fact that these spirit-persons often see only what they *want* to see, which has been fixed or conditioned according to the nature of their own expectations. Thus, in this fixated state of mind, earthbound spirits may be unable to recognize or respond to friends or relatives, or to their loving appeals, depending on the degree of fixation. This situation is, for example, dramatically rendered in the movie *What Dreams May Come* (1998), where Robin Williams descends into the darker realms of the spirit-world and, at the cost of his life, lovingly appeals to his wife who has consigned herself as a suicide to dwell there. At first, because she cannot forgive herself and never expects forgiveness, she cannot recognize her husband at all—she is lost, fixated in despair—but as he perseveres, she is eventually able to respond to his love and to realize finally who he is.

3. Obsessive attachments to persons or places

Spirit-persons with deep, obsessive emotional attachments to particular persons or places on earth may become earthbound if, at the time of death, they are unable psychologically to let go of these. Oftentimes spirit-persons, who may not understand that "death" is really a kind of *birth* into a higher dimension, will tend to cling to those people in whom they are deeply emotionally invested, partly because they fear that nothing they might potentially experience after death could be as valuable or precious as that which they have already experienced in loving relationships on earth. To the extent that such fear dominates these spirits, they are driven by an unearthly obsession. Wickland and Fiore both document this type of psychological obsession, especially in those cases of deceased parents who, out of a feeling of obsessive concern with their children, became *spiritually attached* to a particular child for a long period of time, negatively influencing the child's emotional development. In the following passage, Wickland quotes a deceased mother, who is speaking as an earthbound spirit, via his wife who is the psychic medium:

> "Therefore, be very careful in concentrating your love on one child or just on your own family. Do not put your mind on one child, because when you pass out [die] you will be in hell. You will stay around and disturb that child, and sometimes, as in my case, the child goes insane.
>
> My poor girl was called insane because I was with her and could not get away. I was crying all the time because I wanted only my child. I did not realize I was controlling her. I could not see her."[11]

Admittedly, this quote raises a number of provocative questions, and these will be addressed further on. However, the foregoing at least serves to describe those situations in which spirit-persons become earthbound because they cannot let go emotionally of beloved persons on earth. There is also a *second*, though related way in which spirits may become earthbound here— through the *earth-person's* inability to emotionally let go of a beloved deceased. Fiore, Anderson and numerous others point out that an earth-person's dependent love for, and/or inconsolable grief for, a certain deceased relative or friend may prevent the deceased from going forward after death, and may hold the deceased as captive (or captivated).[12] In extreme cases of this type, the deceased may even be "pulled magnetically" back into the survivor's *aura*, an important phenomenon that will also be discussed at length further on in the answer to Question C.

4.   Physical Addictions: drugs, alcohol, tobacco, food and sex

Spirit-persons who are, again, ignorant of their rightful transition into a higher state of being, may remain tied to the earth plane through physical addictions cultivated when they lived on earth. Because these addictions were the source of their most cherished (and/or compulsive) pleasures during life on earth, these habitual cravings remain psychologically dominant in the life after death; in fact, because of a spirit-person's profoundly amplified sensitivity, the addiction is experienced as even more overpowering than on earth.[13] Dr. Fiore offers an excellent summary of the debilitated situation of these particular earthbound spirits:

> One of the strongest ties that bound spirits to the physical world was addiction—to alcohol, drugs, sex, smoking, even food. If a person died while in the grips of such an addiction, the most overwhelming need felt immediately after death was for the addictive substance or sensation. The spirit was blind to leaving, seeking only to fulfill the compulsion. Spirit guides and relatives were ignored; the Bright Light went unnoticed.
>
> I have treated many of these addicted patients. Spirit addicts tended to cluster around living addicts and the places they frequented, attempting to experience again what was once the dominant theme of their lives. They *did* actually experience it again after possessing the individual. From then on, they exercised their control and had what they wanted when they wanted it![14]

This phenomenon of spirit addicts "possessing" earth-persons is one that needs to be carefully acknowledged inasmuch as it also reveals that the physical addictions of earth-persons are, in fact, psychologically compounded and multiplied by the corresponding addictions of earthbound spirits *attached* to the earth-persons. In other words, one reason why drug and alcohol addictions are often so intractable and incurable is because they are psychically amplified by addicted earthbound spirits. As part of his near-death experience, George Ritchie offers the following extraordinary description of spiritually visiting a bar and witnessing the behavior of spirits craving alcohol:

> I was staring in amazement as the bright cocoon [aura] around the unconscious sailor opened up. It parted at the very crown of his head, and began peeling away from his head, his shoulders. Instantly, quicker than I'd ever seen anyone move, one of the insubstantial beings who had been standing near him at the bar was on top of him. He had been hovering like a thirsty shadow at the sailor's side, greedily following every swallow

the young man made. Now he seemed to spring at him like a
beast of prey. . . . Twice more, as I stared, stupefied, the identical scene was repeated. A man passed out, a crack swiftly
opened in the aureole round him, one of the non-solid people
vanished as he hurled himself at that opening, almost as if he
had scrambled inside the other man.[15]

In yet another part of his near-death experience, Ritchie goes on to
record his astral visitation, accompanied by "Jesus," to an American war-time
(WWII) factory where he witnesses a spirit-woman who is begging an
assembly-line worker, another woman, for a cigarette. But the earthly woman
cannot hear (or see) the pleading of the spirit-woman and, though the spirit-
woman grabs at a lighted cigarette, her hand passes through it and she cannot grasp it.[16]

Some food, drugs and sexuality are, of course, a normal part of human
life. Clearly, however, these can be, and often are, misused. Inasmuch as the
pleasures experienced through food, drugs and sex tend to *replace* or *become
substitutes for* the euphoria naturally inherent in authentic human love (not
to mention God's love), these love-substitutes become addictions.

Even though these addictions are cultivated during earthly life, they
are such strong habits that they continue to block the spirit-person after
death from making his or her rightful transition into the spiritual world. For
instance, while it would be implausible to attribute all overeating or obesity of earth-persons to the psychic influence of spirits addicted to food, it
is nevertheless the situation that such influence may well be present in
those cases of *excessive* obesity or *excessive* preoccupation with eating.
Suffice it to say that there are spirits sufficiently addicted to the experience
of eating physical food (i.e., before they died) that they do seek out people
on earth who are already predisposed to overeating and these earthbound
spirits do form sympathetic, though possessing, bonds with such earth-persons—often entirely unknown to the latter. Fiore documents exactly such
a case in which her patient's desire to diet was continually thwarted by what
was discovered through hypnotherapy to be a dominating earthbound
spirit.[17]

With regard to sexuality and sexual impulses, which lie at the core of
human being, earthbound spirits are also driven to those vulnerable earth-
persons through whom they can act out their obsessions. It is perhaps
important to again point out here that, just as sexuality is often misused during life on earth as a love-substitute, so this misuse of sexuality will often continue, greatly magnified, by earthbound spirits. These attached spirit-persons
seek to insinuate themselves into the sexual desire of earth-persons, who otherwise (if they are already psychologically predisposed in this direction)

may then be compelled into sexual improprieties or immoralities, and even into sexual crimes like rape and incest. Finally, it seems plausible to suggest here that medieval reports of seducing "demons," known as *incubi* and *succubi,* may well be references to earthbound spirits addicted, via their previous life on earth, to the sensations of sexual intercourse.

5.   Revenge and bloodlust

Some spirit-persons become miserably earthbound through their thirst for revenge. Revenge is usually borne out of a deeply preoccupying hatred and is a powerfully fixating emotion. The impulse to revenge is destructive from any perspective. The nasty impulse for revenge that is not consummated on earth is, after death, a kind of ball-and-chain that traps the person as an earthbound spirit. On the one hand, revenge carried out *on earth* serves only to generate serious spiritual (and physical) repercussions, which will have to be indemnified or dealt with by the vengeful person at some later time. On the other hand, the impulse for revenge continuing after death, causing a spirit-person to become earthbound, is usually unquenchable and therefore inextinguishable, though the earthbound spirit may attach itself to the target person of its revenge and create disturbances in that person's life on earth. This situation is, for instance, remarkably documented in the depossession testimony of Linda F. in Appendix A. Here Linda describes her conscious encounter with certain earthbound American slave spirits who, out of vengeful impulses to punish her for her ancestors' crimes against Black slaves, caused profound physical problems and exhaustion for Linda. Wickland also notes that haunted houses are often occupied by spirits seeking revenge for wrongs suffered by them during their earthly lives.[18]

In addition, Wickland brings forth a second very important insight especially regarding the impulse to revenge of those spirit-persons who had been murderers, for instance, during their earthly lives, and who had been executed for their heinous crimes. These spirits retain their criminal intent, only amplified by the desire to revenge their execution. Thus, the executed in particular, and many criminals in general, become hateful earthbound spirits, intent upon possessing vulnerable earth-persons to continue murdering, raping, etc., as Wickland points out here:

> The spirits of many criminals, murderers, those who were executed or are seeking for revenge remain indefinitely in the earth sphere and often endeavor to continue their former activities and to carry out their evil designs through controlling the bodies of mortals who are sensitive to their influence.[19]

Interestingly, this phenomenon would seem to stand as an important argument *against* capital punishment. That is to say, if it is known that executed criminals invariably become trapped as vengeful spirit-persons, intent on psychically attacking vulnerable earth-persons, would it not be wiser to refrain from executing them and instead attempt their rehabilitation, until their natural death? (Clearly, there are no guarantees that they *would* be rehabilitated even within their natural life-span, but at least there would exist the *greater probability* of healing and restoration before death.)

In any case, it is valuable to recognize that, generally, hard-core criminal spirit-persons have no compunction about deliberately trying to possess earth-persons. Such spirits are intensely callous and selfish, reflecting an intractable, conscienceless ignorance. Under certain conditions, extremely sociopathic or psychopathic criminals, like serial murderers, for instance, may sometimes become bloodthirsty earthbound spirits, intent upon locating murderously-inclined earth-persons and amplifying their bloodlust.[20]

6.   Religious fanaticism

Wickland, Fiore and numerous other psychic investigators have commented on the fact that many people who held to a rigidly fundamentalist religious outlook during their lives on earth, after death became fixated as earthbound spirits through the limitation of their dogmatic beliefs. These spirits are usually the most difficult to reach because they have *especially* strictly programmed themselves to acknowledge as real, as true, only those things sanctioned by their *particular* dogma. Wickland offers this telling description of their situation:

> The most difficult to enlighten of the earthbound spirits are the religious fanatics. Dominated in earth life by one narrow, fixed idea, opposed to logical analysis and independent thinking, they are found, after passing out of the physical, in a state of self-hypnosis, ceaselessly repeating their empty "religious" jargon.
>
> Nothing exists for them but their dogmatic creed; they are adamantly set in their self-assurance and it is often many years before they can be brought to a semblance of sanity.[21]

Along these same lines, Wickland is one of the very few psychic researchers to openly recognize that many persons, before death, who held to a mistaken dogmatic belief in *reincarnation,* became earthbound spirits after death in virtue of their unswerving, though mistaken, expectation to reincarnate. As Wickland came to realize, reincarnation not only never takes place, but those earthbound spirits expecting it often create psychological confusion for children on earth.[22]

7.   A sense of unfinished business

This more general category is meant to refer, not so much to the preceding categories (though it doesn't exclude them) as to yet other assorted psychological fixations that might be broadly characterized as "unfinished business." Sometimes spirit-persons may become earthbound out of a mistaken sense of duty to keep a particular *promise* to someone still alive on earth. Or, another example of a fixating sense of unfinished business is dramatized in the movie, *A Stir of Echoes,* where a murdered teenage girl remains earthbound and attached to the premises of the house where she was murdered, in the preoccupied determination that the injustice of her murder should be rectified. In the end, once justice has been traumatically rendered, she is liberated and free to leave. Third, psychic Sylvia Browne relates her visit to an apparently "haunted" office space where she clairvoyantly viewed the environs of an old Spanish mission from the early days of California, complete with earthbound monks in dark robes following their daily routines of praying and ringing bells. Browne notes that this situation revealed the presence of earthbound spirits who had settled into a happy and peaceful routine (a very unusual set of earthbound circumstances)—so much so that they were oblivious to having died, and otherwise chose dutifully to continue their familiar and secure routines.[23]

B.   What is the condition of earthbound spirits in the earth sphere?

Once again, earthbound spirits are simply people who have no physical bodies, and whose consequent disorientation is all the more aggravated by the fact that they are emotionally disturbed (fixated). In fact, one might seriously conceive their environment, the earth sphere, as something like a vast mental hospital,[24] only without anyone to care for the patients because the patients, to a great extent, are emotionally incapable of recognizing that they *are* patients and that there are people who want to help them. That is to say, earthbound spirits either refuse to, or are unable to admit that they have "died," inasmuch as they appear to themselves to be very much alive; they have the same personality, the same likes and dislikes—they think and feel in basically the same way as when they lived on earth.

And, because this is true, whenever earthbound spirits have the opportunity to express themselves through a medium, they always convey that they are *suffering emotionally.* Many of the spirits allowed to speak through Carl Wickland's wife expressed, for instance, that they were wandering restlessly in darkness and had not heard their names spoken for what seemed like years or decades.[25] Other spirits openly admitted that many memories of their lives on earth seemed to be blanked out.[26] Further, in numerous accounts it seems that the sense of the passage of time for earthbound spirits is very vague or almost completely non-existent.[27] Robert Coddington, for instance, discusses this phenomenon of "time stasis" as revealed through his careful investigation of various ghosts:

> In these episodes we have seen how entities that died as children retain a child's consciousness to the present, even though they have existed on the earth plane since their deaths for as long as 70 years. . . . In general, it seems time stops for "earthbound," or "unaware" souls at the moment of death. A similar element of time stasis occurs in other cases in this book, as well. This supports an accepted metaphysical tenet which holds that time in nonphysical realms is, if not nonexistent, at least indeterminate.[28]

Many psychic mediums have commented that the plight of earthbound spirits, especially those involved in tragic accidents and suicide, often leads them from general confusion into a kind of comatose state, as Wickland summarizes here:

> Unenlightened spirits often wander aimlessly for many years in the earth sphere, their lack of knowledge of a higher spirit world, which is attained only through understanding, keeping them in a dreary condition of confusion, monotony and suffering; many remain in the scenes of their earthly lives, continuing their former activities, while others fall into a state of heavy sleep from which they are with difficulty aroused.[29]

The dismal confusion of earthbound spirits is not fully intelligible unless the deeper psychological basis of that confusion, and its resulting fixation, can be examined. Coddington offers the following characterization, employing different terminology which aids in grasping the nature of earthbound emotional fixation:

> The "unaware" ghost seems to be similarly immersed in its own repetitive nightmare of events, now past, oblivious to present reality. It is into this *obsessive dream* that the "medium" can ingratiate himself or herself as a channel. You will find most ghosts in this book first perceived me and other questioners as manifesting in their own scenarios, and our challenge was to convince them that they were *locked in a dream* from which they could willfully awaken and move into their own plane of reality. This requires a persuasive give-and-take of fully verbal dialogue to clarify things for them.[30] [Emphasis added]

Finally, the condition of earthbound spirits might be usefully summarized by recognizing, from this perspective, that there seem to be three distinct classes of earthbound spirits. The first class, which could be termed *fixated and wandering,* includes, among others, all those people who died tragic and usually sudden deaths. The second class, which could be called *fixated and fixed,* may be further subdivided into two distinct types. The first type of earthbound spirit here, and the most psychologically disabled, is the suicide. The suicide is not only severely fixated, often condemned to obsessively reliving his suicidal act over and over again in his mind's eye,[31] but also thereby, to a great extent, the suicide has forfeited his or her motive power, or power of movement—leaving one in an earthbound stasis. This is, by all accounts of psychic mediums, a condition of great hopelessness and misery for suicides. On balance, however, we should probably recognize here that, even in the case of suicides, there are greater and lesser degrees of emotional fixation, according to individual situations.

The second type of "fixated and fixed" earthbound spirit has been resolved by Hans Holzer into two basic categories of "ghosts." The first category includes those persons whose traumatic passing has left them clinging or riveted to the locations of their deaths. Holzer refers to these spirits as "resident ghosts" who, for instance, jealously haunt particular premises (or locations), and whose attitude is generally hostile and even aggressive towards new tenants or visitors.[32] The second and more minor category of ghosts contains what Holzer has termed "stay-behinds." In certain situations, when earth-persons have lived for many years in their homes, and have become deeply attached to their homes and to the lives they lived in their homes, they will refuse to depart from these physical premises after death. A fair example here would be the previously mentioned instance of the Spanish monks seen clairvoyantly by Sylvia Browne. That is to say, "stay-behinds" are so emotionally invested in particular earthly premises that this overrules any counsel or advice they might receive from relatives or friends on the other side. Thus stay-behinds are compelled in their unwillingness to leave a certain residence by a sense of *fearfulness;* as Holzer aptly puts it: "The unknown frightens them. They cling to what they know."[33] In addition, Holzer notes that, unlike resident ghosts, stay-behinds do not resent sharing their beloved premises with new earthly occupants. Their attitude is much more benign—live and let live. Needless to say, that affords little comfort to the earthly residents who are usually quite frightened to encounter the incorporeal residents.

Lastly, the third class of earthbound spirits may be termed *fixated and attached* and refers to those spirits whose emotional fixation has driven them to *attach* themselves, in various ways and for numerous reasons, to persons still living physically on earth. This huge class of earthbound spirits, which eventually includes some of those who started out in the previous two classes, is clearly the most relevant, i.e., consequential, for earth-persons. For this reason, this class will be addressed in considerable detail under the following Question C.

C. In what ways do earthbound spirit-persons influence people who are physically alive on the earth?

The answer to Question A has already made a substantial beginning toward answering the present question. In considering the situations of obsessive, addicted and vengeful earthbound spirits, we have already gleaned some idea of *why* earthbound spirits will attach themselves to earth-persons and then attempt to influence them in various ways. Yet, there are many deeper questions about *how* this *influence via attachment* is carried out—the *modus operandi*—and the *kinds* of influence achieved. While it may not be possible to fathom these issues as completely as we might desire, it is possible to offer more precise, though admittedly speculative, parapsychological insights regarding the nature of the attachment of earthbound spirits.

1. The mode of earthbound influence

It is probably best to begin here by recognizing that the general influence of spirits (not only of earthbound spirits) upon earth-persons can only be carried out if there is some commonality between them—some common base or common interest that they share, e.g., similar character, an addiction, or similar religious beliefs, or even a connection through the same blood lineage, etc. Needless to say, spirit influence, for better or worse, is virtually ubiquitous since all human beings have some things in common. But the *degree* of spirit influence is determined by the intensity of the give-and-take relationship, or channel, between the spirit-person and the earth-person.

This general background explanation is helpful also in grasping the distinction between *obsession* and *possession,* which are like two interconnected sides of the same coin. While possession refers to a psychic invasion from *outside* by some alien personality, obsession refers to the psychological force or condition created from *within* a person that is directed outwards, oftentimes toward discarnate influences.[34] In other words, though obsession and possession may ostensibly be understood as opposite phenomena, obsessive states of mind may serve to create the channel through which possession can take place.

It is important to mention at the outset that the attachment of earthbound spirits that we are discussing here should definitely be understood as a kind of *possession* by these spirits. But this is *not* (in the majority of instances) the same kind of severe diabolical possession that, for instance, Catholic priests are sometimes called upon to address with formal Catholic exorcism. Rather, the possession-via-attachment that we want to discuss here is an everyday phenomenon, extremely widespread, and which generates personality disorders that often go disguised as "normal" behavior for long periods of time, until some precipitating set of circumstances finally reveals how deeply serious these negative earthbound influences have really been, i.e., how much mental suffering or physical disease they have facilitated. This point is impressively rendered in Fiore's book, *The Unquiet Dead.*

In order to begin to understand the mode of possession-via-attachment of earthbound spirits, we need somehow to see things from their point of view. The following brief summary description by Wickland serves our purpose quite well, containing most of the elements we need specifically to discuss here.

> The organism of every human being generates a nervous force and magnetism which surrounds him with an atmosphere of vital emanations and psychic light known as the Magnetic Aura. This aura is visible as a light to earthbound spirits in their condition of darkness, and they may become attracted to persons peculiarly susceptible to their encroachment.
>
> Such spirits are often unable to leave this psychic atmosphere and in the resulting state of confusion . . . although struggling for freedom, they find themselves living the life of the psychic [i.e., the person they are attached to], resenting his presence and bewildered by a sense of dual personality . . . which clearly shows the suffering that spirits may endure when enmeshed in the aura of a mortal.[35]

The first element of discussion must be the nature of the human aura. Many psychics and mediums have explained, as Wickland does here, that earthbound spirits reside in a state of "darkness" (whether it be psychic, psychological, ontological or whatever) and that they are eventually attracted to the "psychic light" of the *auras* of people on earth. While science at the end of the twentieth century (1999) is not yet sophisticated enough to significantly detect the extremely subtle vibrations of the human spirit-self that constitute the human aura, clairvoyant people often readily discern earth-persons' multicolored auras, sometimes together with the earthbound spirits that are attached to them. Esoteric studies suggest that, for all earth-persons, the aura is continuously generated through the give-and-take of energies between energy centers in the human physical self and the corresponding energy centers in the human spirit-self.[36] Earthbound spirits also have auras but these are very dark and, due to the lack of a physical body, their auras cannot readily be regenerated.

What is it like for earthbound spirits to dwell in the earth sphere? To be standing or moving in almost total darkness is, after all, like being blind. Auric light is apparently the only source of illumination for earthbound spirits in the earth sphere and they are readily drawn to the auras of earth-persons. But being attracted to auric light does not mean that earthbound spirits can then readily enter an earth-person's aura and attach themselves within. Attachment can only take place if the earth-person's mental disposition, which largely generates the quality of his or her aura, permits the accommodation of the earthbound spirit. Another way of describing this phenomenon is this: Earthbound spirits reside in a realm of low vibration, psychically speaking. Earth-persons who are emotionally distraught, addicted to drugs, or whose thoughts are sufficiently negatively preoccupied in some way, will generate auras of low vibration. If an earthbound spirit-person encounters such an aura, he or she may enter it, occupy it, and adjust to the experience of living in it—not unlike a parasite.

On the other hand, it is important to mention that people on earth are not only spiritually protected by spirit-guides and angels (which are discussed in other Sections) but they are also protected from earthbound attachments by the strength of their own auras. If an earth-person is healthy—physically, psychologically and spiritually—his or her aura naturally vibrates at a high frequency and serves as a shield against the influence of earthbound spirits. In this regard, Fiore intriguingly suggests that the human aura seems to be something like the spiritual counterpart of our physical immune system:

> The aura is to the emotional-mental-spiritual dimension of a person as the immune system is to the physical body. Just as a weakened immune system leaves the individual susceptible to diseases and infections, so a diminished aura creates a vulnerability to spirit intrusion.[37]

But this, unfortunately, is not the end of the story. Aurically speaking, if an earthbound spirit becomes attached, the possessing spirit's aura intermixes with the earth-person's aura, which then lowers the vibration of the earth-person's aura. This situation often makes the earth-person progressively more vulnerable to further possession by other earthbound spirits, with the consequence that the earth-person's aura vibrates at lower and lower levels with the increasing number of earthbound spirits taking up residence therein.[38] Wickland, encountering the earthbound spirit of Mdme. Helena Blavatsky speaking through his wife (the medium), was told that, while a number of spirits can, in fact, reside simultaneously in one earth-person's aura, only one spirit can control at a time.[39] Perhaps needless to say, this description bears considerable resemblance to the phenomena of schizophrenia where numerous distinct personalities manifest one after the other in succession. An enlightened psychiatry will one day surely determine that schizophrenia occurs, not just as the result of psychological trauma and neurochemical dysfunction, but rather *also* as a consequence of the possessing influence of earthbound spirits—an influence otherwise enabled by the psychological trauma and neurochemical dysfunction.

The second element to be highlighted is the fact that earthbound spirits are attracted to the "psychic light" of earth-persons' auras. In many accounts where earthbound spirits communicate through mediums, these spirits describe wandering in blackness until they encounter a light in the distance, enabling them to feel a great sense of relief. They are immediately drawn to, and into, this light, thinking they will find security, perhaps a resting place, in this auric oasis.

This brings us to the third major representative element in the above passage by Wickland. That is, the auric oasis inevitably proves to be an illusion. The earthbound spirit-person enters the aura, hoping that he or she has found a home of sorts, and for a brief period this location seems re-orienting and comforting. But before long, the earthbound spirit discovers that in becoming attached to the auric light, it is no longer free to move outside of the "magnetic" field of the aura. Quite often, earthbound spirits communicate through mediums that they are "stuck," or "trapped," or "imprisoned" in some earth-person's aura; that they can hear their host talking to other people on earth even when they don't want to hear such things. Consider this testimony of an earthbound husband at first lovingly attached to his wife's aura:

> "The time came when I had to leave [die], and very suddenly I seemed to go into a pleasant sleep of rest, and I woke up—where?
>
> It says in the Bible: 'where your treasure is, there will your heart be also.' My treasure was my dear little wife and when I woke up I found myself in her magnetic aura. . . .
>
> I was in my wife's aura, and could not realize why I should have to go wherever she went, and not be an independent individual as I used to be, and it annoyed me. I felt desperate. I felt that my wife must come with *me*. I did not know where, but I wanted her.
>
> My love for her was so strong that I tormented her against my will, because I had no understanding of the real life [situation] on the other side."[40] [Emphasis added]

Along these same lines, Holzer reports on the remarkable 1961 case of Rita H. of Boston. After rejecting several professional diagnoses of her "personality" problem, she had written to Bishop Fulton Sheen seeking deeper understanding of what she was struggling with. In her letter, she described that, following her long illness and consequent severe depression, she began hearing in her mind *three* distinct voices—two men and a woman, who clearly had their own individual personalities, who were not familiar to Rita at all, and who proceeded to talk to her:

> "They told me they are people who have died and are, naturally, in a bodiless state, and that they heard my despairing thoughts and entered my mind to encourage me. They became trapped there in what they call the 'aura' of my being and cannot release themselves. They fear too that the spirit has an affinity for the flesh. Many times we've been thrown into a near panic. In God's name, I don't know how to release them."[41]

After careful investigation of this case, Holzer concluded that these three distinct personalities were not just "splinters" or suppressed parts of Miss H.'s own personality, and that her testimony was honest and straightforward.

The fourth distinct element is now better understood—that the attached earthbound spirit-person is often plagued with a sense of dual personality. While attached spirits are not able to *see* persons or situations on earth, they have no choice but to know most of the thoughts of their hosts, however irrelevant or frivolous, and to *hear* their hosts talking to other people. In this sense, attached earthbound spirits are forced to adapt to the personality of their host, and otherwise often have no real peace of mind; as a result, they have no real life of their own. To a great extent, they are condemned to live the life of their host—which brings us to the fifth element.

> The final element to be emphasized here is that attached earthbound spirit-persons end up *suffering* deeply while they are enmeshed in an earth-person's aura. While this suffering may not be readily intelligible to us earthly folks, it is, I believe, well summarized by Fiore in the following passage: I view the possessing entities as the true patients. They are suffering greatly, perhaps without even realizing it. Virtual prisoners, they are trapped on the earth plane feeling exactly as they did moments before their deaths, which may have occurred decades before. They do not seem to profit from any positive activities or education that their hosts have experienced throughout their lives since the possession. Moreover, they are keeping themselves from being in the spirit world which would . . . afford them the opportunity to make spiritual progress.[42]

In this way, we should remember that the suffering that occurs through the attachment of earthbound spirits to their earthly hosts is, in fact, a *mutual* suffering. The attached earthbound spirit-person feels imprisoned and harassed by his host's personality which, oftentimes completely unbeknownst to the host, otherwise becomes distorted or impaired because of such earthbound influence.

Finally, the foregoing depicts how the occasion for attachment presents itself to the earthbound spirit in the earth sphere. But it is important, practically speaking, also to mention briefly how the occasion for attachment arises from the standpoint of *earthly circumstances.* In her investigation of possessing spirits, Fiore found that the attachment of these spirit-persons was most likely to occur in certain physical locations—hospitals and nursing homes, funeral homes and cemeteries.[43] Hospitals, in particular, are environments where the auras of very physically ill patients are weakened, facilitating the attachment of earthbound spirits. In addition, funerals, at cemeteries, are oftentimes events at which the bereaved are profoundly emotionally distraught, again yielding opportunity for attachment. Lastly, in addition to the enabling circumstances of various forms of earthly addiction, we should add that sometimes people almost deliberately open themselves to spirit attachment via engaging in channeling or automatic writing, or even through using an Ouija Board.

2.   Earthly results of the influence of earthbound spirits

a)   Suicide, crimes of passion and addictions

Having described the *mode* of influence of earthbound spirits, we can now move into a discussion of various *results* of that influence. It is undoubtedly true that the influence of earthbound spirits plays a significant part in causing many difficult physical and mental aberrations, but we shall address here only a few of the major ones. We can start by recalling some of the effects of spirit influence already mentioned above in regard to suicide, crimes of passion, and addictions.

Suicide, strangely enough, ends up as self-perpetuating. As Fiore, Wickland and numerous others have noted, people who commit suicide quickly discover that they are still alive and so, often remain suicidal after death. If suicidal spirit-persons then become attached to earth-persons, these possessing spirits oftentimes will communicate their suicidal frame of mind to such earth-persons, even compelling *them* to commit suicide.[44] In other words, a kind of chain reaction tends to be set in motion here, and should be recognized as an important result of the influence of earthbound spirits.

We also affirm here that many of the worst crimes committed in society, and down through history, e.g., murder, rape, torture, etc., have been facilitated through the destructive influence of possessing spirits who previously had been criminals during their lives on earth. However, at the same time, we must also acknowledge that it is the possessed earth-person who must take responsibility for having committed these "crimes of passion." By the same token, his "temporary insanity" compelling him to commit these crimes, should be understood as resulting from certain mental and physical conditions which *he is responsible for creating*—conditions which then allowed him to become vulnerable to the influence of possessing spirits. While this affirmation of (earthly) personal responsibility differs from the view espoused by Francezzo (a spirit-person) in the following quote, this passage otherwise serves to confirm that many earthly crimes are compelled via the influence of earthbound spirits:

> In my wanderings upon the earth plane I had learned many ways in which a spirit can still work mischief to those he hates who are yet in the flesh. Far more power is ours than you dream of, but I feel it is wiser to let the veil rest still upon the possibilities the world holds even after death for the revengeful spirit. I could detail many terrible cases I know of as having actually taken place—mysterious murders and strange crimes committed, none knew why or how, by those on earth whose brains were so disordered that they were not themselves responsible for their actions, and were but the tools of a possessing spirit.[45]

Finally, as mentioned above, addicted spirit-persons will attach themselves to earth-persons with the same addictions, thus amplifying the psychological compulsion of the earth-person's addiction and enslaving him or her all the more.

b)   Homosexuality, transexuality and transvestitism

Up until the present time, very few sources have recognized or, for that matter, have even been willing to speculate about the possibility, that homosexuality, transexuality and transvestitism are, to a significant degree, promoted through the influence of attached earthbound spirits. But we concur with Dr. Edith Fiore's findings that possessing entities of the opposite sex are critically responsible for engendering much confusion about sexual identity in their hosts.[46] In extreme cases, this confusion may compel an earth-person, man or woman, into these above-mentioned sexual distortions.

Especially with regard to homosexuality, it is not implausible to consider that a major facilitating earthbound influence would come from those attached spirits who had themselves lived as homosexuals in their lives on earth, and who sought to continue this lifestyle through an earthly host. From one point of view, this would seem to make good sense. And while this description may be valid for certain cases, it is quite thought-provoking to acknowledge the *different* findings of Fiore. In the following passage, Fiore explains that her studies showed it was not a same-sexed spirit-person, but one of the *opposite* sex, that facilitated homosexuality in the host-person:

> One of the causes of homosexuality is possession by spirits of the opposite sex. If the possession began before puberty, heterosexual development often was disrupted and the afflicted grew up believing *they* desired partners of the same sex, when it was the entities who were determining their choices. Every homosexual patient I have done a depossession on has had at least one exceedingly dominating entity of the opposite sex who was determining sexual preference. Often these patients told of feeling they were "trapped" in bodies of the wrong sex.[47]

Having pointed out, however, that earthbound spirits can compel homosexuality in their hosts, we need also to remember here that this situation is never one-sided, but always *reciprocal.* The earthly man or woman should rightfully be understood as responsible for *choosing* a homosexual orientation. While such a statement undeniably flies in the face of mainstream contemporary speculation that homosexual orientation is not chosen, but innate at birth, or perhaps due to genetic predisposition, we nevertheless affirm the importance of individual choice. Homosexual orientation is admittedly a complicated and sensitive issue, but it is not made easier to resolve by denying individual responsibility.

c)   Amnesia

It is certainly the case that amnesia, partial or total, can result from a physical concussion or from brain damage, etc. But other cases of amnesia are less explainable and apparently more mysterious. These are cases where a person suffers emotional trauma, or where a person simply wakes up one day, unable to remember who they are, leaves behind their familiar routines and wanders aimlessly to strange places. Perhaps, sometime later, this person will then recover his normal self, but will not remember any of his recent wanderings. This type of amnesia, which is not as uncommon as one might think, is probably best classified as a kind of psychic aberration due to the influence of attached earthbound spirits. Wickland records a representative case of this type where a young man, in business with his father, woke up early one morning, left home without telling anyone and disappeared. Some weeks later he wrote to his parents, explaining that he had enlisted in the U.S. Navy and would be gone for several years. In due course, the boy's parents asked Dr. Wickland for assistance. In the context of a sitting of members of Wickland's Spiritualist circle, Wickland's wife became the psychic channel through whom the spirit of an earthbound sailor, John Edwards, spoke, explaining that he had become (inadvertently) attached to the young man in question and had led him to enlist in the Navy. After an enlightening dialogue between Dr. Wickland and John Edwards, John felt free to recognize his loving (deceased) relatives' exhortations to transition into the spirit world proper, thereby liberating the young man to recall his previous vocation and to return home to his parents.[48]

d) Mental illness and physical disease

From the foregoing, it is clear that earthbound spirits, given the opportunity, are capable of inducing profound mental disturbance in the earth-person they are attached to. Along these lines, it is also noteworthy that a small but increasing number of psychiatrists are willing to acknowledge spirit influence as an important causative element in mental illness. For instance, British psychiatrist Arthur Guirdham, M.D., in his book, *The Psychic Dimensions of Mental Illness* (1982), expresses his conviction, after 40 years of struggling to heal patients, that most severe forms of mental illness are undoubtedly the result of spirit influence.[49] American psychiatrist Scott Peck, in *People of the Lie* (1983), reported skeptically attending two exorcisms, from which he came away shocked and convinced that "Satan" and/or demonic spirits were indeed real, alien and cruelly possessing personalities.[50]

But, what is perhaps more difficult to grasp is that attached earthbound spirits are capable of inducing or generating *physical ailments* in their hosts. Numerous sources, both mediumistic and shamanistic, acknowledge this reality. For example, the Japanese exorcistic cult, Mahikari, claiming hundreds of thousands of members, affirms that more than 80% of all human illness, both physical and emotional, is due to the influence of possessing spirits.[51]

Wickland, in his chapter on "Psychic Invalidism," relates several stories of people whose ailments were discovered to be directly induced by attached earthbound spirits. Mr. Z suffered an intense nausea for 25 years, during which period he had tried and failed many times to find a physical cure. Finally, he was guided to Dr. Wickland's concentration circle (i.e., regular Spiritualist sitting), where Mrs. Wickland allowed a particular spirit to speak through her, who was readily identified by Mr. Z as an old, and deceased, friend of his. Apparently, Mr. Z had been engaged to the daughter of this spirit-person, though the engagement was eventually called off. Nevertheless, Mr. Z and this man continued as friends, with deep mutual regard. When this man later died of stomach cancer, he was attracted to Mr. Z by virtue of their close friendship. But, as is often the case with earthbound spirits, Mr. Z's friend found himself enmeshed in Mr. Z's aura and had been unable to extricate himself for 25 years. Especially relevant here is the point that, during the 25 years of the earthbound spirit's attachment to Mr. Z, he had unavoidably conveyed to Mr. Z the *nauseous symptoms* of his stomach cancer. Once the spirit could be counseled, via Mrs. Wickland's body, he departed from Mr. Z, who was immediately and permanently cured of the long-standing nausea.[52]

In a second exemplification, Wickland shares the story of Mrs. G, who had been afflicted for seemingly her whole life with profound neck and spinal pain. She had visited many physicians over the years but they had never succeeded in relieving her neck pain. Thus, such pain was apparently in her "mind," but *how*?

Eventually her case came to the attention of the Wicklands and, through Mrs. Wickland, a spirit explained that, as a 16-year-old boy, he had fallen off a horse, broken his back and neck, and had been both paralyzed and in pain for years until he died. Immediately after the dialogue with this boy, other helping spirits (called "guiding intelligences" by Dr. Wickland) stepped in to further elaborate that this young man, after death, had become attached to Mrs. G. when she was a child. He had drifted into her aura, becoming a permanent indweller there and, as a result, had unintentionally communicated to her his physical suffering from the broken back. After Dr. Wickland could address this spirit and direct the boy's attention to those deceased who loved him and were beckoning to him, this young man departed into the spirit-world—and Mrs. G. was miraculously relieved of her life-long neck pain.[53]

The logical question to ask here would be: *How* is it possible that attached earthbound spirits are able to induce the aforementioned physical ailments? Of course, what we are really asking finally reduces to the more essential and perennially problematic question of: *What is the nature of the intrinsic relationship between the human mind and human body or, that is, between the human spirit and flesh?* While we cannot profess to offer here an answer to this critical question that is more definitive than the discussions already presented in earlier Sections of this book, we *can* point to an intriguing clarification given in Theosophical teaching regarding the corporeal effects of earthbound spirits becoming enmeshed within earth-persons' auras. In the following quote, "astral bodies" may be understood generally as the spirit-bodies of (earthbound) spirit-persons, while "etheric bodies" should be taken here as a general reference to earth-persons' auras. Thus, Fiore provides an excellent summary statement here:

> Spirits seem to bring an imprint of their physical bodies
> exactly as they were at death. This affects the living organism
> of the possessees. According to esoteric theory, the spirits'

lower astral bodies interact with the etheric bodies of living people, resulting in a blend of the two. This creates a blueprint for the physical bodies and later manifestations of some of the former physical characteristics of the possessors.

Therefore, possession can result in physical symptoms of all kinds, among them: pains, most frequently headaches, including migraines; PMS with edema (water retention); cramping; lack of energy or exhaustion; insomnia; obesity with resultant hypertension; asthma and allergies; etc.[54]

In addition, Fiore reports that, when the possessing spirit is an elderly person, the symptoms communicated to the possessee are often those of elderly persons, including blurry vision, aches and pains and general tiredness.

In regard to the disease-inducing influence of spirits, the three final sources we will reference here are historically definitive and reveal even more profound aspects of the nature of earthbound attachment. They are 1) New Testament accounts of Jesus' healings-via-exorcism, 2) Emanuel Swedenborg's writings, which are a religious and mystical source, and 3) Unificationist sources, which are religious and shamanistic.

In the New Testament, there are six different recorded instances of Jesus performing exorcisms, all of which are contained in the Synoptic Gospels. Of these six, three of them particularly refer to situations in which Jesus' exorcism accomplished the healing of specific kinds of physical disability, as well as a form of mental dysfunction, though we will address only the two most dramatic narrations here. The first instance, in Mt. 12:22, is related quite briefly and concerns a "blind and dumb" demoniac brought before Jesus who, having cast out what the Pharisees termed a "demon," was able to heal the tormented man "so that the dumb man spoke and saw." The second major instance is found in Mark (Mk. 9:14-29), but is likewise significantly elaborated in Mt. 17:14-21 and Luke 9:37-43. This is the event where a father brings his epileptic son to Jesus:

And when they came to the disciples, they saw a great crowd about them, and the scribes were arguing with them. And immediately all the crowd, when they saw him, were greatly amazed, and ran up to him and greeted him. And he asked them, "What are you discussing with them?" And one of the crowd answered him, "Teacher, I brought my son to you, for he has a dumb spirit; and wherever it seizes him, it dashes him down; and he foams and grinds his teeth and becomes rigid; and I asked your disciples to cast it out, and they were not able." And he answered them, "O faithless generation, how long am I to be with you? How long am I to bear with you?

Bring him to me." And they brought the boy to him; and when the spirit saw him, immediately it convulsed the boy, and he fell on the ground and rolled about, foaming at the mouth. And Jesus asked his father, "How long has he had this?" And he said, "From childhood. And it has often cast him into the fire and into the water, to destroy him; but if you can do anything, have pity on us and help us." And Jesus said to him, "If you can! All things are possible to him who believes." Immediately the father of the child cried out and said, "I believe; help my unbelief!" And when Jesus saw that a crowd came running together, he rebuked the unclean spirit, saying to it, "You dumb and deaf spirit, I command you, come out of him, and never enter him again." And after crying out and convulsing him terribly, it came out, and the boy was like a corpse; so that most of them said, "He is dead." But Jesus took him by the hand and lifted him up, and he arose. And when he had entered the house, his disciples asked him privately, "Why could we not cast it out?" And he said to them, "This kind cannot be driven out by anything but prayer."[55]

Thus, in this passage Jesus is seen unambiguously to exorcize a "deaf and dumb" spirit, an "unclean" spirit that had attached itself to the boy, resulting in a possession becoming shockingly evident in the boy's epileptic seizures.

As indicated in the Opening Quotes to this Section, part of Swedenborg's investigations into spiritual reality led him to recognize clearly the nature and workings of evil spirits. In particular, Swedenborg was well aware that, given the opportunity, such spirits could wreak devastating damage upon both the incorporeal mind and the corporeal body of an earthly human being. While Swedenborg may not have known exactly *how* or *why* evil spirits sought to possess, or colonize, earth-persons, he nevertheless was very cognizant of the fact that this was the aim of many evil spirits, and that possession, in various forms, was a very real phenomenon. Wilson Van Dusen, a major expositor of Swedenborg's writings, explains Swedenborg's understanding of possession in the following remarkable quote:

Both Swedenborg and medieval literature spoke of the aim of spirits to possess and control some part of the patient's body (*Spiritual Diary* [Sections] 1751, 2656, 4910, 5569). Parts involved in my observations have been the ear, eye, tongue, and genitals. Medieval literature speaks of intercourse between a person and his or her possessing spirit, giving these spirits the names "incubi" and "succubi," depending on their sex. One female patient described her sexual relations with her male spirit as both more pleasurable and more inward than normal intercourse. *Swedenborg made it clear that those who enter the affections or emotions enter thereby into all things of the body.* These more subtle possessions are more powerful than simply having voices talking to one, and can easily account for affective psychoses where there is a serious mood change (*Spiritual Diary* 5981). One older German woman was depressed by tiny devils who tormented her in her genital region and made her feel the horror of hell.[56] (Emphasis added)

Thus, Swedenborg and Van Dusen proffer here the insight that certain spirit-persons "enter" the emotions of earthly persons and, from there, are then able to "enter" their bodies. In this way, spirits are able to colonize different parts of the human body. This is, in fact, a provocative insight. Swedenborg understood that, because the human person is foremost a *being of love,* the deepest stratum of human nature was the emotional self, and that, after death, the essentiality that is the emotional self becomes the human spirit-person. In this way, spirits, by their very nature, have direct access into human emotions—if they are given the opportunity. We have seen from the foregoing descriptions in this Section how this phenomenon takes place. But what does Van Dusen *really mean* when he says that spirits can "enter" the physical body via the emotions?

In order to more substantially appreciate what this means, let us examine several key passages where Swedenborg describes the nature of disease-inducing spirit influence. First, the reader should know that the context of these passages is that Swedenborg, as a scientist, sought to investigate certain phenomena by using himself as a kind of guinea pig; that is, he deliberately asked that he could spiritually experience *in himself* the influence of hellish or low spirits—however knowing that he was also guaranteed divine protection from any permanently debilitating effects.

Second, we would note in advance that, interestingly enough, the first four passages we address here seem to take on a kind of Hegelian dialectical structure of *thesis* (first and second passages) and *antithesis* (third passage), which apparently negate or contradict each other, but are really born anew, or subsumed, into a higher union, the *synthesis* (fourth passage).

The first passage we refer to is the Opening Quote to this Section by Swedenborg. Here, Swedenborg describes the "sphere of exhalations" of numerous hellish spirits as consisting of *distorted human cravings,* i.e., arrogance, lasciviousness, adultery, hatred, vindictiveness, belligerence, etc. Swedenborg then says that these spirits, together with their atmospheres of noxious exhalations, "*were allowed to enter into the solid parts of my body"*[57] [emphasis added]. The result was that Swedenborg was seized with pain, tension and disease, which instantly ceased once the spirits were expelled. Thus, the *thesis* here stands as the assertion that spirits actually enter into the physical body proper. In the following quote, Swedenborg gives an even clearer exemplification of this thesis, regarding his encounter with a deviously selfish spirit who was allowed to impose his painful influence within Swedenborg's body:

> There was a particular spirit who had been a consummate adulterer during his physical life. . . . He maintained this practice right into old age. Besides, he was devoted to pleasures, did not help anyone or perform any duty except to advance himself and especially his adulterous ventures.
>
> He was with me for several days. I saw him under my feet, and when his life sphere was communicated to me, wherever he moved he caused pain in the membranes around the bone and the nerves—in the lower surface of the toes of my left foot, for example. And when he was allowed to get out, he caused pain in the parts where he was, especially in the membranes around the bones in my thighs, and also in the membranes in my chest under the diaphragm, and in my teeth, from within.
>
> When his sphere was at work, he also brought on a very severe pain in my stomach.[58]

By contrast, the third passage, while affirming the disease-inducing influence of evil spirits, appears to present an opposite perspective in regard to *how* this is achieved:

> All hellish people impose diseases, the in different ways, because all the hells are involved in cravings and longings for evil. . . . So if hellish people attach themselves, they bring on diseases and ultimately death.
>
> *However, they are not allowed to flow into the actual solid parts of the body, the parts that make up human viscera, organs, and members, but only into cravings and falsities. . . .* Evil spirits have in fact attached themselves to me often and for long periods of time. They have brought on pain and disease proportional to their presence. I have been shown where they were and what they were like, and told where they came from as well.[59] (Emphasis added)

In this passage, then, Swedenborg seems to affirm that spirits are *not actually* allowed into the physical body parts of an earth-person—the *antithesis*. Yet, it is clear that Swedenborg acknowledges that evil spirits do exercise their deleterious influence on specific body parts, even sometimes colonizing, or taking up a kind of residence, in relation to those body parts.

Given the above antithetical positions, we can find their reconciliation, or *synthesis*, in the following fourth passage, where Swedenborg has discerned and is discussing certain kinds of destructive spirits that "relate to fatal head tumors inside the skull" (i.e., brain tumors):

> I mentioned that they [spirits] rush inside the skull and keep going all the way to the medulla spinalis, but it should be realized that this rush of spirits is *an appearance.* They move outside, along *a route that corresponds to the locations inside the body.* This is felt as though the process were happening inside, which is due to the *correspondence.* As a result, their working is readily channelled into the person it is focused on.[60] (Emphasis added)

Here, Swedenborg clarifies that the movement of spirits into the body is "an appearance." Such movement is more correctly conceptualized in terms of the exact correspondence that exists between the physical world and the spiritual world. Underlying Swedenborg's understanding of spiritual reality is his doctrine of correspondence, which has vast implications. Everything existing in the outer (phenomenal) physical world represents, or corresponds to, numerous levels of elements or realities in the inner (causal) spiritual world. One aspect of such a theory of correspondence is that for every organ or element of the human physical body, there is a corresponding spiritual organ or anatomical element. Similarly, every physical disease has its internal counterpart in some kind of emotional violation or excess. Consider here Swedenborg's description of the emotional correspondents of physical disease:

> The reason diseases have their correspondence with these people [in the hells] is that diseases correspond to cravings and passions of the spirit (*animi*), these being their source. In general, the sources of diseases are excess, various kinds of extravagance, pleasures merely physical, and also hatred, vengefulness, licentiousness, and the like. These are destructive of people's inner reaches, and as they are destroyed, the more outward elements are affected, bringing people into disease, and by disease into death.[61]

Hence, the reality which Swedenborg seeks to convey in the above quotes is that spirits can wield their negative influence, not directly in human flesh and organs, but rather against the spiritual counterparts of physical organs and flesh—and it is *this* degenerative influence that eventually manifests in the flesh and physical organs. Similarly, in consequence of certain violative conditions perpetrated by an earth-person, evil spirits may come to colonize, or to desperately indwell particular parts of the spiritual body of this earth-person. And, again, this more permanent and negative residence often communicates devitalizing influences and, depending on the severity of the spiritual violations involved, may eventually issue in serious degenerative diseases that specifically attack individuals (i.e., that are not *epidemic*) like cancer, heart disease, multiple sclerosis, arthritis, lupus, Parkinson's disease, Lou Gehrig's disease, etc., as well as somewhat less serious physical ailments like asthma, epilepsy, allergies, impotence, nausea, vertigo, migraines, insomnia, chronic fatigue syndrome, various kinds of inflammations and rashes, etc.

Does all this imply, then, that a disease like cancer has only spiritual, or emotional, causes? Is the effort to find a physical cure for cancer in vain? — No. Clearly, during earthly life the physical and spiritual are infinitesimally and inseparably intermeshed. It is not wrong to think that cancer has physical "causes," which rightfully justify seeking certain physical "cures." Rather, it would be wrong to believe that the causes are *only* physical and material, thereby failing to acknowledge the causes that are authentically emotional and spiritual. Finally, the question arises: Would a depossession removing attached evil spirits enable, for instance, a remission of one's cancer? The answer we would offer here is: It might. However, on balance, we would also have to say that most severe diseases and diseased conditions are very complicated entities that undoubtedly require *multidimensional* cures.

Swedenborg's writings on hellish spirits inducing disease are instructive because they also serve to suggest what a world *without* sin and excess would be like. Swedenborg himself contemplated this possibility and seemed sure such a disease-less world was God's original intention for humankind:

> But if people had lived good lives, then their more inward elements would be open to heaven, . . . so people would be free of disease. There would be only a decline in extreme old age, when they became children again, but wise children. And then when the body could no longer serve the inner person, the spirit, people would cross without illness from their earthly bodies into the bodies angels have—straight from this world into heaven.[62]

In turning briefly to Unificationist sources, Rev. Sun Myung Moon, founder of the worldwide Unification Movement, has further explained some of the theoretical basis allowing negative spirits to colonize or establish dominion over different parts of the human body. Rev. Moon has pointed out that spirits are easily capable of occupying a "space" the size of an atom.[63] Such an insight not only highlights the radical relativity of "time" and "space" in the spiritual world itself, but serves to suggest that spirit-persons, under certain conditions, are able to dominate regions of various dimensions—from the size of an adult person, to the size of a bodily limb, to the size of an internal organ, and even extending down to cellular and atomic dimensions. This insight, in turn, suggests the possibility that, not just one negative spirit, but whole groups or even myriads of low spirits may become attached *correspondentially* (in the aforementioned Swedenborgian sense) to different parts of the human anatomy, including the blood, the bone marrow or even human DNA.

These insights then afford an apt introduction to the Unificationist sources, which are religious, i.e., grounded in Unification Theology, as well as shamanistic, inasmuch as they speak directly of spirits "on the skin" or "in the body," and describe depossession rituals employing loud sound and bodily pain in order to eject attached earthbound spirits—while also invoking angelic assistance. In particular, Rev. Moon in 1986 sanctioned a Korean woman, Daemo Nim, to undertake the mission responsibility of liberating Unification Church members from the debilitating influences of attached earthbound spirits—thus enabling these members to work more unselfishly and productively in God's providence. Daemo Nim, in order to spiritually qualify herself for this mission, went through profound mortification of her physical body, including a 40-day fast. Soon thereafter, she set up a series of workshops at an available Unification property in Korea, at Chung Pyung Lake, nestled amidst extraordinarily beautiful mountains covered in lush green vegetation. This site is particularly conducive to prayer and spiritual awakening and, in addition, it is a site to which Daemo Nim says she has summoned many angels to help her in removing, and then educating, earthbound spirits.

Each day of the workshop begins with an early morning prayer pilgrimage while hiking up an adjacent mountain. The workshop itself is structured such that, after the prayer walk and breakfast, all attending generally sit on the floor and follow a regimen of simple activities, according to a strict daily schedule. These simple activities may be thought of as a series of depossession practices designed to facilitate the ejection of attached spirits and, as experienced by this author, these rituals consist almost entirely of 1) the non-stop singing of Holy Songs, accompanied by 2) non-stop clapping, punctuated by 3) non-stop *an-sou* (pronounced "on-sue") exercises, for a period of 70 minutes at a session. The participants (sometimes hundreds of people) sit on the floor one behind the other in long columns. There is a lead person up front on the stage who directs the singing and the simultaneous *an-sou* activity, which consists in continuously *hitting,* or slapping, different parts of one's body with either the right hand, left hand, or both hands. If the lead person is hitting his outer thighs, or the back of his head, or his stomach for three minutes, then all the participants follow his example as exactly as possible. When the leader finally shifts to slapping another body part, all participants follow suit. At certain points in the session, the leader will indicate that everyone should slap the back of the person they are sitting behind. Oftentimes the hitting of oneself or the person in front of oneself may become very intense and very painful. In addition, every three or four hours, there is a one-hour period of intensive, out-loud reading of the main Unification theological text, *Divine Principle*. These sessions continue around the clock, separated by only short break times and regular meal periods, until 10:00 p.m.

In the following quote, a participant at one of these workshops, Jorg H., describes what he, and most other attendees as well, understood could be achieved through unstinting participation in the singing and *an-sou* rituals:

> [A]s I mentioned before, [we understood that] the spirits dwelled everywhere in our body, the bone marrow, the bloodstream etc. The intensity of the clapping and singing would make it unbearable to those spirits to stay *inside* the body and bring them to the surface of the skin. Here they would be punished by the person hitting you on the back. The idea was to make the spirits as uncomfortable as possible. Those spirits needed to understand that life anywhere else would be better than staying in the body of this host. . . . Spirits could leave you at any time (but probably not during meal times), not just during the Clapping and Singing sessions. I felt that many of my spirits left me while I was asleep.[64] (Emphasis added)

In his written testimony, Jorg does not claim that he was dramatically healed of some lifelong ailment. He does, however, affirm that during the workshop he had a number of spiritual experiences, and that, upon completing the 40-day workshop, he returned to the United States feeling spiritually much lighter and brighter and, eventually, much more spiritually sensitive to his environment.[65] In addition, he reports that his wife, who participated with him in the Chung Pyung workshop, did, in fact, experience being healed of long-standing bodily pains, as well as unprecedented relief of her asthma. It should be noted, though, that many other participants' experiences in these 40-day workshops were considerably more dramatic than those of Jorg and his wife—such as the experience of Linda F., whose remarkable testimony is included as Appendix A and will be considered shortly.

In discussing the nature of attached earthbound spirits and their ability to induce physical disease, Unification sources are especially significant because they recognize a completely novel *religious* aspect of the phenomenon that we have not yet touched upon here. In order to highlight this new aspect, we are best advised to briefly refer to Unification Theology.

The basic systematic theology of the Unification Church (and larger Unification Movement) is contained in a text entitled *Divine Principle*. *Divine Principle* in a nutshell, not unlike traditional Christian theology, understands God as the God of the Bible, the God of personality who is otherwise the God of Abraham, Isaac and Jacob, and who is first and foremost a God of Love. God's original intention for human beings to live together, with God, in a world of love was thwarted because the original human beings entered into a violation of the nature of love itself, i.e., they participated, together with the archangel Lucifer, in original sin and separated themselves from God—the Fall of Adam and Eve.[66] Thus, the destruction of God's original ideal of love occurs with the advent of sin which, in broadest terms, may be grasped as the violation of original, true relationship—with God, with other human beings, and with all of nature. Consequently, Unification Theology affirms that, across generations, such original violation has become specifically differentiated, or complexified, according to lineage, racial and cultural groupings, and individuality. In other terms, this is to say that *original sin* (the root of sin), passed down through generations, has been translated into several other major distinctive forms, intelligible as *inherited sin, collective sin* and *personal sin.* If original sin is sin we have inherited from the first ancestors, inherited sin then refers to sin spiritually passed down to us by generations of our more immediate ancestors. While collective sin is the sin for which all members of a particular social group are responsible, personal sin refers to violations by each person in his or her own life.

In other words, human beings are both essentially individual *and* essentially relational, or corporate, beings. Stated yet another way, we might say that a human person, as an individual, has individual responsibility and, as a member of a particular lineage, has ancestral or corporate responsibility. Thus, what it really means to be the *spiritual being* that is a fully human being is that we each exist at every moment *simultaneously* as an individual person *and* as the real cosmic representative of our entire unique lineage. The theological point that needs to be grasped here is this: Because the nature of sin is not just *one-dimensional* (individual), so also the nature of the restitution of the above-mentioned forms of sin is necessarily *multidimensional,* i.e., restitution of sin must occur across the span of *lineage,* making such restitution transgenerational, relational and corporate.

Translated further, this means that every person alive on earth, whether or not they are aware of it, represents his or her entire lineage and, as such, has responsibility to try to appropriately atone, not only for personal violations, but also for critical violations committed by his or her ancestors—if possible. Otherwise, one's particularly violative ancestors cannot become liberated and are compelled, oftentimes together with those they have seriously harmed (carrying great resentment), to remain spiritually attached to generations of their descendants. Of course, up until the present time, this religious/shamanistic reality has been very little understood, though the Bible does make brief reference to it in Exodus 34: 6-7.[67]

Against this background, the purpose of the Chung Pyung workshops becomes somewhat more intelligible, a purpose which is also clearly stated in Jorg H.'s testimony:

> Hereditary sin is the sin from our ancestors. This means that
> we are responsible for the sins of our ancestors. The spirits of
> these evil ancestors have been living with us, many of them
> even since our birth, waiting for us to resolve their sins and be
> liberated. On top of that, any spirits who had resentments
> against our ancestors are also "possessing" us. Because they
> were mistreated in whatever way, shape and form by our
> ancestors, they also have a condition [grudge] against us and
> want to get "even." Thus they are waiting for the opportune
> moment to harm us in a similar way they were harmed by our
> ancestors while they were still alive on earth in order to release
> their resentment.[68]

Again, several points are evident here. In this perspective, lineage is understood as a spiritual entity. We who are alive on earth are the key representatives of our lineage because we are the only ones currently possessing physical bodies. As such, we have a special power and authority to accomplish restitution for ancestral sin and, in so doing, to bring about the spiritual/emotional liberation of both our ancestors and those they have violated—who otherwise in many cases remain earthbound spirits attached (aurically and correspondentially) to the body of the target descendant. That such an extraordinary and subtle phenomenon does exist is not easy to discover or demonstrate. But it seems worth recognizing that numerous testimonies of highly intelligent persons of good character and balanced sensitivities (of all different races) who attended these 40-day Chung Pyung workshops, reported remarkable spiritual experiences in which they were able to discern the reality of spirits attached to different parts of their bodies as well as to experience the efficacy of the depossession protocols. A good exemplification of this kind of testimony would be that of Linda F.

Linda F., whose dramatic testimony is included *in toto* as Appendix A, is an intelligent 42-year-old Caucasian American woman who had suffered with numerous, rather severe physical problems throughout her 30's. Ostensibly, there was no proportionate causation for these ailments. Yet, she was often in bad health, oftentimes feeling nauseous, daily experiencing excruciating back pain together with an abiding crook in her neck and spine (preventing her from holding her head upright), feeling bereft of energy on a daily basis, and otherwise feeling so disabled by such a lack of vitality that she thought she might be dying. Furthermore, throughout her whole life, she had never had monthly menstruation, and had been unable to get pregnant for 10 years—before deciding to go to the healing workshop at Chung Pyung Lake in Korea when she was 40 years old.

In addition to the above circumstances, it is important to mention that Linda, as a young girl, grew up in an orphanage where she had very little exposure to Black persons. Later, however, in her 20's, when she chose to join the Unification Church, she had severe difficulty in making friends with and working together with Black members, who almost instantly resented her upon meeting her. Linda, who always tried to express love and care for these Black members, could never understand the hostility she encountered in them, which seemed unwarranted and unfair.

Given this background, the following excerpted testimony by Linda F. seems to us an authentic portrayal of some of the more profound and subtle aspects of earthbound-spirit possession and depossession:

> So, when I went to Chung Pyung Lake, my first experience during the *an-sou,* which is the ceremony done to get rid of spirits, my first experience was that I closed my eyes and I could see a sea of Black people that had been slaves while they were [living] on the earth. And, not all of them, but many of them, especially the ones in front of this sea of people, knew me *intimately.* They *knew* me and I *knew* them, although I had never seen them before in my life. And it occurred to me that they had been *with* me for most of my life, if not all of my life. Because my whole life, I had thought about issues between Blacks and Whites—I had read a lot about slavery and stuff like that—I began this conversation between myself and the black slaves that I could see in front of me. And it was as if I could read their minds, and they could read my mind, and I was saying to them that I didn't want them to feel any more pain—that they had suffered, that their whole lives they had suffered. And in my mind, I went through a check-list of the different kinds of pains that I experienced in my life, and I *realized* as I went through this check-list that these physical problems I had in my lifetime corresponded to assaults that had taken place against their bodies when they were on earth. Like—the fact that my back felt like it was being split across the mid-section—I have no [medically discernible] problem with my back, nothing wrong with my spine, but always in the middle of my back it felt like it was being broken; and that I realized when those slaves were bending over in the fields how

214

their backs felt—and how when I, like I said in the beginning, when I couldn't even rise out of a chair, that my legs would ache and I couldn't even straighten out my feet and I couldn't make my body straighten up even to walk. And I *realized* that this is how their bodies would become after years and years of being stooped over in the fields, working the fields. And I realized my body was experiencing what their bodies had experienced through slavery.

And then—that was the first day—I remember during the *an-sou,* it was so excruciatingly painful to sit on the floor that I wanted to scream and run away—to escape my own body because it hurt so much, my whole body hurt. So, I sat in front of a very large brother and asked him to hit me very hard during the *an-sou.* And I could *see*—in my mind's eye—I could *see* these slaves being liberated. And the whole time, I was thinking to myself and saying to these slaves, in prayer, these slaves that I could see: "Please leave my body." Because of the resentment that they incurred through what happened to them, they were trying to hurt me. They had resentment because of what happened to them, and somehow it was connected to my lineage. And they were trying to hurt *me* because of what was done to *them.* So, I was trying to reason with them, "If you could forgive me, you would be free. You know, hurting me is not going to take your pain away; it isn't." And then I tried to explain: "Your resentment is making you more of a slave *now* than you ever were on earth—because you're enslaving yourself. You could be free, *like that* [snaps fingers], if you forgive and just let it go and *leave* me, and go to a better place where you can be taken care of and where your pains can be healed." And then, many, many of these spirits I could begin to see were coming out of me—slave spirits. And the next day, when I walked up the hill [mountain path] to the Holy Trees to pray, at several of the trees I could *see* these slave spirits, men and women crying and crying and crying. And I was crying, I was sobbing hysterically because there was something between *my* heart and *their* hearts that was resonating the same and it was about forgiveness—that they were grateful to me for [spiritually] liberating them and I was grateful that they could be liberated; they knew that I was genuinely happy for them to be resurrected. And there was some good rapport there. So, that was the first day.

The second day, the same thing happened—my body

started hurting again and I started thinking about my infertility and that made me think about how slaves were treated and the fact that they would be matched up with certain types of Black men to produce a certain type of slave children and that that child would be taken at birth and sold. And then I asked a question: "Is that why I can't have children? Am I being punished, because of what happened to you?" And there was just this icy cold feeling through me when I asked that question. So, then, I started to pray about all the different types of ills that were done to slaves. Another thing was: I had this incredible *thirst,* such that I would drink water all day, all night, and I would have to go to the bathroom 4, 5, 6 times every night because I had this incredible thirst. So, when I was at the Chung Pyung workshop, I thought about that. Yeah, I thought, the slaves must have been very thirsty in the field and couldn't have so much as a cup of water without permission. So, their thirst must have been raging at times. And when they died, the resentment that they had, resentment even over a cup of water. . . . And so, I really repented; I went to the Holy Rock and I took a very large (2-liter) bottle of water and I prayed to the slaves who had suffered from thirst and were even denied so much as a cup of water; and I drank that water, the Holy water, and I said [to them]: "I want each of you to partake of this water, so you can be liberated from your resentment and never feel thirst again." And since that time, I no longer drink water excessively like I used to. It's like something changed in my body, that I no longer needed to drink all the time. Even my husband commented when I came back, that I was not going to the bathroom every 5 minutes, because I no longer had this *obsession* to drink tons of water.

Then, on the third day, I woke up on the third morning and I couldn't *see;* I couldn't see anything. And I went to the *an-sou,* and while doing the *an-sou,* I heard a Black woman, and she was screaming at *me,* at *me personally.* She was saying, she said, "My beloved!"—I didn't know *at first* if she meant her *husband* or her *son*—but she was saying that the person that she loved, the man, was hung by the neck for looking at a white woman. Then, all of a sudden, I felt this incredible pain where I had the [previously mentioned] crookedness in my neck, and I could feel, could see in my mind's eye, there was a Black man, a spirit-man, who had been hung and he wanted to *kill* me. And he was holding on to my neck, where the crooked part was. So, I asked this brother, doing the *an-*

sou on my back, to hit me right here [pointing to the back of her neck] where the lump was. It took all 3 sessions [of *an-sou*], till the end of the day, to get rid of that spirit. And what I realized from that experience was that there were some spirits whose hearts you could easily move, through your repentance, suffering and your love, and they would forgive you and they would leave you. But there were other spirits, whose resentment is so deep and so passionate, that they aren't even satisfied when they kill you. If they wind up killing you, they just go on to your descendants. Because your blood and the blood of your descendants isn't even enough to satisfy the resentment that they have. — So, to get rid of this spirit that was on me was very, very difficult. I'm a very spiritually open person, and I could see the angels pulling, pulling on this Black man who was holding on to my body. Then, I remember that particular *an-sou* because I made this BIG brother sit behind me and he was *an-souing* me *sooooooo* hard, and I was just crying and crying. When it was finally over, and I stood up, it was like I had a new body. I had no pain in my back; I had no pain in my neck; I had no pain in my legs. I thought then that this would last one day, or two days, or three days, but those pains have *never* come back, and to this day, I don't have the lump in my back. But, the most incredible part was I had been there for 40 days. And they do special healing ceremonies for infertile women. I went to that ceremony and, while I was having the *an-sou* done to me, I had a spiritual experience. I saw these women whose children had been taken from them. And you know how Black women's hair is like a corkscrew? It was tied around my reproductive organs, these Black women's hair, cutting off any life to them. And, during the *an-sou*, I could see them [these hairs] being pulled off, one by one by one.—The very next day, I got my period, and I got my period every month after that. And then, one year to the day after that experience, I got pregnant.[69]

In final commentary on the above testimony, we should note first that while Linda's testimony does not detail which of her ancestors committed violations against the Black people that were enslaved, or what became of the ancestor(s), it *does* make clear that the spirits of these Black persons had become attached and earthbound, continuing to be enslaved even after death by their resentment. Resentment, which is destructive enough during earthly life, is a great ball-and-chain to a spirit-person after death. Linda's testimony is valuable inasmuch as it serves to demonstrate that the only authentic liberation of such earthbound spirits is one that must necessarily take place as a liberation of heart and attitude.

D.   How can earthbound spirits become educated and liberated, enabling them to move beyond the earth sphere into the spirit-world proper?

Given the major sources we have referenced so far, let us take stock of their various views regarding the education and liberation of earthbound spirits. Considering these views chronologically, Jesus' exorcisms/depossessions, as recounted in the New Testament, seem to be carried out through his own absolute spiritual authority. Jesus, interestingly enough does not seem to recognize, or at least is not portrayed as being concerned with, any specific need for educating and liberating earthbound spirit-persons; rather, he is concerned with liberating the tortured possessed. But, whereas Jesus apparently casts out the "unclean" spirit in Mark 9 via fiat, he is careful to explain to his disciples that the reason *they* could not successfully cast out this difficult spirit was because such cases required profound prayer (and fasting[70]).

Similarly, Swedenborg does not appear to talk about educating or liberating hellish spirits as such, though he does frequently describe the nature and living conditions of hellish spirits. In particular, as previously noted, Swedenborg recognizes that certain hellish spirits are able to attach themselves to earthly persons and, over time, can facilitate illness in such persons. If these spirits can be expelled, encroaching symptoms of disease will then oftentimes subside and disappear. Swedenborg, it will be remembered, is first of all a scientist and a brilliant observer, and is not readily concerned with exorcism or with the rehabilitation of hellish spirits.

Wickland and Fiore, however, are both concerned to understand the usually desperate plight of attached earthbound spirits and, based upon that understanding, to find a way to break this attachment that is beneficial to both possessor and possessee. As described earlier, Wickland's primary way of approaching earthbound spirits was through his wife, who served as the medium through whom spirits were able to voice their confusion, hostility and despair. It is true that sometimes, before Wickland could effectively address the possessing spirit, such a spirit literally had to be shocked into attention via a form of electroshock therapy—which the spirit-person later typically described as like being hit by "lightning." In any case, Wickland's primary means of educating/liberating earthbound spirits was through directly dialoguing with them, through his wife. In this way Wickland could, in many cases, get these spirits to recognize variously that 1) they were deceased, 2) they had become attached within the auras of earth-persons who, in turn, were being negatively influenced, and 3) that they needed to extricate themselves from their present stagnation by voluntarily hearkening to those deceased who loved them and were otherwise beckoning to them to enter the spirit-world. Wickland often stresses in his counsel to these spirits that they must try to implement *forgiveness,* both for themselves and for others back on earth that they hold a grudge against.[71] Sometimes Wickland explains to particular spirits that in order to achieve liberation, their greatest challenge is to overcome selfishness—through a willingness to care for and serve others, especially considering that this is the central purpose governing life in the spirit-world proper. This counsel is also dramatically voiced (via Mrs. Wickland) by a deceased Methodist minister, William Yates, Sr., who had been a long-standing friend of the Wicklands, and who was one of the few spirit-persons in *Thirty Years Among the Dead* to come through Mrs. Wickland that was not an earthbound spirit:

> When we pass through the material sphere of ether, the sphere around this world, we pass through the sphere in which are most of the spirits of darkness, which we call earthbound spirits.
>
> There all is selfishness and ignorance. These spirits must serve to help themselves to a higher understanding, for they have not served but have been served in their earth lives.
>
> They do not know what it is to live and do for others; they have lived only for self. They are waiting to be served. Their minds have not been developed to do for others.
>
> I wish I could take you to the sphere of suicides, the sphere of the churches, the sphere of the slums, the sphere of the misers, and so on. Here they are in darkness, crying for help. Many of them do not know what to do. They go to mortals and try to control them, upsetting their lives, and they are ignorant of what they are doing.[72]

Interestingly, Fiore's approach is very similar to Wickland's in that it relies on direct dialoguing with attached earthbound spirits as the basic means to educating them. However, whereas Wickland gained his opportunity to address directly such spirits through his mediumistic wife, Fiore utilizes a methodology of hypnotherapy, which also has the effect of closing down the host's personality so that the attached spirit-person is free to speak through the host. In any case, Fiore is thereby enabled to talk directly with the possessing entity, who can then be compassionately informed regarding the deleterious effects of his/her attachment and, on this basis, who can eventually choose of his/her own accord to depart from the host person and move into the supportive environment of the spirit-world proper. In this way, Fiore has carried out many successful depossessions, bringing healing reorientation to both patients, i.e., the earthbound spirit and its host.

In her book, Fiore further provides "General Instructions" for conducting a depossession of *oneself*—especially in those cases where a person has a strong intuition of being interfered with by earthbound spirits. In these situations, Fiore recommends a certain sequence of depossession procedures: You should begin with a prayer, followed by the careful visualization of white light surrounding oneself for self-protection. After this preparation, you can then directly, verbally address the earthbound spirit, explaining first that he or she has died, i.e., making clear to the spirit-person that his or her own physical body has died and that now s/he continues to exist as an incorporeal spirit; that he or she has become attached to you, is experiencing physicality through *your* physical body, and is creating problems for you on earth; and, finally, that he or she needs to understand that his/her rightful destination is to move into the Light and thereby into the spirit-world, where this spirit will readily discover that he or she actually has a perfect, luminous body. To conclude, one should send the spirit away with either a Christian blessing and prayer, or otherwise with any sincere prayer or affirmation.[73]

One of the most powerful means of addressing earthbound spirits is to pray for them. Wickland and Fiore, as well as many contemporary psychics, affirm the liberating and healing effects of prayer upon earthbound spirits. Psychic medium James Van Praagh, for instance, comments on this phenomenon in the following passage, noting that prayer serves to comfort and guide such disoriented souls:

> Fortunately, the prayers and loving thoughts from family and friends on earth for such souls help to change the auric atmosphere of depression and torture into one of healing and love. That's why it is so important to pray for those who pass over. Eventually, these souls will become aware of their higher spiritual natures and will begin to seek a way out of their situations. There are many on the other side of life whose sole responsibility is to assist these trapped victims and lovingly escort them to areas where they can receive proper comfort for their mental torture.[74]

Both Wickland and Fiore approach earthbound spirits by first attempting to instruct and educate them and, in this way, help them to realize that they should, without fear and with the assistance of more enlightened souls, choose to relinquish any attachments they have to an earthly host and move into the spirit-world proper. Thus, the order of the process here is education, depossession and liberation. However, the Unificationist methodology described earlier reverses the initial two stages of this process—accomplishing depossession first, and then education leading to liberation. As we have seen, the Chung Pyung retreats are structured to provide a kind of depossession regimen incorporating rigorous prayer/singing/*an-sou*/scriptural study/prayer—which generates a spiritually intense vibrational milieu that rouses and disturbs attached spirits. Following these events, the Korean shaman-like teacher, Daemo Nim, employs her considerable spiritual authority (recognized as granted by God) to evict attached spirits from their earthbound residence while at the same time directing them to attend educational seminars in the spirit-world. Further, inherent in her direction is the promise to these spirit-persons that, if they faithfully attend these seminars, and are consequently able to relinquish their resentment and to achieve new understanding of God and God's love, they can become fully liberated to dwell in the spirit-world.

Conclusion

We have deemed the foregoing investigation into the nature of earthbound spirit-persons as critically important because the truth is that there are millions of these tortured souls stuck in the earth-sphere. As we have seen, many of these remain unattached, emotionally disoriented and wandering in various degrees of darkness. Many others become insalubriously attached to earth-persons, and we have attempted here to examine the meaning and extent of such attachment by recognizing, first, that an attached earthbound spirit becomes attached within the *aura* of an earth-person; second, that attachment within the aura is a *correspondential* attachment, or an attachment to a part of the aura that corresponds to some particular anatomical element of the human physical body; and third, that such correspondential attachment can and does occur sometimes *across generations* within a particular lineage.

In closing, we would agree with Fiore, from a practical standpoint, that research should be undertaken to elucidate the role that spirits play in human life. From a therapeutic perspective, we would further agree with her that information on possession-via-attachment, as well as alternatives for depossession, should be made public, so that people may educate and protect themselves from the unfortunate realities of spirit interference.[75] Lastly, from an innermost spiritual perspective, we would suggest that, not only all varieties of earthbound spirit-persons, but also all human beings living physically on earth, cry out for emotional healing—the spiritual healing of the human heart, which can only, finally, be achieved through the experience of God's love.

NOTES

Section 1

1. Emanuel Swedenborg, *The True Christian Religion* (London: The Swedenborg Society, 850, 1984), 792.
2. Sun Myung Moon, *Master Speaks, 3 & 4, 1965* (Transcribed Notes, 1965).
3. Peter Thompkins & Christopher Bird, *The Secret Life of Plants* (New York: Harper & Row, Publishers, 1984), p. 26.
4. Moon, *Exposition of the Divine Principle* (New York: The Holy Spirit Association for the Unification of World Christianity, 1966), pp. 47-48.

Section 2

1. Emanuel Swedenborg, *Arcana Coelestia* 994 (Standard Edition).
2. Paramahansa Yogananda, *Autobiography of a Yogi* (Los Angeles: Self-Realization Fellowship, 1972), p. 481.
3. This catastrophic fire is described, for instance, in a 1763 letter written by philosopher Immanuel Kant to Charlotte Von Knobloch, excerpted in George Trobridge's *Swedenborg: Life and Teaching,* revised by Richard H. Tafel (New York: Swedenborg Foundation, Inc., 1992 [1901]), pp. 109-110.
4. Sun Myung Moon, *Exposition of the Divine Principle* (New York: The Holy Spirit Association for the Unification of World Christianity, 1996), pp. 36-37.
5. Peter Thompkins & Christopher Bird, *The Secret Life of Plants* (New York: Harper & Row, Publishers, 1972, 1984), p. 136.
6. *Ibid.*, p. 141.
7. Robert A. McDermott, ed., *The Essential Steiner* (San Francisco: Harper & Row, 1984), p. 40 (excerpted from Hans Gebert, "About Goetheanistic Science," *Journal for Anthroposophy* [Spring 1979], pp. 45-46).

Section 3

1. Emanuel Swedenborg, *Heaven and Hell* (trans. by George F. Dole) (New York: Swedenborg Foundation, Inc., 1979), 463.
2. Anthony Borgia, *Life in the World Unseen* (London: Psychic Press, Ltd., 1954), p. 144.
3. Sun Myung Moon, *The Divine Principle—Study Guide* (New York: The Holy Spirit Association for the Unification of World Christianity, 1973), p. 49.

4. Swedenborg, *The Spiritual Diary* (Cambridge: University Press, 1977), vol. 1, 140.
5. Malachi Martin, *Hostage to the Devil* (San Francisco: Harper Collins *Publishers*, 1992 [1976]), p. 308.
6. *Heaven and Hell* 462b-463.

Section 4

1. Emanuel Swedenborg, *Earths In The Universe* (London: The Swedenborg Society, 1970 (1869)), 125.
2. Anthony Borgia, *Life in the World Unseen* (London: Psychic Press, Ltd., 1954), p. 24.
3. Sun Myung Moon, "Individual Course of Life" (1/20/80 speech), p. 6.
4. Moon, *Unification Thought* (New York: Unification Thought Institute, 1973), p. 80.
5. Paramahansa Yogananda, *Autobiography of a Yogi* (Los Angeles: Self-Realization Fellowship, 1972), p. 478.
6. Moon, "The Necessity for the Day of Victory of Love" (1/15/84 speech) in *God's Will and the World* (New York: The Holy Spirit Association for the Unification of World Christianity, 1985), p. 662.

Section 5

1. Anthony Borgia, *Life in the World Unseen* (London: Psychic Press, Ltd., 1954), p. 154.
2. Robert Monroe, *Journeys Out of the Body* (New York: Doubleday, 1977), p. 175.
3. Elisabeth Kübler-Ross, *On Life After Death* (Berkeley, California: Celestial Arts, 1991), p. 30 (excerpted from a 1982 speech entitled "Living and Dying").

Section 6

1. Samuel M. Warren, *A Compendium of the Theological Writings of Emanuel Swedenborg* (New York: Swedenborg Foundation, Inc., 1979 [1875]), p. 21 (trans. of Swedenborg's *Divine Love and Wisdom* 319-320).
2. Sun Myung Moon, *Exposition of the Divine Principle* (New York: The Holy Spirit Association for the Unification of World Christianity, 1996), p. 47.
3. Emanuel Swedenborg, *Heaven and Hell* (trans. by George F. Dole) (New York: Swedenborg Foundation, Inc., 1979), 89.
4. *A Compendium of the Theological Writings of Emanuel Swedenborg* (excerpt

from *Divine Love and Wisdom* 321).

5.   Moon, *Master Speaks, 3 & 4, 1965* (Transcribed Notes, 1965).

6.   Swedenborg, *Divine Love and Wisdom* (trans. by George F. Dole) (West Chester, Pennsylvania: Swedenborg Foundation, Inc., 1985), 288.

7.   Moon, "Mainstream of the Dispensation of God" (11/19/78 speech), p. 14.

Section 7

1.   Emanuel Swedenborg, *Heaven and Hell* (trans. by George F. Dole) (New York: Swedenborg Foundation, Inc., 1979), 112.

2.   Sun Myung Moon, *Exposition of the Divine Principle* (New York: The Holy Spirit Association for the Unification of World Christianity, 1996), p. 46.

3.   *Ibid.*

4.   Swedenborg, *Arcana Coelestia* 69 (Standard Edition).

Section 8

1.   D. Scott Rogo, *Leaving the Body* (New York: Fireside, Simon & Schuster, 1983), pp. 173-74.

2.   Sun Myung Moon, *Master Speaks, 3 & 4, 1965* (Transcribed Notes, 1965).

3. Anthony Borgia, *Life in the World Unseen* (London: Psychic Press Ltd., 1954), p. 123.

4.   Emanuel Swedenborg, *The Universal Human* 4225, in George F. Dole, ed. and trans., *Emanuel Swedenborg: The Universal Human and Soul-Body Interaction* (in The Classics of Western Spirituality series) (New York: Paulist Press, 1984), p. 109.

5.   Paramahansa Yogananda, *Autobiography of a Yogi* (Los Angeles: Self-Realization Fellowship, 1972), p. 479.

6.   Borgia, *Life in the World Unseen*, p. 57.

7.   Swami Panchadasi, *The Astral World: Its Scenes, Dwellers, and Phenomena* (Chicago, IL: Advanced Thought Publishing, 1915 [The Book Tree, 2000]), p. 8.

8.   Robert Monroe, *Journeys Out of the Body* (New York: Doubleday, 1977), p. 76.

9.   Gary Zukav, *The Seat of the Soul* (New York: Fireside, Simon & Schuster, 1990), p. 97.

10. Roger Wescott, "Toward an Extraterrestrial Anthropology" in *Cultures Beyond the Earth*, ed. by Magoroh Maruyama and Arthur Harkins (New York: Vintage Books, 1975), p. 17.

11. It seems worthwhile here to share a description of a friend's experience while under the influence of the psychedelic, psilocybin. This friend related that, while in a fully conscious, non-hallucinatory, though hypersensitive state of awareness, he experienced his field of vision become differentiated into two

distinct dimensional perspectives—the first was that of normal sight, with
everything appearing in its conventional orientation; the second perspective,
however, which appeared more or less transparently superimposed upon the
first, was the extremely lucid seeing of a man and woman walking together,
oriented at a 45-degree angle to his otherwise normal field of vision. This general kind of experience of "interdimensional traffic" has been narrated to the
author by at least four or five different people at different times and, while
these accounts don't necessarily prove anything in themselves, they *do* seem
suggestive of the possibility that reality is far more multidimensional than
most people are accustomed to believing, and further, that access to such
other dimensions lies in the appropriate (and not at all necessarily drug-
induced) transformation of human consciousness.

12.   Craig R. Lundahl, Ph.D. and Harold A. Widdison, Ph.D., *The Eternal
Journey: How Near-Death Experiences Illuminate Our Earthly Lives* (New
York: Warner Books, Inc., 1997), p. 130.

13.   Emanuel Swedenborg, *Earths in the Universe* 127 (London: The Swedenborg
Society, 1860, 1970), p. 68.

14.   Lundahl and Widdison, *The Eternal Journey: How Near-Death Experiences
Illuminate Our Earthly Lives,* p. 166.

15.   Yogananda, *Autobiography of a Yogi,* p. 478.

16.   Betty J. Eadie, *Embraced by the Light* (California: Gold Leaf Press, 1992), pp.
87-88.

17.   Swedenborg, *Earths in the Universe* 6, p. 3.

18.   *Ibid.* 47, p. 22.

19.   Borgia, *Life in the World Unseen,* p. 123.

20.   *Ibid.*

21.   Monroe, *Journeys Out of the Body,* p. 78.

22.   Swedenborg, *The Universal Human* 4041, pp. 95-96.

23   Emanuel Swedenborg, *Heaven and Hell* 29 (trans. by George F. Dole) (New
York: Swedenborg Foundation, Inc., 1979), p. 49.

24.   Swedenborg, *Heaven and Hell* 38, p. 53. Swedenborg here seems to be distinguishing between *quantitative* levels, which are properly characterized by
numerical amounts, and *qualitative* levels, which cannot be described by
numerical differences, since they are of different *characters* and are not quan-
titatively comparable.

25.   Joong Hyun Pak and Andrew Wilson, *True Family Values* (New York: Holy
Spirit Association for the Unification of World Christianity, 1996), pp. 148-
156.

26.   In *Heaven and Hell* (553.2), Swedenborg offers this description of the
appearance of those residing in the hells:
"In general, their faces are frightful, lifeless as corpses. Some are black, some
like fiery little torches, some swollen by pimples, distorted veins, and sores.
Many have no visible face, but only something hairy or bony instead; with

some, only teeth stand out. Their bodies are grotesque, and their speech apparently arises from anger or hatred or revenge because each one talks out of his own false nature and has a voice quality that stems from his evil nature. In short, all of them are reflections of their own hells."

27. This point refers to one of the major differences between Unification theology and traditional Christian theology. Unification theology teaches that God originally intended Jesus to become the incarnation of such unconditional *parental* love through having married and become a parent in his own right during his life on earth—a life-course hoped for but tragically prevented by the crucifixion.

Section 9

1. Anthony Borgia, *Life in the World Unseen* (London: Psychic Press Ltd., 1954), p. 42.

2. Emanuel Swedenborg, *The True Christian Religion* (London: The Swedenborg Society, 1850, 1984), 280.5-6.

3. Sun Myung Moon, "The Way of Original Form" (6/8/80 speech) (New York: The Holy Spirit Association for the Unification of World Christianity), pp. 15-16.

4. Craig R. Lundahl, Ph.D. and Harold A. Widdison, Ph.D., *The Eternal Journey: How Near-Death Experiences Illuminate Our Earthly Lives* (New York: Warner Books, Inc., 1997), p. 118.

5. Anthony Borgia, *Here and Hereafter* (Midway, Utah: M.A.P., 1995), p. 108.

6. Robert Monroe, *Journeys Out of the Body* (New York: Doubleday, 1977), p. 74.

7. Hildegard of Bingen, *Liber Vitae Meritorum* (Pitra,1882), p. 75 in Matthew Fox and Rupert Sheldrake, *The Physics of Angels* (New York: HarperCollins Publishers, Inc., 1996), p. 145.

8. Matthew Fox and Rupert Sheldrake, *The Physics of Angels* (New York: HarperCollins Publishers, Inc., 1996), pp. 146-47.

9. Emanuel Swedenborg, *Conjugial Love* (London: The Swedenborg Society, 1970), 521.

10. Emanuel Swedenborg, *Arcana Coelestia* 1886 (Standard Edition).

11. Emanuel Swedenborg, *Heaven and Hell,*trans. by George F. Dole (New York: Swedenborg Foundation, Inc., 1979), 2.

12. Emanuel Swedenborg, *Spiritual Diary* 5102.

13. *Arcana Coelestia* 6624.

14. *Ibid.* 1757.

15. *Heaven and Hell* 243.

16. *Arcana Coelestia* 322.

17. *Spiritual Diary* 1482.

18. *Arcana Coelestia* 803.2.
19. *Ibid.* 1640.2.
20. Emanuel Swedenborg, *Divine Providence* 224.3 (Standard Edition).
21. *Heaven and Hell* 245.
22. *Spiritual Diary* 5564.
23. *Ibid.* 4342; Swedenborg's description here has a direct contemporary corollary in the description by Robert Monroe of "NVC" ("nonverbal communication") or, that is, the form of totalistic communication employed by "other intelligent species" that Monroe encountered in his remarkable out-of-body explorations. Like Swedenborg's holistic "cogitative speech," NVC seems to operate via instantaneous thought transmission of multitudes of sensory details as well as personal attitudes and feelings, etc., in regard to a particular situation, person or object:

"All other intelligent species use what we now call nonverbal communication (NVC). It is something far more than what we label body language, telepathy, remote viewing, and the often mystical or religious connotations so commonly applied to a tiny part of NVC. We say a picture is worth 1,000 words. A color picture is worth 10,000 words. A moving color picture is worth 50,000 words, perhaps, and a talking moving color picture is worth 100,000 or more words in the transmission of information and/or communication.

NVC takes a quantum jump beyond a talking moving color picture. It is direct instant experience and/or immediate knowing transmitted from one intelligent energy system and received by another."

—Robert Monroe, *Far Journeys* (New York: Doubleday, 1985), pp. 71-72. Monroe further conjectures, not implausibly, that NVC should be applicable to specifically human communication, as well as to interacting with "other intelligent species." In this, he affirms that NVC definitely exists as a *practical, human* potentiality which, if it could somehow be developed and utilized among human beings, would allow them to immediately access, and otherwise share, the fullness of each other's life experiences. Not unlike Rev. Moon's assertion that, in the future, clairvoyance and clairaudience will become as prevalent in human culture as television and radio are today, Monroe exemplifies the practical significance of NVC in this passage:

"If I were proficient at NVC and my son was also trained in the technique, I could pass along to him, in very short order, all of the education and experience that I have gathered that he might desire or that might be of use to him. It would not be the absorption of words simply received in serial form, but an instantaneous, or nearly so, transmission absorption of the entire event— including my emotional reaction, what my five senses perceived, and the interpretations and conclusions that I gleaned from the experience."
Ibid., pp. 72-73.

24. *Arcana Coelestia* 1641.
25. *Ibid.* 1637-38.

26. In fairness, we should acknowledge here, again, that Swedenborg generally believed and held that the population of angels in the spiritual world originally came from the human race, and he does not seem to partake in any way of the more traditional Christian notion that angels were originally created by God to exist as a unique, non-human order of purely spiritual (incorporeal) beings.

27. E.g., in *Divine Providence* 34.3:
     "One who understands the elevation and perfecting of these degrees can see to an extent why angelic wisdom is said to be ineffable. So ineffable, indeed, is it, that a thousand ideas in the thought of angels in their wisdom can present only a single idea in the thought of men in their wisdom, the other nine hundred and ninety-nine ideas being unutterable, because they are supernatural. Many a time have I been given to know this by living experience."

28. That such profound subtlety of thought is possible is a reality that I also feel I, Kerry Pobanz have glimpsed and can testify to from my personal experience with altered states of consciousness. If I were to encapsulate my insight from such experience, I would suggest that reality seems accessible to thought in "chunks"; the more developed one's thought or mind is, the larger the chunks of reality that become comprehensible to it, and the less adequate that words are to communicate those chunks, resulting finally in total ineffability.

     The comprehending of "chunks" that I speak of here refers to the grasping of meaning, of many different, progressively more expansive levels of meaning. For instance, on the most external level of meaning, one may see and hold an apple that he is about to eat. At this level, one simply is conscious of, perhaps, being hungry and wanting to satisfy his hunger, and this is the meaning the apple has for him. Yet, as one moves into and through progressively more internal states of consciousness of the apple, one experiences reality in progressively larger chunks: Beyond the appetitive appreciation of the apple, one may move to the recognition that it is, in fact, a MacIntosh apple; next, that it grew on a particular MacIntosh tree where it had once been picked in a certain way at a specific time of year; next, that the MacIntosh tree arose from a particular seed, planted and nurtured in a particular way in a specific season in a certain apple orchard on a certain farm; next, that the farm itself was built or created according to the purpose or desire of a particular farmer, etc. Thus, what the apple *means,* beyond satisfying one's hunger, can be experienced via the indeterminate and inarticulable multidimensionality of levels of meaning that inhere in the apple's provenance, all of which levels are actually comprehensible to human consciousness and all of which *ultimately* can be traced back to God. This is also to say that human consciousness, in its original, uninterrupted connection to God, would accomplish comprehension of these many levels of meaning, not sedulously one after the other, but essentially simultaneously.

29. *The True Christian Religion* 280.8.

30. *Arcana Coelestia* 3345.

31. *Spiritual Diary* 2137-2141.
32. *Heaven and Hell* 234.
33. *Spiritual Diary* 1479.
34. *Heaven and Hell* 239.
35. *Arcana Coelestia* 1646.
36. *Heaven and Hell* 241. Specifically, Swedenborg writes in his Diary on March 3, 1748:

    "Although angels do not manifest themselves to man by means of speech, still in order that I might perceive how they express their thoughts even by speech and discourse, I have heard them talking, being at the time transmitted into a state not unlike that of good spirits, so that I might perceive that the angels were speaking through the good spirits and according to their meanings. Their speech is quick, flowing like smooth water. There are words, indeed, but they are, as it were, continuous, or rather, the ideas are continued like a stream in which is the thought which quickly falls into words with me. In short, there is, as it were, a stream of ideas to which the words correspond, but they do not adhere to them. When I answered, I observed that my speech was broken, that is, divided by the words and of another sound, not fluent, thus not heavenly; wherefore I was at once distinguished from them because I was not such as they were. Thus angelic discourse, when spoken, is the infilling sense of the words taken together, in those cases in which the words do not suffice."
    Spiritual Diary 1146

37. *Arcana Coelestia* 3219, 6615.
38. *Heaven and Hell* 258-264; *Spiritual Diary* 5579.
39. Sun Myung Moon, "The Way of Original Form" (6/8/80 speech), pp. 15-16.
40. *Heaven and Hell* 244.

Section 10

1. Emanuel Swedenborg, *Conjugial Love* 46, [1768] (as quoted in Wilson Van Dusen, *The Presence of Other Worlds* (West Chester, Pennsylvania: The Swedenborg Foundation, 1994 [1974]), pp. 109-110.
2. M. Scott Peck, *In Heaven as on Earth: A Vision of the Afterlife* (New York: Hyperion, 1996), p. 58.
3. Sang Hun Lee, *Life in the Spirit World and on Earth* (New York: Family Federation for World Peace and Unification, 1998), pp. 67-68.
4. George Ritchie, *My Life After Dying* (Norfolk, Virginia: Hampton Roads, 1991), p. 92.
5. Emanuel Swedenborg, *Conjugial Love* (London: The Swedenborg Society, 1970 [1768]), 48.
6. *Ibid.,* 44.3.
7. *Ibid.,* 44.8.

8. *Ibid.*, 44.9.

9. Robert Monroe, *Journeys Out of the Body* (New York: Doubleday, 1977), p. 196.

10. *Ibid.*, p. 193.

11. Don and Linda Pendleton, *To Dance With Angels* (New York: Windsor Publishing Corp., 1990), p. 209.

12. *Life In The Spirit World and on Earth,* pp. 33-34.

13. *Ibid.*, pp. 67-68.

Section 11

1. St. Thomas Aquinas, *Summa Theologica,* v. 1, Question 50, Art. 1, in *Great Books of the Western World,* ed. by Robert M. Huchins (Chicago: Encyclopedia Britannica, 1952), vol. 19, p. 269.

2. Rudolf Steiner, *Spiritual Beings in the Heavenly Bodies and in the Kingdoms of Nature* (Hudson, NY: Anthroposophic Press, 1992 [1912]), pp. 65-66.

3. Jacques Vallee, *Dimensions* (New York: Ballantine Books, 1989), pp. 96, 120.

4. Sun Myung Moon, *Master Speaks* (Nos. 3 & 4), 1965.

5. Matthew Fox and Rupert Sheldrake, *The Physics of Angels* (New York, NY: HarperCollins*Publishers* (HarperSanFrancisco), 1996), p. 1.

6. Paramahansa Yogananda, *Autobiography of a Yogi* (Los Angeles, California: Self-Realization Fellowship, 1972 [1946]).

7. It is also interesting to see that this notion is espoused by a contemporary psychic medium like Sylvia Browne. As part of the teaching in her newly founded gnostic religion (called "Novus Spiritus"), she independently corroborates, at least in part, Swedenborg's vision of the planetary *structure* of the spirit-world:
   "An "Other Side" surrounds each inhabited planet for the long-lasting residence of created entities. It is an environment of love and peace without "death," where awareness and knowledge are heightened and one evolves intellectually and lovingly with the "veil" lifted. . . .
   Other dimensions are nothing more than the Other Side. Each planet that contains life has its own Other Side."
   (From: Sylvia Browne, *God, Creation and Tools for Life* [Carlsbad, CA: Hay House, Inc., 2000], p. 70.)

8. Moon, *Master Speaks* (3 and 4).

9. Matthew Bunson, *Angels A to Z* (New York, NY: Three Rivers Press, 1996), p. 227.

10. *Ibid.*, p. 226.

11. Aquinas, *Summa Theologica,* v. 1, Question 111, Art. 2.

12. Emanuel Swedenborg, *Arcana Coelestia* 5992 (Standard Edition).

13. Bunson, *Angels A to Z,* p. 124.

14. *Ibid.*, pp. 212-214.
15. Pierre Jovanovich, *An Inquiry into the Existence of Guardian Angels* (New York: M. Evans and Company, Inc., 1993), pp. 340-341.
16. Joseph F. Smith, quoted in *Journal of Discourses*, vol. 22, p. 351, in J. Heinerman, *Guardian Angels* (Salt Lake City, Utah: Joseph Lyon & Associates, 1988), p. 24.
17. Anthony Borgia, *Life in the World Unseen* (London: Psychic Press, Ltd., 1954), pp. 175-176.
18. George Anderson and Andrew Barone, *Lessons from the Light* (New York: Berkley Books, 2000), p. 266.
19. Sylvia Browne and Antoinette May, *Adventures of a Psychic* (Carlsbad, CA: Hay House, Inc., 1998 [1990]), pp. 23-24.
20. See Section 9 in this book on the nature of thought and language in the spiritual world.
21. Bunson, *Angels A to Z*, p. 164.
22. James Hastings, ed., *Encyclopaedia of Religion and Ethics* (New York: Scribner, 1955), p. 617.
23. Gustav Davidson, *A Dictionary of Angels* (New York: The Free Press, 1967), p. 64.
24. 3 Enoch 14:4, 17:3, 20:1-2 in *The Old Testament Pseudepigrapha*, ed. by J. H. Charlesworth (New York: Doubleday, 1983).
25. Davidson, *A Dictionary of Angels*, p. 192.
26. 3 Enoch 8-10.
27. In the theology of Greek Orthodox Christianity, for instance, one finds the notion that: God became man in order that man could become God.
28. Gen. 2:16 gives God's commandment to Adam and Eve in Eden: "You may freely eat of every tree of the garden, but of the tree of the knowledge of good and evil you shall not eat, for in the day you eat of it you shall die." Unificationists understand, with very plausible scriptural support, all the elements of the Genesis story of Adam and Eve's transgression in the Garden to be symbolic: the serpent represents the archangel Lucifer promoting deception; the Tree of Life represents Adam in his ideal, perfected state, having grown into the mature manhood that would enable him to stand in complete unity with God; the Tree of the Knowledge of Good and Evil, as bilaterally symmetrical, represents Eve, though in her present immature state, still in the process of growth to divine womanhood; given that trees multiply via the seeds contained in their fruit, the "fruit" is a symbol for human love yielding multiplication; the *fruit* of the Tree of the Knowledge of Good and Evil is a symbol for the *love of immature Eve;* and finally, *eating the fruit* of the Tree of the Knowledge of Good and Evil refers to having sexual intercourse. Thus, God's commandment to Adam and Eve was not a harsh dictate to ruthlessly enforce their obedience, but was, rather, a Father's loving, appropriate direction to his children not to enter into a sexual relationship during their years of

growth to full physical and spiritual maturity.

The sexual interpretation of the human fall is, of course, not unique to Unification teaching. One need only remember that even in Genesis itself, the description of "knowing" a woman, which partakes of the same Hebrew root as "knowledge" in the "Tree of *Knowledge* of Good and Evil," is an unambiguous reference to having sexual relations (see, e.g., Gen. 4:1). Further, as Theologian Young Oon Kim points out:

"The sexual interpretation of the Fall has been one of several views advocated by rabbinic commentators, apocalyptic writers, early Christian sectarians, and several modern Biblical scholars. There are also numerous hints in the early Greek church fathers, suggesting that the sexual explanation of Adam's sin was fairly widespread in the formative period of the Christian movement." (Young Oon Kim, *Unification Theology* [New York, NY: The Holy Spirit Association for the Unification of World Christianity, 1980], p. 113.)

29. One may reasonably wonder how it is possible for an angel and a human being to have a sexual relationship. The first thing we must understand here is that, while Adam and Eve possessed both physical and spiritual bodies, the archangel, as incorporeal, possessed only a spiritual body. Second, it should be noted that Adam and Eve, as pristine human beings in the Garden of Eden, had full use of their five spiritual senses, correspondent to their five physical senses. One consequence of this was that Adam and Eve were naturally clairvoyant and clairaudient, and could both see and socially relate to Lucifer just as easily as they could see and relate to each other. Another point should also be noted here, which is generally not appreciated: *the sense of touch between two spiritual bodies is just as substantial as the sense of touch between two physical bodies, if not more so.* Thus, in the last analysis, Lucifer and Eve were free to develop their relationship, not only through sight and conversation, but also finally in the very substantial act of sexual consummation by means of their spiritual bodies. In other words, the sexual fall on the spiritual plane was just as real and devastating as was the sexual fall on the physical plane. The net result was that God's original, full ideal of True Love became compromised, as it were, through the primordial misuse of sexual love.

30. John 12:31 refers to Satan as "the ruler of this world"; 2 Cor. 4:4 names Satan as "the god of this world."

31. Sun Myung Moon, *Exposition of the Divine Principle* (New York: The Holy Spirit Association for the Unification of World Christianity, 1996), pp. 53-65 (Note: This is the entirety of Chapter 2, which provides the systematic theological explanation of the nature and significance of the event of the Human Fall).

32. The Fall was an emotionally devastating event, both for human beings and for God. How can this primordial Fall ever be rectified? How can God's heart, angels' hearts and the hearts of humanity be healed? The Messiah is the one who comes with the healing authority to grant salvation.

33. F. R. Tennant, *The Sources of the Doctrines of the Fall and Original Sin* (New York: Schocken Books, 1968), p. 176.

34. 1 Enoch 6-7.

35. Dionysius the Pseudo-Areopagite, *The Celestial Hierarchy*, 337A, in *Pseudo-Dionysius: The Complete Works*, trans. by Colm Luibheid (in The Classics of Western Spirituality series) (New York: Paulist Press, 1987), p. 188.

36. *Ibid.*, 257B (p. 170).

37. *Ibid.*, 205B-260B (pp. 161-170).

38. *Ibid.*, 237A (p. 173).

39. *Ibid.*, 304A-304B (pp. 178-179).

40. *Ibid.*, 336A-336B (pp. 187-188).

41. Fox and Sheldrake, *The Physics of Angels*, p. 75.

42. Bunson, *Angels A to Z*, p. 233.

43. *Ibid.*, p. 286.

44. *Ibid.*, p. 225.

45. *Ibid.*, p. 53.

46. Emanuel Swedenborg, *Heaven and Hell*, trans. by George F. Dole (New York: Swedenborg Foundation, Inc., 1979 [1758]), 312.4.

47. *Ibid.*, 311.2.

48. *Divine Love and Wisdom* 140, trans. by George F. Dole (West Chester, PA: Swedenborg Foundation, 1994 [1763]). (See also, *Heaven and Hell* 311-316, and *Divine Providence* 27.)

49. *Arcana Coelestia* 2203 (Standard Edition).

50. Taking this a step further, Swedenborg teaches not only that each angel is a person, and a microcosm of heaven, but that this is because *heaven itself* is in the form of a person:
    "The entire heaven, made up of myriads of angels, is like a person in its overall form. The same holds true of every community, larger or smaller. Further, this is why an angel is a person, an angel actually being a heaven in its smallest form." (*Divine Love and Wisdom* 19.)

51. Swedenborg, *Arcana Coelestia* 6135.

52. *Heaven and Hell* 75.

53. *Ibid.*, 184-186.

54. *Arcana Coelestia* 5576.

55. *Heaven and Hell* 162.

56. *Ibid.* 192.

57. *Ibid.* 269.2.

58. *Ibid.* 267.

59. *Divine Love and Wisdom* 202.

60. *Ibid.*

61. *Heaven and Hell* 267.

62. *Ibid.* 391.

63. *Ibid.* 387-394.

64. *Ibid.* 229.
65. *Arcana Coelestia* 8118.
66. *Ibid.* 10384.
67. *Divine Love and Wisdom* 188.
68. Robert A. McDermott, ed., *The Essential Steiner* (San Francisco, CA: Harper & Row, Publishers, 1984), pp. 6-12.
69. The previous English translations of this work have been titled: *Knowledge of the Higher Worlds and Its Attainment.*
70. Steiner, *Spiritual Beings in the Heavenly Bodies and in the Kingdoms of Nature,* p. 16.
71. The following discussion represents a selective summary of Steiner's Lectures 1-7, out of the complete set of ten lectures contained in *Spiritual Beings in the Heavenly Bodies and in the Kingdoms of Nature.*
72. *Ibid.,* pp. 29-30.
73. *Ibid.,* p. 49.
74. *Ibid.,* p. 66.
75. Though it is not germane to the present discussion, the offspring of the exusiai, dynamis and kyriotetes are, according to Steiner, *the group-souls of plants and animals or,* that is, the group-souls informing all individual plants and animals:
    ". . . [O]ccult vision of the second stage finds in the beings of the plant and animal kingdoms, spiritual beings who are not, as in humanity, individual spirits in individual human beings; but we find groups of animals, groups of plants that are of like form, ensouled by a common soul being. These we call group-souls, and these group-souls are the detached offspring of the beings of the second hierarchy, just as nature spirits are the offspring of the third hierarchy." (*Spiritual Beings in the Heavenly Bodies and in the Kingdoms of Nature,* pp. 78-79.)
76. *Ibid.,* pp. 81-82.
77. *Ibid.,* p. 83.
78. Again, for our purposes in this section, we have chosen not to enter into a detailed discussion of the spiritual offspring of the second and third hierarchies. The reader is invited instead to read the full text of this series of ten lectures fully elaborating Steiner's systematic angelology, contained in *Spiritual Beings in the Heavenly Bodies and in the Kingdoms of Nature.*
79. *Ibid.,* p. 120.
80. *Ibid.,* p. 121.
81. James Daugherty, *William Blake* (New York: The Viking Press, 1960), p. 104.
82. *Ibid.,* pp. 75-76.
83. W. Y. Evans-Wentz, *The Fairy Faith in Celtic Countries* (Buckinghamshire, Great Britain: Colin Smythe Limited, 1977 [1911]), p. 242.
84. *Ibid.,* p. 18.
85. Mary T. Browne, *Life After Death* (New York: Ballantine Books, 1994), p. 52.

86. Ted Andrews, *Enchantment of the Faerie Realm* (St. Paul, Minnesota: Llewellyn Publications, 1993), p. xii.

87. Dora van Gelder, *The Real World of Fairies* (Wheaton, Illinois: Theosophical Publishing House, 1999 [1977]), p. 13.

88. From Lecture 2 of a lecture cycle given in Vienna, Austria, September 1923, entitled "Anthroposophy and the Human Gemüt" in Stewart C. Easton, *Man and World in the Light of Anthroposophy* (Spring Valley, New York: The Anthroposophic Press, 1975), p. 310.

89. Van Gelder, *The Real World of Fairies,* pp. 51, 54.

90. Evans-Wentz, *The Fairy-Faith in Celtic Countries,* pp. 59-66.

91. *Ibid.,* p. 11.

92. Van Gelder, *The Real World of Fairies,* p. 145.

93. Francezzo (transcribed by A. Farnese), *A Wanderer in the Spirit Lands* (West Grove, PA: AIM Publishing Company, 1993), p. 99.

94. Andrews, *Enchantment of the Faerie Realm,* p. 51.

95. Easton, *Man and World in the Light of Anthroposophy,* p. 286.

96. Marjorie Spock, *Fairy Worlds and Workers* (Hudson, NY: Anthroposophic Press, 1980), p. 13.

97. Andrews, *Enchantment of the Faerie Realm,* p. 35.

98. *Ibid.,* pp. 22-23.

99. Spock, *Fairy Worlds and Workers,* pp. 17-18.

100. Andrews, *Enchantment of the Faerie Realm,* p. 37.

101. Spock, *Fairy Worlds and Workers,* p. 19.

102. Andrews, *Enchantment of the Faerie Realm,* pp. 94, 98.

103. Van Gelder, *The Real World of Fairies,* p. 154.

104. Spock, *Fairy Worlds and Workers,* p. 20.

105. Andrews, *Enchantment of the Faerie Realm,* p. 43.

106. *Ibid.,* p. 8.

107. Dorothy Maclean, *To Hear the Angels Sing* (Hudson, NY: Lindisfarne Press, 1990 (1980), p. 64.

108. Van Gelder, *The Real World of Fairies,* pp. 170-176.

109. Andrews, *Enchantment of the Faerie Realm,* p. 29.

110. Michael Lindemann, *UFOs and the Alien Presence: Six Viewpoints* (Santa Barbara, CA: The 2020 Group, 1991), p. 10.

111. Whitley Strieber, *Communion* (New York, NY: Avon Books, 1987), pp. 226-227.

112. Vallee, *Dimensions,* p. 144.

113. Ruth Montgomery, *Aliens Among Us* (New York: Ballantine Books [Fawcett Crest], 1986), p.153.

114. Yogananda, *Autobiography of a Yogi,* p. 478.

115. Moon, *Master Speaks* (Nos. 3 & 4).

116. In the period from 1987-2000, Strieber published the following books (in chronological order), which address the nature and significance of the

"Visitor" phenomenon:

(1) *Communion* (New York, NY: Avon Books, 1987).

(2) *Transformation* (New York, NY: Beech Tree Books [William Morrow], 1988).

(3) *Breakthrough* (New York, NY: HarperCollins*Publishers,* 1995).

(4) *The Secret School* (New York, NY: HarperCollins*Publishers,* 1997).

(5) *The Communion Letters* (New York, NY: HarperPrism, 1997).

(6) *Confirmation* (New York, NY: St. Martin's Press, 1998).

117. Strieber, *Breakthrough,* pp. 136-142.

118. Richard L. Thompson, *Alien Identities* (San Diego, CA: Govardhan Hill Inc., 1993), p. 217.

119. *Ibid.,* pp. 267, 283.

120. *Ibid.,* p. 308.

121. This was communicated to the author in 1986 by a person who had reliably heard it from those Unification Church leaders closely connected to Rev. Sun Myung Moon at that time.

122. Raymond E. Fowler, *The Watchers* (New York: Bantam Books, 1990), p. 119.

123. *Ibid.,* p. 163.

124. Strieber, *Breakthrough,* p. 91.

125. See discussion in Section 8 of this book.

126. Thompson, *Alien Identities,* p. 217.

127. For those who are interested to read further about specific, actual encounters with the UFO-beings referred to here as "hairy dwarfs," see Timothy Good, *Alien Base: The Evidence for Extraterrestrial Colonization of Earth* (New York, NY: Avon Books, 1998), pp. 169-175.

128. Vallee, *Dimensions,* p. 146.

129. Andrews, *Enchantment of the Faerie Realm,* p. 14.

130. Raymond E. Fowler, *The Andreasson Affair* (Englewood Cliffs, New Jersey: Prentice-Hall, 1979), pp. 143-144.

131. Thompson, *Alien Identities,* p. 396.

132. John E. Mack, *Passport to the Cosmos: Human Transformation and Alien Encounters* (New York, NY: Crown Publishers, 1999), pp. 169, 184.

133. *Ibid.,* p. 156.

134. *Ibid.,* pp. 158-160.

135. *Ibid.,* p. 185.

136. *Ibid.,* p. 194.

137. *Ibid.,* p. 155.

138. *Ibid.,* p. 269.

139. Interestingly, Whitley Strieber also comes to this conclusion through his painstaking analysis of the UFO-abduction phenomenon. The following excerpt is from a 1998 letter from Strieber to Michael and Ian Baldwin, and also endnoted in John Mack's book, *Passport to the Cosmos,* p. 290: "I do not differentiate between the physical and spiritual worlds. "The spiri-

tual" is simply a matter of seeing better. But there is no break between the spiritual and the physical. This is why I see the exposure of implants as a spiritual act—the act of a spiritual rebel, really. To me, the placing of an object in the body is the placing of an object in the soul. And so I am deeply concerned with the meaning of these objects, because they must necessarily affect the whole self, from the trembling mortality to the highest serene edge."

140. Gary Kowalski, *The Souls of Animals* (Walpole, New Hampshire: Stillpoint Publishing, 1991), pp. 55-56.
141. *Ibid.,* p. 58.
142. *Ibid.,* p. 67.
143. *Ibid.,* p. 68.
144. *Ibid.,* p. 87.
145. *Ibid.,* pp. 90-91.
146. Francezzo, *A Wanderer in the Spirit Lands,* p. 97.
147. Jan Price, *The Other Side of Death* (New York: Faucett Columbine, 1996), p. 39.
148. George Anderson and Andrew Barone, *Lessons from the Light,* p. 305.
149. Emanuel Swedenborg, *Soul-Body Interaction* 15, in George F. Dole, ed. and trans., *Emanuel Swedenborg: The Universal Human and Soul-Body Interaction* (in The Classics of Western Spirituality series) (New York: Paulist Press, 1984), pp. 247-248.
150. Moon, *Master Speaks* (Nos. 3 & 4).
151. Emanuel Swedenborg, *Apocalypse Explained* 1199, quoted in *The Swedenborg Concordance,* ed. and trans. by Rev. J. F. Potts (London: University Printing House, Cambridge, 1976 [1888]), vol. 1, pp. 192-193.
152. *Ibid.,* 1200.

Section 12

1. Sylvia Cranston, ed., *Reincarnation: The Phoenix Fire Mystery* (Pasadena, California: Theosophical University Press, 1994,1997), p. 170.
2. *Ibid.,* p. 220.
3. Paul Edwards, *Reincarnation: A Critical Examination* (Amherst, New York: Prometheus Books, 1996), pp. 12-13.
4. Young Oon Kim, *The Divine Principles* (San Francisco, California: The Holy Spirit Association for the Unification of World Christianity, 1960), pp. 93-94.
5. Steven Rosen, *The Reincarnation Controversy* (California: Torchlight Publishing, Inc., 1997), p. 2.
6. Geoff Viney, *Surviving Death* (New York: St. Martin's Press, 1993), p. 230.
7. Rosen, *The Reincarnation Controversy,* p. 6.
8. Viney, *Surviving Death,* p. 232.
9. *Ibid.,* pp. 240-241.

10   *Ibid.,* p. 245.

11.   *Ibid.,* pp. 284-286.

12.   Peter Washington, *Madame Blavatsky's Baboon* (New York: Schocken Books, 1995), p. 129.

13.   Ian Stevenson, *Twenty Cases Suggestive of Reincarnation* (Charlottesville, Virginia: University Press of Virginia, 1974, 1966), p. x.

14.   Edwards, *Reincarnation: A Critical Examination,* p. 261.

15.   *Ibid.,* pp. 248-249.

16.   Mark Woodhouse, *Paradigm Wars: Worldviews for a New Age* (Berkeley, California: Frog, Ltd., 1996), p. 146.

17.   Morey Bernstein, *The Search for Bridey Murphy* (Pocketbook paperback reprint, 1978), p. 259.

18.   Woodhouse, *Paradigm Wars,* pp. 139-140.

19.   Edwards, *Reincarnation: A Critical Examination,* p. 229.

20.   Viney, *Surviving Death,* p. 266.

21.   Hans Küng, together with Josef van Ess, Heinrich von Stietencron, and Heinz Bechert, *Christianity and the World Religions: Paths of Dialogue with Islam, Hinduism, and Buddhism* (Garden City, New York: Doubleday & Co., 1986), p. 233.

22.   Edwards, *Reincarnation: A Critical Examination,* p. 235.

23.   *Ibid.,* p. 291.

24.   *Ibid.,* p. 287.

25.   Rifat Sonsino and Daniel B. Syme, *What Happens After I Die? —Jewish Views of Life After Death* (New York, New York: UAHC Press, 1990), p. 51.

26.   Küng, *Christianity and the World Religions,* pp. 235-236.

27.   *Ibid.,* p. 232.

28.   *Ibid.,* p. 233.

29.   *Ibid.,* p. 234.

30.   *Ibid.,* pp. 234-235.

31.   Stevenson, *Twenty Cases Suggestive of Reincarnation,* p. 333.

32.   Geoff Viney also notes, however, that while this scheme explains the aspect of how such memories may enter the mind, it does not have the power to account for carry-over birthmarks often discernible in Stevenson's cases. It seems worth suggesting here that these birthmarks, which Stevenson claims are not adequately explained by any other hypothesis than reincarnation, might, in fact, be accounted for along the lines of the appearance of the "stigmata" in numerous Christian saints. The stigmata, so it seems, appear as a consequence of a saint's extreme identification with the person of the crucified Jesus. This identificatory unification with the deceased Jesus is sufficiently potent to yield an actual conformation of the flesh of the saint with what was the originally crucified flesh of Jesus, i.e., to yield the psychic appropriation of the stigmata. Thus, why might it not be possible for a strong psychic connection between a deceased person (in the spirit-world) and a baby in the womb,

or an infant on earth, to result in some kind of correlative birthmark? This explanation does not at all seem far-fetched once we recognize the profound connection between mind and body.

33. Woodhouse, *Paradigm Wars,* p. 151.

34. Stevenson, *Twenty Cases Suggestive of Reincarnation,* p. 339.

35. Nicholas P. Spanos, Evelyn Menary, Natalie J. Gabora, Susan C. Dubreuil and Bridget Dewhirst, "Secondary Identity Enactments During Hypnotic Past-Life Regression: A Sociocognitive Perspective," *Journal of Personality and Social Psychology,* 1991, Vol. 61, No. 2, pp. 308-20, in Arvin Gibson, *Journeys Beyond Life* (Bountiful, Utah: Horizon Publishers & Distributors, Inc., 1994), p. 240.

36. Betty Eadie, *Embraced by the Light* (California: Gold Leaf Press, 1992), p. 93.

37. Stevenson, *Twenty Cases Suggestive of Reincarnation,* p. 343.

38. *Ibid.*

39. Rupert Sheldrake, *The Presence of the Past: Morphic Resonance and the Habits of Nature* (New York, New York: Vintage Books, 1989), p. xviii.

40. *Ibid.,* p. 221.

41. *Ibid.*

42. Edwards, *Reincarnation: A Critical Examination,* p. 262.

43. Stevenson, *Twenty Cases Suggestive of Reincarnation,* pp. 376-377.

44. *Ibid.,* pp. 382-383.

45. Carl A. Wickland, M.D., *Thirty Years Among the Dead* (National Psychological Institute, 1924), p. 333.

46. *Ibid.,* pp. 352-353.

47. Emanuel Swedenborg, *Heaven and Hell,* trans. by George F. Dole (New York: Swedenborg Foundation, Inc., 1979), 256.

48. Wickland, *Thirty Years Among the Dead,* p. 346.

49. Sonsino and Syme, *What Happens After I Die?,* p. 49.

50. *Ibid.,* p. 53.

51. Young Oon Kim, *World Religions: Living Religions of the Middle East* (New York, New York: Golden Gate Publishing Co., 1976), pp. 44-45.

52. Kim, *The Divine Principles,* p. 92.

53. Sun Myung Moon, "Individual Course of Life," speech given 1/20/80, p. 10.

54. Viney, *Surviving Death,* pp. 290-291.

55. Sun Myung Moon, *Exposition of the Divine Principle* (New York, New York: Holy Spirit Association for the Unification of World Christianity, 1996), pp. 133-151.

56. Revised Standard Version, *Harper Study Bible* (Grand Rapids, Michigan: Zondervan Bible Publishers, 1976).

57. *Ibid.*

58. Moon, *Exposition of the Divine Principle,* pp. 175-223.

59. Sun Myung Moon, *Earthly Life and Spirit World II* (printed by Family

Federation for World Peace and Unification International, in Canada, 1998), pp. 177-178.

60. Mary T. Browne, *Life After Death* (New York: Ballantine Books, 1994), p. 103.

61. Sun Myung Moon, *Master Speaks* (Nos. 3 & 4, 1965).

Section 13

1. Carl Wickland, M.D., *Thirty Years Among the Dead* (National Psychological Institute, 1924), p. 132.

2. Angie Fenimore, *Beyond the Darkness* (New York: Bantam Books, 1995), p. 124.

3. Bruce M. Metzger and Michael D. Coogan, eds., *The Oxford Companion to the Bible* (New York: Oxford University Press, 1993), p. 161. However, in fairness, it should be noted that the theologians of ancient Israel generally believed that God alone had the authority to terminate life.

4. See the Centers for Disease Control (CDC) website, under "suicide" (*http://www.cdc.gov/ncipc/factsheets/suifacts.htm*), for these statistics and many others regarding suicide in the United States.

5. Betty Eadie, *Embraced by the Light* (California: Gold Leaf Press, 1992), p. 70.

6. James Van Praagh, *Talking to Heaven* (New York: Dutton, 1997), p. 111.

7. *Ibid.,* p. 103.

8. George Ritchie, *Return from Tomorrow* (Grand Rapids, Michigan: Fleming H. Revell, 1978), pp. 58-59.

9. Joel Martin and Patricia Romanowski, *Our Children Forever: George Anderson's Messages from Children on the Other Side* (New York: Berkley Books, 1994), p. 224.

10. Sun Myung Moon, *Leaders' Address (5/1/65)* (New York: The Holy Spirit Association for the Unification of World Christianity, 1980), p. 305.

11. Arvin Gibson, *Journeys Beyond Life* (Bountiful, Utah: Horizon Publishers, 1994), p. 82.

12. Van Praagh, *Talking to Heaven,* p. 100.

13. Wickland,*Thirty Years Among the Dead,* p. 134.

14. Francezzo (transcribed by A. Farnese), *A Wanderer in the Spirit Lands* (West Grove, PA: AIM Publishing Company, 1993), p. 184.

15. Joel Martin and Patricia Romanowski, *We Don't Die: George Anderson's Conversations with the Other Side* (New York: Berkley Books, 1988), p. 242.

16. Mary T. Browne, *Life After Death* (New York: Ballantine Books, 1990), p. 112.

17. Martin and Romanowski, *We Don't Die: George Anderson's Conversations with the Other Side,* p. 242.

18. Melvin Morse, M.D., *Closer to the Light* (New York: Ballantine Books, 1990), p. 185-86.
19. Browne, *Life After Death,* p. 128.
20. *Ibid.,* p. 116.
21. Pierre Jovanovic, *An Inquiry into the Existence of Guardian Angels* (New York: M. Evans and Company, Inc., 1995), p. 94.

Section 14

1. See Plutarch's *Moralia.*
2. Emanuel Swedenborg, *The Universal Human,* 5715, in George F. Dole, ed. and trans., *Emanuel Swedenborg: The Universal Human and Soul-Body Interaction* (in The Classics of Western Spirituality series) (New York: Paulist Press, 1984), pp. 216-217.
3. George Ritchie, *My Life After Dying* (Norfolk, Virginia: Hampton Roads, 1991), p. 23.
4. Edith Fiore, Ph.D., *The Unquiet Dead: A Psychologist Treats Spirit Possession* (New York: Ballantine Books, 1988), pp. 3-4.
5. *Ibid.,* p. 154.
6. James Van Praagh, *Reaching to Heaven* (New York, New York: Dutton, 1999), p. 44.
7. George Ritchie, *Return from Tomorrow* (Grand Rapids, Michigan: Fleming H. Revell, 1978), p. 61.
8. Emanuel Swedenborg, *Heaven and Hell,* trans. by George F. Dole (New York: Swedenborg Foundation, Inc., 1979), 427.
9. Carl Wickland, M.D., *Thirty Years Among the Dead* (National Psychological Institute, 1924), p. 219.
10. Fiore, *The Unquiet Dead,* p. 29.
11. Wickland, *Thirty Years Among the Dead,* p. 291.
12. Fiore, *The Unquiet Dead,* p. 112.
13. See, e.g., Francezzo (transcribed by A. Farnese), *A Wanderer in the Spirit Lands* (West Grove, Pennsylvania: AIM Publishing Company, 1993), p. 52.
14. Fiore, *The Unquiet Dead,* p. 32.
15. Ritchie, *Return from Tomorrow,* pp. 60-61.
16. *Ibid.,* pp. 56-57.
17. Fiore, *The Unquiet Dead,* p. 42.
18. Wickland, *Thirty Years Among the Dead,* p. 110.
19. *Ibid.,* p. 116.
20. It is important here to point out that most evil spirit-persons, after death, will become consigned to the lowest levels of Hell in the spirit-world where, to a great extent, they have no power to influence people on earth. However, under certain conditions, some evil spirit-persons will become trapped in the earth sphere as

earthbound spirits, who then may aggressively try to possess earth-persons.

21. Wickland, *Thirty Years Among the Dead,* p. 275.
22. *Ibid.,* p. 333.
23. Sylvia Browne and Antoinette May, *Adventures of a Psychic* (Carlsbad, California: Hay House, Inc., 1998), pp. 144-145.
24. In fact, one of the earthbound spirits interviewed by Wickland offered the description of the earth sphere as "the worst ward in an insane asylum" (*Thirty Years Among the Dead,* p. 55).
25. *Ibid.,* pp. 60, 227.
26. *Ibid.,* pp. 79, 108, 277.
27. *Ibid.,* p. 101.
28. Robert H. Coddington, *Earthbound: Conversations with Ghosts* (New York, New York: Kensington Books, 1997), p. 78.
29. Wickland, *Thirty Years Among the Dead,* p. 68.
30. Coddington, *Earthbound: Conversations with Ghosts,* pp. 16-17.
31. See Section 13 in this book addressing the spiritual consequences of committing suicide.
32. Hans Holzer, *Ghosts* (New York: Black Dog & Leventhal Publishers, Inc.,1997), p. 631.
33. *Ibid.*
34. Hans Holzer, *Psychic: True Paranormal Experiences* (New York: SMITH-MARK Publishers, 1999), p. 208.
35. Wickland, *Thirty Years Among the Dead,* pp. 90-91.
36. This certainly seems plausible enough given, for instance, the Unificationist understanding that the spirit-self develops via the give and take of elements with the physical self and, in particular, grows brighter and more well-defined as it receives positive vitality elements through one's physical body. See Section 1 for a fuller description of this process.
37. Fiore, *The Unquiet Dead,* p. 109.
38. *Ibid.,* p. 110.
39. Wickland, *Thirty Years Among the Dead,* p. 356.
40. *Ibid.,* p. 223.
41. Holzer, *Psychic,* pp. 203-204.
42. Fiore, *The Unquiet Dead,* pp. 11-12.
43. *Ibid.,* pp. 110-112.
44. Wickland, *Thirty Years Among the Dead,* p. 132; Fiore, *The Unquiet Dead,* p. 39.
45. Francezzo (transcribed by A. Farnese), *A Wanderer in the Spirit Lands* (West Grove, Pennsylvania: AIM Publishing Company, 1993), p. 52.
46. Fiore, *The Unquiet Dead,* p. 36.
47. *Ibid.,* p. 43.
48. Wickland, *Thirty Years Among the Dead,* pp. 176-184.
49. Arthur Guirdham, *The Psychic Dimensions of Mental Health*

(Wellingborough: Thurstone Press, 1982), in Fiore, *The Unquiet Dead*, p. 171.

50. M. Scott Peck, M.D., *People of the Lie: The Hope for Healing Human Evil* (New York: Simon and Schuster, 1983), pp. 182-211.

51. A. K. Tebecis, *Mahikari, Thank God for the Answers at Last* (Tokyo: L. H. Yoko Shuppan, 1982) in Fiore, *The Unquiet Dead*, p. 173.

52. Wickland, *Thirty Years Among the Dead*, p. 187.

53. *Ibid.*, pp. 188-193.

54. Fiore, *The Unquiet Dead*, pp. 36-37.

55. Mark 9:14-29, *Revised Standard Version*.

56. Wilson Van Dusen, *The Presence of Other Worlds: The Psychological/Spiritual Findings of Emanuel Swedenborg* (West Chester, Pennsylvania: Chrysalis Books, 1974), p. 132.

57. Swedenborg, *The Universal Human* 5715, in George F. Dole, ed. and trans., *Emanuel Swedenborg: The Universal Human and Soul-Body Interaction.*

58. Swedenborg, *ibid.*, 5714.

59. *Ibid.*, 5713.

60. *Ibid.*, 5717.

61. *Ibid.*, 5712.

62. *Ibid.*, 5726.

63. Sun Myung Moon, *Master Speaks, 3 & 4*, 1965 (transcribed notes, 1965).

64. Jorg H.'s written testimony (January 7, 1997) of his experience of attending the 40-day workshop (8/1/96 - 9/9/96) at Chung Pyung Lake in Korea, pp. 8, 10.

65. *Ibid.*, p. 11.

66. Sun Myung Moon, *Exposition of the Divine Principle* (New York: The Holy Spirit Association for the Unification of World Christianity, 1996), pp. 47-48.

67. Exodus 34:6-7 (*Revised Standard Version*): The Lord passed before him, and proclaimed, "The Lord, the Lord, a God merciful and gracious, slow to anger, and abounding in steadfast love and faithfulness, keeping steadfast love for thousands, forgiving iniquity and transgression and sin, but who will by no means clear the guilty, visiting the iniquity of the fathers upon the children and the children's children, to the third and fourth generations."

68. Jorg H.'s testimony, p. 2.

69. Excerpt from transcripted testimony of Linda F., given in 5/99 interview with the author.

70. The New King James Version also includes mention of "fasting," in Mark 9:29: "So He said to them, "This kind can come out by nothing but prayer and fasting,"

71. Wickland, *Thirty Years Among the Dead*, p. 102.

72. *Ibid.*, pp. 358-359.

73. Fiore, *The Unquiet Dead*, pp. 126-130.

74. Van Praagh, *Reaching to Heaven*, p. 155.

75. Fiore, *The Unquiet Dead*, p. 155.

APPENDIX A

Transcript of Linda F. Testimony (5/99)

Linda: Shall I start from the beginning? It's important because of the problems, the physical problems. The reason I want to tell the physical problems is because, when I had the spiritual experiences with spirits that had been possessing me my whole life—had been with me—those physical problems disappeared; which is why it's important that I tell about the physical problems.

So, as I was saying—I never had my period, I couldn't get pregnant—the doctors said there was no physical reason for that; they insisted that it was all in my head—my spine is curved; at one time, the top of my neck was shaped like an "L" stuck out and it impaired everything. I couldn't hold my head upright. When I was very, very young there was a very strange accident when I was shot in the eye with an arrow, a toy arrow, and I was blinded in my right eye. Many physical things happened to me.

Two years ago, I was 40 years old and my health was so bad that I felt like I was going to die. I don't say that lightly—I mean, I literally felt like I was being killed. I felt like I had no energy; every part of my body hurt, especially my back, my lower back and it was a *time thing*; most of the day I would be pretty OK and then early evening, late evening, I couldn't even walk. Just to get up to go get a drink of water was excruciating. I couldn't straighten my body up. So, I felt, because I'm a spiritual person, that there was something inside of me trying to kill me and it was scaring me very badly. And my husband, who is not a spiritual [spiritually-open] person at all, agreed to send me to Chung Pyung Lake [spiritual retreat] for spiritual healing. So, even though it cost a lot of money, and even though my husband doesn't believe in such things, because he was so afraid for what he saw happening to me, he willingly sent me there.

And, upon arriving at Chung Pyung Lake, I immediately felt a difference in the spirit-world, in the land which is Chung Pyung, as opposed to everywhere else I had ever been. And what struck me right away was how much more my pain increased when I got there—so much so that, as anyone knows who has been to Chung Pyung Lake—you sit on the floor for long periods of time, clapping and singing songs, and trying to relieve yourself of spiritual entities who are bothering you. So, that being said, I want to get to the point in my life that—since I was a young child, I've always felt this *closeness* with Black people. I was raised in an orphanage and it was a predominantly white orphanage; it was an all-white orphanage. And I remember the day that a young Black girl came to our orphanage. She was the only Black person I had ever seen up until that time. But I remember liking her right away and we paired off and became friends, and were (then) ostracized by all the other white children in the orphanage.

Even when I left the orphanage, I never had anything to do with Black people again. This was something I thought about, dreamed about—this problem between the Whites and the Blacks. And when I was old enough to try to *make* friends, Black friends, I realized it was not an easy thing to do; there were a lot of problems. And also when I joined the Unification Church, I had many problems with Blacks, even though I felt in my heart I liked them. Whenever they would meet me, they would instantly take a dislike to me—a serious, sever dislike to me, which I could never understand because I had never done anything *to them.*

So, when I went to Chung Pyung Lake, my first experience during the *an-sou,* which is the ceremony done to get rid of spirits, my first experience was that I closed my eyes and I could see a sea of Black people that had been slaves while they were [living] on the earth. And, not all of them, but many of them, especially the ones in front of this sea of people, knew me *intimately.* They *knew* me and I *knew* them, although I had never seen them before in my life. And it occurred to me that they had been *with* me for most of my life, if not all of my life. Because my whole life, I had thought about issues between Blacks and Whites—I had read a lot about slavery and stuff like that—I began this conversation between myself and the black slaves that I could see in front of me. And it was as if I could read their minds, and they could read my mind, and I was saying to them that I didn't want them to feel any more pain—that they had suffered, that their whole lives they had suffered. And in my mind, I went through a check-list of the different kinds of pains that I experienced in my life, and I *realized* as I went through this check-list that these physical problems I had in my lifetime corresponded to assaults that had taken place against their bodies when they were on earth. Like—the fact that my back felt like it was being split across the mid-section—I have no [medically discernible] problem with my back, nothing wrong with my spine, but always in the middle of my back it felt like it was being broken; and that I realized when those slaves were bending over in the fields how their backs felt—and how when I, like I said in the beginning, when I couldn't even rise out of a chair, that my legs would ache and I couldn't even straighten out my feet and I couldn't make my body straighten up even to walk. And I *realized* that this is how their bodies would become after years and years of being stooped over in the fields, working the fields. And I realized my body was experiencing what their bodies had experienced through slavery.

And then—that was the first day—I remember during the *an-sou,* it was so excruciatingly painful to sit on the floor that I wanted to scream and run away—to escape my own body because it hurt so much, my whole body hurt. So, I sat in front of a very large brother and asked him to hit me very hard during the *an-sou*. And I could *see*—in my mind's eye—I could *see* these slaves being liberated. And the whole time, I was thinking to myself and saying to these slaves, in prayer, these slaves that I could see: "Please leave my body." Because of the resentment that they incurred through what happened to them, they were trying to hurt me. They had resentment because of what happened to them, and somehow it was connected to my lineage. And they were trying to hurt *me* because of what was done to *them*. So, I was trying to reason with them, "If you could forgive me, you would be free. You know, hurting me is not going to take your pain away, it isn't." And then I tried to explain: "Your resentment is making you more of a slave *now* than you ever were on earth—because you're enslaving yourself. You could be free, *like that* [snaps fingers], if you forgive and just let it go and *leave* me, and go to a better place where you can be taken care of and where your pains can be healed." And then, many, many of these spirits I could begin to see were coming out of me—slave spirits. And the next day, when I walked up the hill [mountain path] to the Holy Trees to pray, at several of the trees I could see these slave spirits, men and women crying and crying and crying. And I was crying, I was sobbing hysterically because there was something between *my* heart and *their* hearts that was resonating the same and it was about forgiveness—that they were grateful to me for [spiritually] liberating them and I was grateful that they could be liberated; they knew that I was genuinely happy for them to be resurrected. And there was some good rapport there. So, that was the first day.

The second day, the same thing happened—my body started hurting again and I started thinking about my infertility and that made me think about how slaves were treated and the fact that they would be matched up with certain types of Black men to produce a certain type of slave children and that that child would be taken at birth and sold. And then I asked a question: "Is that why I can't have children? Am I being punished, because of what happened to you?" And there was just this icy cold feeling through me when I asked that question. So, then, I started to pray about all the different types of ills that were done to slaves. Another thing was: I had this incredible *thirst*, such that I would drink water all day, all night, and I would have to go to the bathroom 4, 5, 6 times every night because I had this incredible thirst. So, when I was at the Chung Pyung workshop, I thought about that. Yeah, I thought, the slaves must have been very thirsty in the field and couldn't have so much as a cup of water without permission. So, their thirst must have been raging at times. And when they died, the resentment that they had, resentment even over a cup of water. . . . And so,

I really repented; I went to the Holy Rock and I took a very large (2-liter) bottle of water and I prayed to the slaves who had suffered from thirst and were even denied so much as a cup of water; and I drank that water, the Holy water, and I said [to them]: "I want each of you to partake of this water, so you can be liberated from your resentment and never feel thirst again." And since that time, I no longer drink water excessively like I used to. It's like something changed in my body, that I no longer needed to drink all the time; even my husband commented when I came back, that I was not going to the bathroom every 5 minutes, because I no longer had this *obsession* to drink tons of water.

Then, on the third day, I woke up on the third morning and I couldn't see, I couldn't see anything. And I went to the *an-sou*, and while doing the *an-sou*, I heard a Black woman, and she was screaming at *me*, at *me personally*. She was saying, she said, "My beloved!" — I didn't know *at first* if she meant her *husband* or her *son*—but she was saying that the person that she loved, the man, was hung by the neck for looking at a white woman. Then, all of a sudden, I felt this incredible pain where I had the [previously mentioned] crookedness in my neck, and I could feel, could see in my mind's eye, there was a Black man, a spirit-man, who had been hung and he wanted to *kill* me. And he was holding on to my neck, where the crooked part was. So, I asked this brother, doing the *an-sou* on my back, to hit me right here [pointing to the back of her neck] where the lump was. It took all 3 sessions [of *an-sou*], till the end of the day, to get rid of that spirit. And what I realized from that experience was that there were some spirits whose hearts you could easily move, through your repentance, suffering and your love, and they would forgive you and they would leave you. But there were other spirits, whose resentment is so deep and so passionate, that they aren't even satisfied when they kill you. If they wind up killing you, they just go on to your descendants. Because your blood and the blood of your descendants isn't even enough to satisfy the resentment that they have. — So, to get rid of this spirit that was on me was very, very difficult. I'm a very spiritually open person, and I could see the angels pulling, pulling on this Black man who was holding on to my body. Then, I remember that particular *an-sou* because I made this BIG brother sit behind me and he was *an-souing* me *soooooooo* hard, and I was just crying and crying. When it was finally over, and I stood up, it was like I had a new body. I had no pain in my back; I had no pain in my neck; I had no pain in my legs. I thought then that this would last one day, or 2 days, or 3 days, but those pains have *never* come back, and to this day, I don't have the lump in my back. But, the most incredible part was I had been there for 40 days. And they do special healing ceremonies for infertile women. I went to that ceremony and, while I was having the *an-sou* done to me, I had a spiritual experience. I saw these women whose children had been taken from them. And you know how Black women's hair is like a corkscrew? It was tied around my reproductive organs, these Black women's hair, cutting off any life to them. And, during the *an-sou*, I could see them [these hairs] being pulled off, one by one by one. — The very next day, I got my period, and I got my period every month after that. And then, one year to the day after that experience, I got pregnant.

So, I know that these experiences are real, because there is a physical manifestation before, then there's the spiritual liberation, and then there's the physical manifestation of having been liberated from these things [physical problems] that were tormenting me. Also, when I went back home to my husband, he was in awe—he's not a spiritual [spiritually open] person at all, and it's very difficult to convince him that you're having a spiritual experience. But he could see that there was an absolute difference, not only physically, but *emotionally*. —Spirits also can affect your emotions—because if I was happy, I would be extremely *high* happy, and if I was sad, I would be extremely low. But, if I became *angry*, it was almost like *murderous* anger, like a murderous rage. Because I often would get angry, then I was obsessed with this murderous rage, to the point where I was alienated from the people who loved me, like my husband. Like, you know it's something coming *over* you; when I say the words "coming over me," I literally mean spirits come to you, possess you, and magnify your feeling of rage. And when I got liberated finally from it, the slave rage, the rage that those slaves felt—then, when I became angry after that, it was a very normal anger and I began to heal the relationship with my husband, because I no longer became bloodthirsty in rage, or murderous. And so, that's another way I feel that spirits can influence you—by what you think and by what you feel and even in your physical body.

Kerry: I was going to ask you, Linda, about this whole phenomenon, because when I was there, Daemo Nim explained something about how, I guess, a number of Americans were being attacked, or possessed in some way, by Black people [spirits]. And I was wondering if she explained that any further, why that would be the case.

Linda: Well, when a person, I believe, as I understand it, when a person dies with resentment, you're not free to travel in the spirit-world, but you become *earthbound* by resentment. And so, in order to extract revenge, for how they feel they were abused, then they *hound* the person and even the descendants of the person who abused them.

So, I knew for many years, that I had this problem in my lineage with Black people. I remember three times I was beaten up in the Unification Church, by Black sisters, who would get possessed for seemingly no reason and totally unprovoked by me, and would beat me up. And, the first one was an experience where, one night, all of the sisters were asleep and every one of us that same night dreamt about me. I had a dream that Black people were attacking me and trying to kill me. The sisters next to me had dreams that a Black person had attacked me and I was laying in my bed bloody. The sister who did the actual attacking had a dream she tried to kill me. The very next day, without any of us telling each other our dreams—because it was early morning—I walked into the kitchen; I saw that sister who actually did hit me, who later hit me, and there was something horrible about her face. She looked like she was in a murderous rage and she wanted to attack me. I took one look at her face, and I turned around and I walked out. That's *all* I did. She followed me into the living room and just started beating me. And I didn't hit her back—for 2 reasons: 1) Because she *was* Black, and 2) she had just had an operation on her face and I didn't want to hurt her. I just stood there dumbfounded that she was beating me. But after that happened—the brothers pulled her off me—we all started talking and then all the dreams came out; all the sisters started saying, "Oh my God, I can't believe this happened because I had a dream." And when we then told each other our dreams, it was foreshadowed that that would happen.

Another time, with another Black sister, a very similar thing. From the moment I met her, she just hated me—and I could feel this hatred. And, what makes it more painful is the fact that I want to love them [Black people]. Do you know what I mean? If I didn't care, or I hated them, or had resentment, it wouldn't be so bad because I could just say, "Well, screw you!" and I could just ignore them. But I actually wanted to be their friends; I wanted to like and *love* them. And so it hurt even more that they were rejecting me and hating me for no apparent reason. The 3 times that this happened, it was totally unprovoked as it was in the first, and they beat me up.

Have you read the book, *The Unquiet Dead*? You should definitely read it. It's incredible. Actually, I read that book before I went to Chung Pyung Lake, and it really helped me because it talked about spiritual possession. It talked about how spirits affect your life, and how, once they leave—you can entice them to leave—your life changes.

[Kerry makes assorted comments on spiritualist investigator, Carl Wickland, M.D., and his wife, Anna (psychic medium), addressing earthbound spirits in 1920; Wickland's transcript of the earthbound spirit of Madame Blavatsky denying reincarnation; and Wickland's explanation of how spirits who believed in reincarnation during their earthly lives, after death fulfill their expectation to return via illegitimately insinuating themselves into earthly children's auras, creating deep spiritual problems for both themselves as well as for the children they are possessing.]

Even I can tell you that I had experiences walking down the street and I would think to myself: "I wonder what it would be like to be a Black woman instead of a White woman?" And, all of a sudden, I could feel this—it was almost as if I could look down and see that my skin was Black. And I felt like I was a *Black* woman. And that, somehow, everyone was looking at me differently; I know they weren't but I could feel it. You know what I am saying? I had the experience that I was actually a Black woman. If I believed in reincarnation, then I would have believed that I had been a Black woman or a Black slave before I was myself. But because I know about "returning resurrection," I know it's just another spirit that's come to me with her situation, her problems.

Kerry: That book, *The Unquiet Dead*—isn't the author Edith Fiore?

Linda: I don't know. I don't remember . . . but the book's fascinating.

Kerry: This is the fascinating thing to me—that there are these incredible dynamics, dynamics of relationship, that go on between people on earth and people in the spiritual world—the lower spiritual world, the higher spiritual world—but, up until now, it's been so indiscernible, so unknowable.

Linda: Because we don't know of the existence of the spirit-world, or believe in it because we're too modern, then they [spirits] actually have a lot more power and authority over what we think and feel, and over what we do, what happens to us, than they do once we know the situation and can deal with it. I didn't actually know, for instance, that I had Black slaves attached to me who were actually trying to hurt me and even kill me. I didn't know that *truly* until I went to Chung Pyung Lake and I could literally see them and I could hear them, just like I can see and hear you. They were as real as you are.

Kerry: Well, I've never really had experiences with spirits in that way, you know. But I've had a lot of other, different kinds of spiritual experiences. I've met spiritual guides in dreams and things like that. But I'm not really clairvoyant or clairaudient, as far as I know.

Linda: Well, it's not a picnic—especially if you're ignorant, and I'm pretty ignorant most of the time.

Kerry: Emanuel Swedenborg, for instance, was a scientist up to 53 years old. He was a hard-core scientist, analytic thinker and everything, the whole nine yards. Then, he wanted to really plumb the secrets of the universe and the nature of the mind, and the more he did, the more he realized that human beings were essentially spiritual beings. So, then, he had to go through a whole transfiguration of his psyche. Over a period of time, the spirit-world led him, the angels—and then he finally had a certain breakthrough where he could remain constantly in touch with the world of the spirits. And he traveled freely into all the different parts of the spirit-world and wrote it all down. But, the thing is, there was this one incident in Swedenborg's life: Swedenborg had a certain reputation, in his later years, for being a psychic in Europe. People would come to him for various sorts of reading, you know. — I mean, this guy spanned the entire spectrum of human consciousness, from hard-core scientist to absolute psychic. He was this incredible character. . . .

Linda: I tried to read some of his stuff, but he's so intellectual that he's hard for me to follow sometimes.

Kerry: Yeah, a lot of people experience that about his writing. But the thing is, there was this one incident in his life where this guy came to him. He greatly admired Swedenborg and had read a lot about him and his writings. And he asked Swedenborg if he might be able to develop the same kind of spiritual openness as Swedenborg himself had. And Swedenborg said to him: "No, you don't want to do that. This is the road to madness." And, in this way, Swedenborg really discouraged the person. But Swedenborg says directly that, if it were not for being protected by angels, he would be ceaselessly spiritually attacked by the lower spiritual world.

REFERENCES AND SUGGESTED READING

Anderson, George and Barone, Andrew. *Lessons from the Light: Extraordinary Messages of Comfort and Hope from the Other Side.* New York: Berkley Books, 2000.

Andrews, Ted. *Enchantment of the Faerie Realm: Communicate with Nature Spirits and Elementals.* St. Paul, Minnesota: Llewellyn Publications, 1993.

_____. *How to Meet & Work with Spirit Guides.* St. Paul, MN: Llewellyn Publications, 1993.

_____. *How to See & Read the Aura.* St. Paul, MN: Llewellyn Publications, 1993.

Berman, Phillip L. *The Journey Home.* New York: Pocket Books (Simon and Schuster), 1996.

Bogg, John S. *Glossary of Terms and Phrases Used by Swedenborg.* Bryn Athyn, PA: The Swedenborg Association, 1994 (1915).

Borgia, Anthony. *Life in the World Unseen.* London: Psychic Press, 1984 (1954).

_____. *More About Life in the World Unseen.* London: Psychic Press, 1984 (1956).

_____. *Here and Hereafter.* Utah: M.A.P., 1995.

Brinkley, Dannion. *Saved by the Light.* New York: Villard Books, 1994.

_____. *At Peace in the Light.* New York, HarperCollinsPublishers, 1995.

Browne, Mary T. *Life After Death.* New York: Ballantine Books, 1994.

Browne, Sylvia. *God, Creation and Tools for Life.* Carlsbad, CA: Hay House, Inc., 2000.

_____. and May, Antoinette. *Adventures of a Psychic.* Carlsbad, CA: Hay House, 1998.

Bruyere, Rosalyn L. *Wheels of Light.* New York: Simon & Schuster, 1994 (1989).

Bunson, Matthew. *Angels A to Z: A Who's Who of the Heavenly Host.* New York, NY: Three Rivers Press, 1996.

Burnham, Sophy. *A Book of Angels.* New York, NY: Ballantine Books, 1995 (1990).

Cannon, Dolores. *Between Death and Life: Conversations with a Spirit.* Huntsville, AR: Ozark Mountain Publishers, 1995 (1993).

Charlesworth, J.H. *The Old Testament Pseudepigrapha.* New York, NY: Doubleday, 1983.

Coddington, Robert H. *Earthbound: Conversations with Ghosts.* New York: Kensington Publishing Corp., 1997.

Cranston, Sylvia. *Reincarnation: The Phoenix Fire Mystery — An East-West dialogue on death and rebirth from the worlds of religion, science, psychology, philosophy, art and literature.* Pasadena, CA: Theosophical University Press, 1994 (1977).

Daugherty, James. *William Blake.* New York, NY: The Viking Press, 1960.

Davidson, Gustav. *A Dictionary of Angels—including the fallen angels.* New York: The Free Press, 1971 (1967).

Dole, George F., ed. and trans. Emanuel Swedenborg: *The Universal Human and*

Soul-Body Interaction. (The Classics of Western Spirituality series) New York, NY: Paulist Press, 1984.

Doore, Gary. *What Survives? Contemporary Explorations of Life After Death.* Los Angeles, CA: Jeremy P. Tarcher, 1990.

Eadie, Betty J. *Embraced By The Light.* Placerville, CA: Gold Leaf Press, 1992.

_____. *The Awakening Heart: My continuing journey to love.* New York: Pocket Books, 1996.

Easton, Stewart C. *Man and World in the Light of Anthroposophy.* Spring Valley, NY: The Anthroposophic Press, 1982 (1975).

Edward, John. *One Last Time: A Medium Speaks to Those We Have Loved and Lost.* New York: Berkley Books, 1998.

Edwards, Paul. *Reincarnation: A Critical Examination.* Amherst, NY: Prometheus Books, 1996.

Evans-Wentz, W.Y. *The Fairy-Faith in Celtic Countries.* Buckinghamshire, Great Britain: Colin Smythe Limited, 1977.

Fenimore, Angie. *Beyond the Darkness: My Near-Death Journey to the Edge of Hell and Back.* New York: Bantam, 1996.

Fiore, Edith. *The Unquiet Dead: A Psychologist Treats Spirit Possession.* New York: Ballantine Books, 1987.

Fowler, Raymond E. *The Andreasson Affair.* Englewood Cliffs, NJ: Prentice Hall, 1979.

_____. *The Watchers: The Secret Design Behind UFO Abduction.* New York: Bantam Books, 1990.

Fox, Matthew and Sheldrake, Rupert. *The Physics of Angels: Exploring the Realm Where Science and Spirit Meet.* New York: HarperCollinsPublishers, 1996.

Francezzo. (transcribed by A. Farnese) *A Wanderer in the Spirit Lands.* West Grove, PA: AIM Publishing Co., 1993.

Gibson, Arvin S. *Journeys Beyond Life: True Accounts of Next-World Experiences.* Bountiful, Utah: Horizon Publishers, 1994.

Good, Timothy. *Alien Base: The Evidence for Extraterrestrial Colonization of Earth.* New York, NY: Avon Books, 1998.

Kowalski, Gary. *The Souls of Animals.* Walpole, New Hampshire: Stillpoint Publishing, 1991.

Luibheid, Colm, trans. *Pseudo-Dionysius: The Complete Works.* (The Classics of Western Spirituality series) New York, NY: Paulist Press, 1987.

Harner, Michael. *The Way of the Shaman.* New York: HarperSanFrancisco, 1990 (1980).

Heinerman, Joseph. *Guardian Angels.* Salt Lake City, Utah: Joseph Lyon and Associates, 1985.

Holzer, Hans. *Ghosts: True Encounters With the World Beyond.* New York: Black Dog & Leventhal Publishers, 1997.

_____. *Psychic: true paranormal experiences.* New York: SMITHMARK Publishers, 1999.

Jovanovich, Pierre. *An Inquiry into the Existence of Guardian Angels.* New York: M. Evans and Company, 1995.

Kim, Young Oon. *The Divine Principles.* San Francisco, CA: The Holy Spirit

Association for the Unification of World Christianity, 1963 (1960).

_____. *Unification Theology*. New York, NY: The Holy Spirit Association for the Unification of World Christianity,1980.

_____. *Unification Theology and Christian Thought*. New York, NY: Golden Gate Publishing Co., 1976 (1975).

_____. *World Religions* (vol. 1 of 3). New York, NY: Golden Gate Publishing Co., 1976.

Kübler-Ross, Elisabeth. *On Death and Dying*. New York: Touchstone, Simon and Schuster, 1997 (1969).

_____. *On Life After Death*. Berkeley, CA: Celestial Arts, 1991.

Küng, Hans. *Eternal Life: Life After Death as a Medical, Philosophical and Theological Problem*. Garden City, NY: Doubleday & Co., 1984.

_____. *Christianity and the World Religions: Paths to Dialogue with Islam, Hinduism and Buddhism*. Garden City, NY: Doubleday & Co., 1986.

Kuthumi and Kul, Djwal. *The Human Aura*. Corwin Spring, MT: Summit University Press, 1996 (1971).

Lee, Sang Hun. *Essentials of Unification Thought*. Japan: Unification Thought Institute, 1992.

_____. *Life in the Spirit World and on Earth*. New York: Family Federation for World Peace and Unification, 1998.

_____. *Unification Thought*. New York, NY: Unification Thought Institute, 1973.

Lindemann, Michael. *UFOs and the Alien Presence: Six Viewpoints*. Santa Barbara, CA: The 2020 Group, 1991.

Lundahl, Craig R. and Widdison, Harold A. *The Eternal Journey: How Near-Death Experiences Illuminate Our Earthly Lives*. New York: Warner Books, 1997.

Mack, John E. *Abduction: Human Encounters with Aliens*. New York, NY: 1995 (1994).

_____. *Passport to the Cosmos: Human Transformation and Alien Encounters*. New York, NY: Crown Publishers, 1999.

Maclean, Dorothy. *To Hear the Angels Sing: An Odyssey of Co-Creation with the Devic Kingdom*. Hudson, NY: Lindisfarne Press, 1990 (1980).

Martin, Joel and Romanowski, Patricia. *We Don't Die: George Anderson's Conversations with the Other Side*. New York: Berkley Books, 1989 (1988).

_____. *Our Children Forever: George Anderson's Messages from Children on the Other Side*. New York: Berkley Books, 1994.

Martin, Malachi. *Hostage to the Devil: The Possession and Exorcism of Five Americans*. New York: HarperSanFrancisco, 1992 (1976).

Maruyama, Magoroh and Harkins, Arthur, eds. *Cultures Beyond the Earth: The Role of Anthropology in Outer Space*. New York, Vintage Books, 1975.

McDermott, Robert A. *The Essential Steiner: Basic Writings of Rudolf Steiner*. San Francisco, CA: Harper and Row, 1984.

Montgomery, Ruth. *Aliens Among Us*. New York, NY: Ballantine Books, 1986.

Moody, Raymond. *Reunions: Visionary Encounters with Departed Loved Ones*. New York: Villard Books, 1993.

Monroe, Robert A. *Journeys Out of the Body*. New York: Bantam Doubleday Dell Publishing, 1971.

_____. *Far Journeys*. New York: Bantam Doubleday Dell Publishing, 1984.

_____. *Ultimate Journey*. New York: Doubleday, 1994.

Moon, Sun Myung. *Earthly Life and Spirit World I*. Washington, D.C.: Family Federation for World Peace and Unification International, 1998.

_____. *Earthly Life and Spirit World II*. Washington, D.C.: Family Federation for World Peace and Unification International, 1998.

_____. *Exposition of the Divine Principle*. New York: The Holy Spirit Association for the Unification of World Christianity, 1996.

_____. *God's Will and the World*. New York: HSA-UWC, 1985.

_____. *The Divine Principle Study Guide*. New York: HSA-UWC, 1973

Morse, Melvin. *Closer to the Light*. New York: Villard Books, 1990.

Myss, Caroline. *Anatomy of the Spirit: The Seven Stages of Power and Healing*. New York: Harmony Books, 1996.

Pak, Joon Hyun and Wilson, Andrew. *True Family Values*. New York: HSA-UWC, 1996.

Peck, Scott. *People of the Lie: The Hope for Healing Human Evil*. New York: Simon and Schuster, 1983.

_____. *In Heaven as on Earth: A Vision of the Afterlife*. New York: Hyperion, 1996.

Potts, John Faulkner—translator, editor and compiler. *The Swedenborg Concordance* (6 vols., covering more than 5000 pages). Great Britain: University Printing House, Cambridge, 1976 (1888).

Price, Jan. *The Other Side of Death*. New York: Faucett Columbine,1996.

Rawlings, Maurice. Beyond Death's Door. New York: Bantam Books, 1979 (1978).

_____. *To Hell and Back*. Nashville, Tennessee: Thomas Nelson Publishers, 1993.

Ritchie, George G. *Return from Tomorrow*. Grand Rapids, MI: Fleming H. Revell, 1995 (1978).

_____. *Ordered to Return: My Life After Dying*. Charlottesville, VA: Hampton Roads Publishing Co., 1998.

Rogo, D. Scott. *Man Does Survive Death*. Secaucus, NJ: The Citadel Press, 1977 (1973).

Rosen, Steven. *The Reincarnation Controversy: Uncovering the Truth in the World Religions*. Badger, CA: Torchlight Publishing, 1997.

Russell, Jeffrey Burton. *A History of Heaven: The Singing Silence*. Princeton, NJ: Princeton University Press, 1997.

Sharp, Kimberly Clark. *After the Light: The Spiritual Path to Purpose*. New York: Avon Books, 1996.

Sheldrake, Rupert. *The Presence of the Past: Morphic Resonance and the Habits of Nature*. New York: Vintage Books, 1989.

Sigstedt, Cyriel Odhner. *The Swedenborg Epic: The Life and Works of Emanuel Swedenborg*. London: The Swedenborg Society, 1981.

Smith, Huston. *Forgotten Truth: The Primordial Tradition*. New York: Harper and Row Publishers, 1976.

Sonsino, Rifat and Syme, Daniel B. *What Happens After I Die? Jewish Views of Life After Death*. New York: UAHC Press, 1990.

Spock, Marjorie. *Fairy Worlds and Workers.* Hudson, NY: Anthroposophic Press, 1980.

St. Clair, Marisa. *Beyond the Light: Files of Near-Death Experiences.* New York: Barnes & Noble Books, 1997.

Steiner, Rudolf. *How to Know Higher Worlds.* Hudson, NY: Anthroposophic Press, 1994 (1909).

_____ . *Life Between Death and Rebirth.* Hudson, NY: Anthroposophic Press, 1968.

_____ . *Spiritual Beings in the Heavenly Bodies and in the Kingdoms of Nature.* Hudson, NY: Anthroposophic Press, 1992 (1912).

_____ . *Life Beyond Death.* London: Rudolf Steiner Press, 1995.

Stevenson, Ian. *Twenty Cases Suggestive of Reincarnation.* Charlottesville, VA: University Press of Virginia, 1995 (1966).

Storm, Howard. *My descent into death and the message of love which brought me back.* Hammersmith, London: Clairview Books, 2000.

Strieber, Whitley. *Communion: A True Story.* New York, NY: Avon Books, 1987.

_____ . *Transformation: The Breakthrough.* New York, NY: Beech Tree Books, 1988.

_____ . *Breakthrough: The Next Step.* New York, NY: HarperCollins Publishers, 1995.

_____ . *The Secret School: Preparation for Contact.* New York, NY: HarperCollins Publishers, 1997.

_____ . *Confirmation: The Hard Evidence of Aliens Among Us.* New York, NY: St. Martin's Press, 1998.

Strieber, Whitley and Ann. *The Communion Letters.* New York, NY: HarperPrism, 1997.

Swami Panchadasi. *The Astral World: Its Scenes, Dwellers and Phenomena.* Chicago: The Book Tree, 2000 (1915).

Swedenborg, Emanuel. *Conjugial Love.* (trans. by A.W. Acton) London: The Swedenborg Society, 1970 (original, 1768).

_____ . *Divine Love and Wisdom.* (trans. by G.F. Dole) West Chester, PA: Swedenborg Foundation, 1994 (original, 1763).

_____ . *Divine Providence.* (trans. by W.F. Wunsch) New York: Swedenborg Foundation, 1986 (original, 1764).

_____ . *Earths In The Universe.* London: The Swedenborg Society, 1970 (first printing, 1860).

_____ . *Heaven and Hell.* (trans. by G.F. Dole) New York: Swedenborg Foundation, 1973 (original, 1758).

_____ . *Journal of Dreams.* (trans. by J.J.G. Wilkinson, Commentary by Wilson Van Dusen) New York: Swedenborg Foundation, 1986 (first printing, 1859).

_____ . *The Spiritual Diary* (vol. I). (trans. by A.W. Acton) Great Britain: Cambridge University Press, 1977 (original 1745).

_____ . *The Spiritual Diary* (vol. III). (trans. by G. Bush and J.H. Smithson) New York: Swedenborg Foundation (first published, 1843; original, 1746-1748).

_____ . *Spiritual Life / The Word of God.* (trans. by J.C. Ager) New York: Swedenborg Foundation, 1972 (first U.S. printing, 1896).

_____ . *The True Christian Religion.* (vols. I & II) (trans. by J.C. Ager) New York: Swedenborg Foundation, 1984 (original, 1771).

Thompson, Richard L., *Alien Identities: Ancient Insights into Modern UFO Phenomena.* San Diego, CA: Govardhan Hill, Inc., 1993.

Tompkins, Peter and Bird, Christopher. *The Secret Life of Plants.* New York: Harper Colophon, 1984 (1973).

Trobridge, George. *Swedenborg: Life and Teaching.* (Revised by Richard Tafel, Sr. and Richard Tafel, Jr.) New York: Swedenborg Foundation, 1992 (1907).

The URANTIA Book. Chicago, Illinois: The URANTIA Foundation, 1995 (1955).

Vallee, Jacques. *Passport to Magonia: On UFOs, Folklore and Parallel Worlds.* Chicago, Illinois: Contemporary Books, Inc., 1993.

_____ . *Dimensions: A Casebook of Alien Contact.* New York, NY: Ballantine Books, 1989.

Van Gelder, Dora. *The Real World of Fairies: A First-Person Account.* Wheaton, Illinois: Theosophical Publishing House, 1999 (1977).

Van Dusen, Wilson. *The Presence of Other Worlds: The Psychological/Spiritual Findings of Emanuel Swedenborg.* West Chester, PA: Chrysalis Books, 1994.

Van Praagh, James. *Talking to Heaven: A Medium's Message of Life After Death.* New York: Dutton, 1997.

_____ . *Reaching to Heaven: A Spiritual Journey Through Life and Death.* New York: Dutton: 1999.

Viney, Geoff. *Surviving Death: Evidence of the Afterlife.* New York: St. Martin's Press, 1993.

Washington, Peter. *Madame Blavatsky's Baboon: A History of the Mystics, Mediums, and Misfits Who Brought Spiritualism to America.* New York: Schocken Books, 1995 (1993).

Wesselman, Hank. *Spiritwalker: Messages from the Future.* New York: Bantam Books, 1995.

_____ . *Medicinemaker: Mystic Encounters on the Shaman's Path.* New York: Bantam Books, 1998.

White, Stewart Edward. *The Unobstructed Universe.* Ohio: Ariel Press, 1988 (1940).

Wickland, Carl A., M.D. *Thirty Years Among the Dead.* Newcastle Publishing Company Inc. (USA), 1974 [National Psychological Institute (USA), 1924]

Wilson, Ian. *The After Death Experience.* New York: William Morrow, 1987.

Woodhouse, Mark B. *Paradigm Wars: Worldviews for a New Age.* Berkeley, CA: Frog, Ltd., 1996.

Yogananda, Paramahansa. *Autobiography of a Yogi.* Los Angeles, CA: Self-Realization Fellowship, 1972 (1946).

Zaleski, C. *Otherworld Journeys: Accounts of Near-Death Experience in Medieval and Modern Times.* Oxford: Oxford University Press, 1987.

Zoeteman, Kees. *Gaiasophy: The Wisdom of the Living Earth.* Hudson, NY: Lindisfarne Press, 1986.

Zukav, Gary. *The Seat of the Soul.* New York: Fireside (Simon and Schuster), 1990 (1989).